Inside Kinship Care

of related interest

Kinship Care
Fostering Effective Family and Friends Placements
Elaine Farmer and Sue Moyers
ISBN 978 1 84310 631 9
eISBN 978 1 84642 803 6
Quality Matters in Children's Services series

Nurturing Attachments Training Resource
Running Parenting Groups for Adoptive Parents and Foster or Kinship Carers
Kim S. Golding
ISBN 978 1 84905 328 0
eISBN 978 0 85700 665 3

Life Story Work with Children Who are Fostered or Adopted
Creative Ideas and Activities
Katie Wrench and Lesley Naylor
ISBN 978 1 84905 343 3
eISBN 978 0 85700 674 5

Direct Work with Vulnerable Children
Playful Activities and Strategies for Communication
Audrey Tait and Helen Wosu
Foreword by Brigid Daniel
ISBN 978 1 84905 319 8
eISBN 978 0 85700 661 5

Young People Leaving Care
Supporting Pathways to Adulthood
Mike Stein
ISBN 978 1 84905 244 3
eISBN 978 0 85700 505 2

Why Can't My Child Behave?
Empathic Parenting Strategies that Work for Adoptive and Foster Families
Amber Elliott
Foreword by Kim S. Golding
ISBN 978 1 84905 339 6
eISBN 978 0 85700 671 4

Inside Kinship Care

Understanding Family Dynamics and
Providing Effective Support

Edited by David Pitcher

Forewords by Professor Bob Broad and Sir Mark Potter

Jessica Kingsley *Publishers*
London and Philadelphia

First published in 2014
by Jessica Kingsley Publishers
73 Collier Street
London N1 9BE, UK
and
400 Market Street, Suite 400
Philadelphia, PA 19106, USA

www.jkp.com

Library of Congress Cataloging in Publication Data
Inside kinship care : understanding family dynamics and providing effective support /
edited by David
Pitcher ; foreword by Professor Bob Broad.
     pages cm
 Includes bibliographical references and index.
 ISBN 978-1-84905-346-4 (alk. paper)
 1. Kinship care. 2. Foster children--Services for. 3. Foster children--Family
relationships. I. Pitcher,
David.
 HV873.I57 2014
 362.73'3--dc23
                          2013023991

British Library Cataloguing in Publication Data
A CIP catalogue record for this book is available from the British Library

ISBN 978 1 84905 346 4
eISBN 978 0 85700 682 0

Printed and bound in Great Britain

*This book is dedicated to Jean Stogdon OBE,
social pioneer, co-founder of Grandparents Plus
and a tireless advocate for kinship care.*

.

Contents

Part 2 Intervention and Support

Part 3 International Contexts

Foreword

Professor Bob Broad

Today in the world of child welfare is an especially unprecedented time of uncertainty and financial austerity for families and local authorities as the role of the state is being further reduced as a result of political ideology. It is no surprise therefore that despite or because of the increasing numbers of children being removed into care, and because of the budgetary pressures placed on local authorities, the notion that families can and should 'look after their own' more, as an alternative to state care, has re-emerged. Kinship care is therefore both a pragmatic and ideological response.

It is within this context that this welcome and timely book *Inside Kinship Care* fulfils and indeed exceeds the promise of its title by providing a range of professional, psychological and therapeutic insights. The editor David Pitcher has put together an eclectic collection of newly commissioned social work, social policy and psychological chapters to aid readers' understanding and appreciation of kinship care in its broader sense. He is well placed through his practice, research and knowledge to bring together these experts in their respective fields.

At its heart formal kinship care, or kinship care where the state is statutorily involved, is a deceptively simple notion, namely that family and friends care for a child in those circumstances where that child can no longer live with their birth parent(s) as a result of welfare concerns.

Yet in terms of policy and practice, formal kinship care often falls into the gap between public and private, into the space between it being a public service and a family duty. This role ambiguity results in kinship carers – usually older relatives (maternal grandparents) – often feeling emotionally exploited since they feel they are keeping the family together, largely at their own expense, and in so doing usually at the expense to their health and wellbeing. They may also struggle on, exhausted because they do not want their grandchild or grandchildren to be placed into or returned to local authority care and will therefore put the child's interests before their own, out of duty.

Indeed as if needing to legitimise general carers' needs the British Medical Association published its recommendations this year about the importance of providing carers suffering from depression with counselling. Of course depression has social, financial and community dimensions as well as clinical ones yet this counselling initiative, though limited and somewhat overdue, is most welcome.

A devastating combination of financial hardship on families, demographic changes and a further re-evaluation of the social contract between the state, its institutions and its citizens have led to a revisiting of the 'privatised family' of the 1980s. Governments continue to fail to value, acknowledge and invest in kinship care, resulting in considerable and unnecessary pressures on these carers in terms of their finance, health and wellbeing, and family relationships. Nevertheless despite these structural problems the international research findings summarised here confirm that outcomes for children living in kinship care and children's views of kinship care are predominantly positive as they highly value living with a family member despite wanting more contact with their birth parent(s).

Perversely, despite or because of ever increasing numbers of children coming into care local authorities seem reluctant and/or unwilling to invest in kinship care, the latest child placement 'kid on the block' with the same status and standing of other placement options. Thus kinship carers find themselves battling with intransigent and reluctant local authorities, themselves under pressure from seemingly endlessly restructuring, downsizing and lacking transparency and consistency. More broadly in the UK and also in the USA, as a direct result of more children being assessed as being on the threshold of care combined with a shortage of foster carers, different types of formal kinship care are expanding as another placement type, and in an ad hoc way, being added onto existing organisational structures without the associative budgets, transparent policies and responsibilities one might expect and that are needed.

At the local level the reluctance and unwillingness of hard-pressed authorities to provide transparent, entitlement-based kinship care policies can arise both from a fear of 'opening the floodgates' of financial payments to kinship carers and more fundamentally from there not being a universal kinship carers' allowance, or carers' entitlement made payable either through the tax or welfare system. A number of groundbreaking legal cases in the UK have been successfully fought on behalf of kinship carers against local authorities and the funding of kinship care is improving as a result. There will also be unanticipated consequences of these legal cases as local authorities become more cautious about the costs of different child placement options. In the UK the carers lobby continues to assert and extend its influence to enable different types of carers to be better recognised and funded and the energetic Kinship Care Alliance exerts an influence and authority over kinship care policy matters.

So against this ever-changing background and context for kinship care this book illuminates a range of important practice and policy issues from the UK – and also from the USA, New Zealand and South Africa – where key issues about recognition or lack of recognition of kinship carers' needs are often remarkably similar.

It is most welcome in this book that 'ways forward for kinship care' are identified so that readers are not left simply reading about known problems but also different solutions and new approaches. It is also important to note that at the international level kinship care is regarded more as another type of 'out-of-home' care thereby continuing to attract welcome and necessary guidance from the United Nations and others in order to safeguard children so that out-of-home care does not become out-of-home exploitation. The research evidence demonstrates that kinship carers both value and are frustrated by the actions and inactions of social services, and this may partly be the result of unrealistic expectations by carers, and partly by a lack of clarity, resources and prioritisation by local authorities. In order to safeguard, support and nurture children in kinship care and their carers and make it a more consistent, valuable and supported experience, government, local authorities, the voluntary sector and social workers need to take this book's valuable understandings and perspectives to the next level of understanding and appreciation.

The essence of this important, positive publication is its varied and coherent range of insights into kinship care, its evidence base, its practice examples, and its therapeutic understandings and messages about what living in kinship care is really like for children and their families as well as the professionals and organisations working with them.

Professor Bob Broad, PhD
Weeks Centre for Social and Policy Research
London South Bank University

Foreword

Sir Mark Potter

Soon after my retirement as President of the Family Division and Head of Family Justice (in which capacity I was also Chair of the inter-disciplinary Family Justice Council) I was privileged to be invited to chair the Advisory Group of a much needed research project conducted by the University of Bristol and funded by the Lottery Fund and the charity Buttle UK. Its ambitious aim was to provide so far as possible a comprehensive picture of the nature, extent and efficiency of *informal* kinship care arrangements in respect of children cared for by relatives and friends, and to compare their 'outcomes' with those in respect of looked after children placed by Children's Services with relatives or friends approved as formal kinship foster carers.

The first part of the study, which used Census microdata to examine the extent and nature of kinship care in the UK, was published in April 2011 (*Spotlight on Kinship Care* by Shareen Nandy and Julie Selwyn). Based on data from the 2001 census (the necessary data from the 2012 census is not yet available) the study found that at least 173,000 children were being raised by family members other than their parents. Of these, more than 90 per cent were cared for under agreements informally made outside the ranks of looked after children, and with limited and usually short-term support from Children's Services. The study also demonstrated that kinship carers formed three main distinct groups: (a) grandparents; (b) siblings and (c) other relatives such as aunts, uncles or cousins and that such carers disproportionately lived in poverty, such poverty being contributed to by the burden of care for the child(ren) concerned.

The second part of the study (*The Poor Relations? Children and Informal Kinship Carers Speak Out* by Julie Selwyn, Elaine Farmer, Sarah Meakins and Paula Unisey, 2013) reported early this year. It builds on the 2011 work and is the product of multiple interviews with kinship carers and children. It makes a number of recommendations for the alleviation and improvement of support for kinship carers, many of whom have their own problems. These are not limited to the problem of poverty, but involve the need for practical as well as financial help and the availability of advice on the management of children's behaviour, including the opportunity for respite care of younger children.

It is against that background that I welcome the authorship and production of this authoritative volume on every significant aspect of kinship care. Not only do the contributors cover the field with a welcome absence of jargon. They do so with evident humanity and the shared purpose of concern for the carers as well as the looked after children. In my view the book should be required background reading for the family judiciary as well as children's lawyers, social workers and others concerned with the provision and implementation of Children's Services.

The chapters get off to a flying start with the forceful and moving contribution of Amy O'Donohoe, whose personal story and account of her difficulties as a juvenile in persuading professionals that she meant what she said are both moving and persuasive of the need to accord weight to the voice of the child.

The book then proceeds, chapter by chapter, to set out a variety of perspectives, provided by a number of distinguished and experienced contributors who are experts in their field. It is not my role in this introduction to summarise the contributions, a task deftly and succinctly performed in the 'Introduction' and 'Epilogue' by David Pitcher of Cafcass who, together with Professor Elaine Farmer and Sarah Meakings also supplies the chapter on 'Siblings and Kinship Care'. However, in my own capacity as a grandparent, as well as a former judge with frequent cause to appreciate the resolutive intervention of grandparents in care cases, it is interesting to note the confirmation and endorsement of their beneficial role by experts and practitioners alike in several of the chapters.

The contribution of Nicholas Banks ('What do White Kinship Carers need to consider when caring for Children of Black "Mixed Race"?') is an illuminating reminder that more than empathy and good intentions are necessary to cope successfully with the cultural issues likely to arise in such cases.

There are also international contributions of interest from Australia and New Zealand ('Australia and New Zealand: Assessing Parenting Capacity in Kinship Care'), South Africa ('Kinship Care among Families affected by HIV in South Africa') and the United States ('The Views of Children in Kinship Care, their Caregivers and Birth Parents: Key Themes from the United States').

It is important and interesting to note that three decades of research confirm that kinship care arrangements in the US are generally more stable and, on most behavioural and care indicators, more successful than in cases where the children are placed in foster care with non-relatives. So far as I am aware, there is nothing in the research material generated over a single decade in the UK to suggest that the position here is any different.

This book is welcome as a comprehensive and highly readable compendium of chapters which together comprise an up to date study of kinship care.

Sir Mark Potter,
former President of the Family Law Division
and former Head of Family Justice

Introduction

David Pitcher

Twenty years ago, a crack cocaine epidemic on the West coast of America brought the issue of kinship care to prominence (Minkler and Roe 1993). It is perhaps from this time that kinship care has been recognised as a distinct phenomenon (for a discussion of the term and its origins, see Scannapieco and Hegar 1999, p.2), different, and yet similar, to other forms of substitute care for children. Different, because of the bonds of loyalty within families; and similar, because many of the children involved have complex emotional and behavioural needs. Kinship care might therefore now be seen as one generation old.

Families, and perhaps especially grandmothers (Hill and Hurtado 2012) have always looked after their own vulnerable young family members. This may be due to a crisis, such as bereavement or maltreatment, or by deliberate design, such as when children are cared for by grandparents and others for economic reasons. For example, children in the Caribbean were commonly brought up by grandparents when their parents left the community to find work or to study (Russell-Brown, Norville and Griffith 1996). Kinship care in its current sense involves professionals, on behalf of the state, being tasked to regulate the quality of the care provided, and at the same time promoting a form of care that does not disrupt identity and family continuity. Meanwhile, 'informal' kinship care continues as it always has done, and forms a background for more 'formal' kinship care.

Defining kinship care

The term 'kinship care' is now in wide use among social care professionals, but is not common in ordinary language, or indeed among 'kinship carers' themselves. Sometimes the expression 'family and friends care' is also used. The two terms are synonymous and their use is really a matter of personal or agency preference. There is no one comprehensive and universally agreed definition of what kinship care is, although there are many broadly overlapping definitions, some of which appear in this book.

Kinship care has come to include the following elements:

1. A child is cared for *within his or her own family network*. This includes blood relatives, such as aunts, uncles, grandparents and siblings, and also people who are already connected to (and ideally trusted by) the child, either in their own right (for example, parents of their own friends), or as friends of their parents. It can include godparents, neighbours and non-related family members (Argent 2007). In the United States, it can also mean members of the same Native American tribe. The same thinking can be seen elsewhere including, potentially, in the United Kingdom (Cemlyn 2008). However, kinship care is not taken to include unrelated people who were formerly in a parental role, such as current or former step-parents. The definition might include a child who is cared for by a distant relative who he or she has never previously met (Lutman, Hunt and Waterhouse 2009).

2. Such care is *full time*, so kinship care does not apply to carers who have a child at weekends, but it would include a child who is placed with kin and who is cared for by his or her mother or father overnight or holiday contact, or for periods of respite care.

3. Care is, or is intended to be, *for a significant period of time*, such that the carer takes on a parental role rather than a caretaking role, with all of the psychological adjustments that this calls for.

4. Implicit in the concept of kinship care is that the child is being cared for *as a response to a family adversity or upheaval*, so that the child would otherwise need substitute care outside of the network (Pitcher 2002). Thus, kinship care would include a child whose parent had died, was imprisoned or was incapacitated through drugs, but not a child whose parent had gone on an extended holiday. If a child has a parent who is working away, a lot would depend on the longer-term intentions nature of the arrangement made. Such an arrangement might become a kinship placement in the child's experience. Family adversity might be related to the behaviour of the child concerned (Department for Education 2011).

Within kinship care, a parent may be involved at different levels, depending on their willingness, availability or any assessed risk (Gleeson and Seryak 2010; Goodman and Silverstein 2001). A child's mother or father may even live with the family, but be taking a back step to the principal parent figure. The potential for confusion can be seen, and such is the experience of many children.

5. Kinship care may be 'formal', that is arranged by a body representing the state; or it may be 'informal', arranged by the family itself. The former is sometimes referred to as 'kinship foster care'. In either case, the state may be obliged to provide some level of approval or support (Broad 2004; Department for Education 2011) which, rightly or wrongly (Hunt and Waterhouse 2012), will differ according to legal status. Of course, some arrangements are unknown to the state; but, were help to be sought, kinship care status would be an important consideration in deciding the agency's level of response.

A kinship care arrangement may be subject to a variety of legal orders (including there being no order), in which there are varying balances of power and responsibility between the carers, the original parents and the state. From 2002 (effective from December 2005), the United Kingdom has had the provision of Special Guardianship, a status (unlike a Residence Order) that is not available to a birth parent. Adoption is a frequently used legal order in the United States in kinship cases, but is almost never used now in the United Kingdom for placement within the family. Kinship care is one of a number of types of care available to a child, alongside fostering with professional carers, and adoption with non-friends and family. In the United Kingdom, the United States and elsewhere, it is almost always stated explicitly that kinship care should be the first option. Of course, once a child has been placed for a while with non-kin foster parents they often become kin to that child (Department for Education 2011), and Special Guardianship Orders are frequently made to foster carers who wish to assume a less highly regulated form of family life.

By breaking kinship care down into its constituent elements it may be seen that there is a central concept, with distinctive psychological and sociological implications, but also that the definition is a little 'fuzzy around the edges', in that it encompasses a wide variety of actual experiences, but excludes others.

The biggest proportion of kinship carers consists of grandparents (Broad, Hayes and Rushworth 2001), and in particular maternal grandmothers (Pitcher 2002). This is recognised to be the case internationally (UNICEF 2008). As a result, the literature almost treats kinship care and care by grandparents as synonymous. The implications for this are discussed throughout this book.

The place of this book

In the first generation of kinship care, much important work has been done by scholars, policy makers and kinship carers themselves to help kinship care be recognised and understood in a way that it has never been before. We have excellent descriptions of the experiences of kinship carers and, to a lesser extent, of other family members (Broad 2004; Farmer and Moyers 2008). Special Guardianship forms a solid legal basis for kinship care in the United Kingdom, and it is slowly attracting case law. The support needs of kinship carers, while not always met, are much better known through the work of Grandparents Plus, The Family Rights Group, and the Grandparents' Association. The next task, I suggest, is to look clearly at what is going on 'inside' families.

Anyone who has worked with children who are placed with grandparents or other relatives, or where such a placement is proposed, will know just how complex the issues can be. This is well put by Brynna Kroll (2007, p.6) in the context of parental substance misuse:

> The family could be seen as both the cause of the problems, and the solution to them… Grandparents are a powerful force for change, and a significant source of support, providing a protective mantle for both children and parents. In some families, however, they may assume a different role at times – smokescreens, obfuscators, repositories of secrets.

This mixed picture will be familiar, and will remain with us. Much of the literature and legislation, however, presents a somewhat idealised picture of kinship care. This may be necessary for campaigning or for sending clear messages, but there is also a need to come to terms with the psychological complexities and, at times, contradictions within kinship care placements. With some notable exceptions (e.g. Barratt and Granville 2006; Broad 2001; Doucette-Dudman 1996; Greeff 1999), it is less easy to see this in the literature and, especially, not easy to see how these factors can be addressed and balanced. Yet without this families cannot be properly understood or helped to understand themselves. Assessments will fail to be properly informative and support may risk missing the real issues. Such an in-depth understanding is available in the literature on adoption, and on non-relative foster care. As I was planning this book, I asked a group of experienced practitioners what, having been given training in kinship care and access to the existing literature, they still did not feel they understood. Their responses included:

- What is the right kind of support and training to provide, especially long term?

- What do adults who were brought up in kinship care say about their experience?

- How can a grandparent switch to a new role, both for their child and their grandchild?

- How can a family's narrative best be incorporated into a written assessment?

The purpose of this book is to bring together a variety of perspectives that can help us to understand the complex dynamic of kinship care. The mix of styles and views is inevitably varied. I have asked each contributor to link kinship care with a particular theoretical model, or a particular issue, or describe kinship care in a particular setting. The aim is to provide an element of cross-fertilisation: not only will the literature on kinship care be enriched by these perspectives, but a variety of disciplines will be helped to understand kinship care. In some of the areas, kinship care has never been considered in a specific way. Other authors can look back on the last generation of formal kinship care and draw new insight from this. All the contributors, many of whom are known to me personally as highly skilled practitioners, take a new perspective on kinship care and make recommendations for further exploration of the issues. I hope that this volume will be a seedbed for future research and exploration.

Every day, families, courts, social workers and many others are wrestling with the multiple issues which are presented within kinship care. These issues will never become simple because the hopes, frustrations, anger and love are at the heart of people's identity, in the white heat of the 'family crucible' (Napier and Whitaker 1978). Yet these contributions can deepen our understanding of these issues and provide clues to effective help.

An outline of this book

Any treatment of kinship care must surely begin with the actual experience of those involved, especially that of children and young people. In the existing literature, there are many comments and quotes from interviews with children, but few extended narratives. I was keen to begin this book with such an account. Amy O'Donohoe was brought up in kinship care, and being now a student of English, is able to write about her experiences in a direct and unmediated way. She is old enough to look back on her childhood, but close enough to it for it not to have lost its immediacy. Amy describes being on the receiving end of the child protection system, including some misjudgements by professionals. She also describes her thoughts about being a young carer herself, and what it is really like to have to become part of a new family. Amy's account is a remarkable one, and I hope that it will become a resource for researchers, policy makers and students of social work.

An understanding of kinship care must be embedded in an understanding of how families support each other more generally. This can be seen in the history of most kinship care arrangements, where grandparents may have tried to support their grandchild at home initially, or where a child is cared for full time at certain times. Sadie Young explores the range of family support for one particular group of people – parents with intellectual disabilities. The 'three generational family' has often been criticised (for the classic example of this see Rappaport 1958) though it is the family form in which most people have always lived, and continue to live. While this can be a supportive arrangement, misunderstandings can arise around the question of who is the primary carer for the child. Drawing on many years of work with some of the most complex cases before the courts, Sadie strikes a cautionary note, and brings clarity to an area which is very familiar to practitioners, but rarely addressed in the literature.

Relationships between siblings touch every aspect of kinship care. Children may be cared for by a parent's sibling, or by an elder sibling of their own. They may also have to form sibling-like relationships with children in their new family, to whom they formerly related as a young uncle, aunt or cousin. However, the existing literature (which in itself is somewhat scanty) has never been brought to bear on kinship care. In our third chapter, Sarah Meakings, Elaine Farmer and I begin by looking at the way in which sibling relationships work. We then apply this to what may be going on specifically in the kinship care context. To illustrate this, we draw on a very recent study in which members of 80 families were interviewed.

If siblings are important, the continuing influence of mothers is clear throughout the literature and to anyone who works with kinship families, or is part of one. It would hardly be an exaggeration to say that the attitude of a mother towards a placement, especially if the carer is her own mother, has the power to make or break it. Mothers may be in a particularly difficult position because their own loss may be compounded with expectations of mothers within our society (Gustafson 2005). Erica Flegg looks at the experience of mothers, in particular when a child is placed by the authorities with her own mother. Erica addresses the generational factors within the family, and highlights the way in which any failings on the mother's part can become magnified by the social workers' own psychological processes. Such mothers, who are already likely to be in a vulnerable position, experience further humiliation and shame. Properly informed therapeutic work can bring about a much healthier situation for everyone.

Kinship care is, by very definition, all about the 'wider family'. A child in kinship care still has a wider family, although a reconfigured one. The attitude of the child's wider family is often overlooked by professionals, but it can have an important influence not only in terms of practical support, but also of how the placement is thought of. Jeanne Ziminski draws on her own research and experience as a systemic family therapist to examine this. Jeanne thinks about what 'family' can mean, and how theoretical understandings can enhance professional practice.

We now turn to some of the processes which are designed to help families, beginning with safeguarding. Andrew Turnell and Susie Essex describe an approach to working with the whole network of family and friends in a way that makes sense to the people who are actually involved, and this approach contains within it the power to establish strong, properly informed kinship care placements where these are necessary. Andrew and Susie challenge the approach based on undue control by professionals, and show how a focus on what has been working well can be used even in times of acute crisis, when it is easy for professionals to see nothing but the problems. Susie uses the concept of 'cross-stitching' to look at how concerns and strengths can be acknowledged together, in a way that 'honours' the family. These ideas have been widely used and tested by the authors and others, and the chapter contains practical ideas and tools for working with children and families who are around them.

When cases involving kinship care are before the courts and become particularly complex or contested, a clinical psychologist is sometimes appointed in order to provide an 'expert report'. Anna Gough is one such expert, and her assessments are highly regarded. Here, Anna shows how she approaches a kinship assessment and how her particular discipline of clinical psychology can deepen our understanding of the processes at work within a family, and at the same time how the work can be therapeutic in itself. Anna provides an original analysis of her role, which will be of real interest to all those involved in the court process and beyond.

The concepts of permanence and of attachment have become widely used and accepted in the literature on fostering and adoption. Strangely, says John Simmonds, these fundamental insights seem not to feature in thinking about kinship care. Perhaps we are used to relatives 'helping out', and indeed many families approach kinship care with the thought of it being a provisional arrangement until the child is able to return to his or her parents. This has resulted in serious misunderstandings with agencies. John encourages us to consider how a child entering a kinship placement may well have an immediate need for a psychologically and legally secure family, while family members may be struggling to deal with loss and uncertainty. John also raises important ideas about what kind of support families need to manage this successfully.

When kinship care is discussed, the emphasis is usually on the stability of placements, when compared with non-relative care (Farmer 2009; Lutman et al. 2009). Yet kinship placements do break down, and sometimes painfully so for all involved. Of course, if a kinship placement does break down, it brings the added potential risk to the child of being permanently estranged from a birth family. Children in non-family placements can, and do, find their way back to their birth families and often receive some support. A young person who is estranged from his or her family because of a placement breakdown in a kinship placement really can be on their own. If we are going to support children and their families, we need to understand the dynamics of placement breakdown within kinship placements, and to develop a way of thinking about them.

Tom Hawkins considers two cases in which he was involved where issues within family relationships, which were not foreseen at the time of placement, led to the breakdown, or possible breakdown, of these placements. In so doing, Tom also reinforces many of John Simmonds' observations about permanence and attachment from the previous chapter.

Much has been written about psychodynamic theory and its insights remain foundational. However, little has been written that links these insights to the complex world of kinship care. Furthermore, psychodynamic thinking carries about it something of a mystique. Graham Music and Geraldine Crehan enable us to get an inside view into how a psychoanalytically informed intervention might be carried out, taking into account the particular issues inherent within kinship care. Graham and Geraldine take us carefully through a case study, showing how they refuse to dismiss difficult and painful experiences, but rather see them as the essential part of an effective piece of work.

From the early days of kinship care in the United States, support groups for grandparent carers have been an important feature, not least because of the work of the Child Welfare League of America (CWLA) and the American Association of Retired Persons (AARP). With some exceptions, this has been less the case in the United Kingdom and elsewhere. Some practitioners have found it difficult to get groups started, or if started, to understand their dynamics. Jackie Wyke of the Grandparents Association sets groups in their overall context of support, and discusses some of the issues that have faced their particular form of group, the 'grandparent and toddler group'. Jackie suggests ways in which our understanding of support groups might be deepened.

When looking at attachment and permanence, John Simmonds pointed out to us how insights that have long become standard in non-relative care have scarcely affected kinship care; Nick Banks identifies another such area. Racially matched and sensitive foster and adoptive placements are now assumed. However, there are many children of mixed race who are cared for by white grandparents who may well not have had the opportunity to understand racially sensitive thinking. Nick shows how 'commonsense' attitudes such as 'children are children, aren't they?' can completely miss the experience that mixed race (see Nick's introduction for a discussion of this term) children have, which is often built up of multiple but invisible incidents of 'micro-aggression'. Nick does not leave us there, but points to ways in which white grandparents can relate empathetically to their mixed race grandchildren.

We conclude by looking at kinship care in three international contexts, beginning with Australia and New Zealand. Formal kinship care begins with assessment, and how such assessments should be undertaken has been the source of much debate (see, for example, Burnette 1997; Scannapieco 1999). Should they be different to the assessment of other carers, and if so, why? It is appropriate to have a contribution from Australia, as New Zealand and Australia have been prominent in promoting kinship care, both by legislation and innovative practice, perhaps as a response to an earlier history of insensitivity to the needs of indigenous families.

Marilyn McHugh and Paula Hayden examine the way in which assessing kinship placements – which form a 'vast continuum' – is approached, and how the distinction can be made between 'enabling', as opposed to 'approving', families to care. What are the key elements that need to be present? The authors describe the Winangay Assessment, a unique, strength-based resource which has been developed specifically for Aboriginal families.

No one can have failed to be struck by the scale of the HIV/AIDS epidemic that hit sub-Saharan Africa and elsewhere beginning in the 1990s (McGeary 2001). This resulted in a huge increase in kinship care (Daniel 2004a, 2004b), both by grandparents and by siblings, including so-called 'child headed households'. It is striking that the experience of these kinship carers and those working with them has not been linked more with that of kinship care in the West. What challenges have been faced? What lessons have been learned? I firmly believed that no treatment of kinship care would be complete without hearing about the southern African experience. Caroline Kuo, Lucie Cluver and Don Operario have collaborated to provide a comprehensive analysis of kinship care as it is worked out in South Africa, including a discussion of the psychological and economic consequences. The chapter also describes what systems have been developed in South Africa to protect kinship caregivers. The chapter concludes that many interventions have yet to be evaluated. I hope that we will increasingly learn from each other.

If our current understanding of kinship care began in the United States, it is fitting that our treatment should end there. Jim Gleeson provides an overview of what has been learned since the early days, beginning with an invaluable analysis of children's views. Jim then provides a view from the perspective of the carers, which includes a very interesting discussion about the continuing importance of parents. Jim's contribution leaves us with a sense of being completely up-to-date. I find the picture he gives is an optimistic one, as he concludes with 'the hopes and dreams that children, parents and caregivers have for each other'.

In this book, we see a cross-fertilisation of different strands of thought and experience: different theoretical perspectives, the views of different generations, and a variety of geographical settings. These will be cross-fertilised further as they link with your experience and those of other readers. Kinship care will always be with us, and it will always be a source of ever more finely tuned enquiry. At the end of this book, I will suggest some areas for further research that have emerged from these chapters.

References

Argent, H. (2007) *Kinship Care: What it is and What it Means.* London: BAAF.

Barratt, S. and Granville, J. (2006) 'Kinship Care: Family Stories, Loyalties and Binds.' In J. Kenrick, C. Lindsey and L. Tollemache (eds) *Creating New Families: Therapeutic Approaches to Fostering, Adoption and Kinship Care.* London: Karnac.

Broad, B. (ed.) (2001) *Kinship Care: The Placement Choice for Children and Young People.* Lyme Regis: Russell House Publishing.

Broad, B. (2004) 'Kinship care for children in the UK: messages from research, lessons for policy and practice.' *European Journal of Social Work 7*, 211–227.

Broad, B., Hayes, R. and Rushworth, C. (2001) *Kith and Kin: Kinship Care for Vulnerable Young People.* London: National Children's Bureau and Joseph Rowntree Foundation.

Burnette, D. (1997) 'Grandparents raising grandchildren in the inner city.' *Families in Society 78*, September–October, 489–501.

Cemlyn, S. (2008) 'Human rights and gypsies and travellers: an exploration of the application of a human rights perspective to social work with a minority community in Britain.' *British Journal of Social Work 38*, 1, 153–173.

Daniel, M. (2004a) 'A new place in the family.' *Professional Social Work* May 2004, 12–13.

Daniel, M. (2004b) 'Kinship care in Botswana.' *Professional Social Work* June 2004, 18–19.

Department for Education (2011) *Family and Friends Care: Statutory Guidance for Local Authorities.* London: Her Majesty's Stationary Office.

Doucette-Dudman, D. with LaCure, J. (1996) *Raising Our Children's Children.* Minneapolis, MN: Fairview Press.

Farmer, E. (2009) 'Placement stability in kinship care.' *Vulnerable Children and Youth Studies 4*, 2, 154–160.

Farmer, E. and Moyers, S. (2008) *Kinship Care: Fostering Effective Family and Friends Placements.* London: Jessica Kingsley Publishers.

Gleeson, J.P. and Seryak, C.M. (2010) '"I made some mistakes…but I love them dearly." The views of parents of children in informal kinship care.' *Child and Family Social Work 15*, 87–96.

Goodman, C. and Silverstein, M. (2001) 'Grandmothers who parent their grandchildren: affective relations across three generations and implications for psychological well-being.' *Journal of Family Issues 22*, 557–578.

Greeff, R. (ed.) (1999) *Fostering Kinship: An International Perspective on Kinship Foster Care.* Aldershot: Ashgate.

Gustafson, D.L. (ed.) (2005) *Unbecoming Mothers: The Social Production of Maternal Absence.* New York: The Haworth Clinical Practice Press.

Hill, K. and Hurtado, M. (2012) 'Human reproductive assistance.' *Nature 483*, 8 March, 160–161.

Hunt, J. and Waterhouse, S. (2013) *'It's Just Not Fair!' Support, Need, and Legal Status in Family and Friends Care.* Family Rights Group/Oxford Centre for Family Law and Policy.

Kroll, B. (2007) 'A family affair? Kinship care and parental substance misuse: some dilemmas explored.' *Child and Family Social Work 12*, 84–93.

Lutman, E., Hunt, J. and Waterhouse, S. (2009) 'Placement stability for children in kinship care: a long-term follow-up of children placed in kinship care through care proceedings.' *Adoption and Fostering 33*, 3, 28–39.

McGeary, J. (2001) 'Death stalks a continent.' *Time Magazine,* 12 February.

Minkler, M. and Roe, K. (1993) *Grandmothers as Caregivers: Raising the Children of the Crack Cocaine Epidemic.* Thousand Oaks, CA: Sage.

Napier, A. and Whitaker, C. (1978) *The Family Crucible.* New York: Harper and Row.

Pitcher, D. (2002) 'Placement with grandparents: the issues for grandparents who care for their grandchildren.' *Adoption and Fostering 26*, 1, 6–14.

Rappaport, E.A. (1958) 'The grandparent syndrome.' *Psychoanalytic Quarterly 27*, 518–538.

Russell-Brown, P.A., Norville, B. and Griffith, C. (1996) 'Child Shifting: A Survival Strategy for Teenage Mothers.' In J.L. Roopnarine and J.Brown (eds) *Caribbean Families: Diversity among Ethnic Groups.* Greenwich, CT: Ablex.

Scannapieco, M. (1999) 'Formal Kinship Care Practice Models.' In R. Hegar and M. Scannapieco (eds) *Kinship Foster Care.* Oxford: Oxford University Press.

Scannapieco, M. and Hegar, R. (1999) 'The Cultural Roots of Kinship Care.' In R. Hegar and M. Scannapieco (eds) *Kinship Foster Care.* Oxford: Oxford University Press.

UNICEF (2008) *Working Paper: Alternative Care for Children in Southern Africa: Progress, Challenges and Future Directions.* Nairobi: UNICEF.

PART 1

Family Perspectives

CHAPTER 1

Entering Kinship Care

A Young Person's Story

Amy O'Donohoe

The funny thing about growing up in a bad situation is that for the most part you don't realise that anything is wrong. I certainly never questioned the near constant presence of alcohol and police, or thought that sitting in the pub all day was strange. Although things got progressively worse as I grew, I don't think I noticed how toxic my mother and stepfather's lifestyles had become. Life was difficult, much more difficult than I should ever have had to deal with, but I never thought it had gone too far. At least, it didn't seem it before my mother fell pregnant. In a brutal change of situation, my selfish and innocent way of seeing the world was ripped away; everything which had previously seemed bearable to me now became a threat to my unborn sister – and I had no way to protect her. I spent nine painful months watching my mother's drinking become worse than I remember before, and when my sister was born (miraculously, with nothing obvious wrong with her) our home life somehow got even worse.

It was more than unfortunate that (due to another eviction) when my sister was born, our family was living in a one bedroom pub. With a constant flow of alcohol our parents never stopped drinking, and became steadily more violent towards each other. They made less and less effort to care for us. When my sister wasn't being showed off in the pub, I tried to look after her upstairs. Having no knowledge of how to care for a baby, I had serious difficulty coping with my home and school life. The only normality I had in those days was the weekly visits to my aunt's house. It was an afternoon of peace, a decent meal and a chance to do my homework. It was a chance to act my age. When my brother and I were younger, my aunt looked after us whenever she could, making sure we were fed and OK. It was a regular occurrence that the police would take us to our aunt's house when there had been a particularly bad argument. I remember her making us fish fingers or chips in the early hours of the morning because we hadn't been fed. We would stay and be looked after for a few days until the argument had blown over, and then we'd have to go back to our mother's until the next time. Looking back now, I can see that my aunt was always trying to find ways to look after us. I didn't realise it at the time, but I really did rely on those afternoons to keep me afloat.

In the nine months following my sister's birth, our family life grew unbearable. We moved from the pub to a small house, but our mother continued to drink extensively and fell into depression. I looked after my sister for the majority of the time, and at the same time I was trying to hide knives and razors and making sure our mother wasn't hurting herself. I often found her with gashes on her wrists, and once I confronted her about cutting herself in less conspicuous places like her shoulders or thighs. Sometimes I had no chance to notice until she had cut herself so deeply that the blood stained her clothes and pooled on the floor. My relationship with my mother soured as I realised that she refused to put anything or anyone before herself and her drinking. She acted like she hated me, and so I hardened myself to it and hated her back. Instead of being upset around her I cried on my way to school, I cried in the toilets, I stayed after school and made detours on the way home. In fact the only reason I didn't leave or tell any authority of our situation was the fear of losing my brother and sister. To me it would have been much better to stay and cope with what we had than risk having my siblings torn apart just so I could have an easier life.

Our life continued to spiral. I argued constantly with our mother while trying to look after everyone, and I honestly couldn't see how it could ever get better. So it was terrifying, and oddly a relief, when an argument broke out when my brother and I were away from home and the question of child protection was finally raised. My mother was arrested for harming my sister in front of the police, and for the first time my brother and I had the choice to be somewhere else. Our aunt, who was in a panic thinking something had happened to us during the fight, found us at our friend's. She took us in, and gave us the chance to stay with her while she tried to sort things out for us. Even though none of us were under the impression it was to be a permanent placement, our lives started to change.

There were many issues that we had to overcome with the initial placement with our aunt. It was after all only a temporary placement. We all feared for my sister's welfare, and the introduction of social services was no easy thing to accept when they seemed determined to make staying with our aunt impossible. As it was such an unexpected turn of events, our aunt had been able to make no preparations for our stay. She lived in a small three bedroom house with my two cousins, and though they were not lacking in space there was no room for two extra teenagers. We made do with what we had – my brother and I slept on my younger cousin's floor – but unsurprisingly we quickly got under each other's feet. More than once my cousin and I argued about the room we all shared, and as there was nowhere to get away from each other tensions ran high. It took a long time for me and him to get on again. I understood that it was hard for him, but I was too worried about myself and my siblings to care that his life had changed as well. I was selfish and self-absorbed – it's an unfortunate product of feeling like you have the weight of the world on your shoulders at 14 years old. It took time but eventually our relationship changed. We started to accept our new situation and acted more like brother and sisters than cousins who had been forced upon each other. I didn't like to think about what my cousins were giving up at the time; it was easy to mull over bigger things without looking at what my family did to help my siblings and me. Considering what us living with them meant they hardly complained at all; they made a difficult time much easier than it might have been.

As well as the problem with space, living with my aunt meant an entirely new style of living. I would be lying if I said it was easy for any of us to get used to. Though I was incredibly grateful to my aunt for taking us in, I resented being treated like the child I was when I hadn't had rules or structure in my entire life. It took a very long time to accept that I didn't have to look after myself. I pushed against it, not realising how much I needed to be cared for. It took a lot of getting used to, but eventually after many arguments I began to see my aunt as the parental figure. In truth, I spent most of the beginning months with my aunt worrying about my sister and my mother. I was so used to worrying about them at home that I found it difficult to get out of that mind-set while living with my aunt. I feared for my sister's health and for our mother's happiness. I didn't think she would be able to cope without us being there and would hurt herself even worse than before. I knew she had tried to kill herself, and it seemed only a matter of time before she would succeed. At the beginning of the move we had letterbox contact with her, but the letters we received from our mother were cold and angry, and said nothing to ease my mind. It was easier to have no contact at all then deal with her barbed comments.

The few months that followed our initial move were difficult. The social care system was something none of us were prepared for. My aunt spent most of her time researching aspects of social services and family and friend carers. She found advocates for my brother and me, spoke to people who had been in a situation like ours, and started to fight social services for the things we were entitled to. When I think back to that time, all I remember is a blur of professionals asking me to talk about the same things again and again. I started to feel disassociated with my own experience; I started to explain everything that happened as if I had watched it in a film or read it in a book to stop me breaking down every time I spoke about it. I don't remember most of what happened in my childhood now; it's a shock every time I look through the old paperwork.

At every opportunity we asked social services how my sister was doing. They said that she was living in a pub with her father (my stepfather), and that despite our worries and the information we had given them, they had no reason to remove her. It was heart-breaking knowing the environment she was in and the neglect she would definitely be facing. In the middle of the night, four months after the move to our aunt's house, we received the phone call we had all been waiting for. An argument had broken out between our mother and stepfather, the police had been contacted, and my sister was placed in my aunt's care. My sister was filthy, her hair was matted, she was far too thin, and she was overly weary. I don't think my aunt or I will ever forget that night: she was both the saddest and most wonderful sight I had ever seen and will ever see. That night my aunt, my sister and I stayed in the same bed, and when I woke up I felt happier then I had in months. It seemed like life was starting to move in the right direction. It was something all of us needed.

My aunt made a point of taking all the responsibilities for my sister. My immediate impulse was to jump back into the role I played while with my mum, and though it was difficult to accept, it started to fade. At first I didn't understand why it had to change, as I was happy to help look after my sister. But I know my aunt was doing the right thing, she was forever trying to make me realise I wasn't the adult I had been forced to be. For two weeks we felt like we were floating, in a daze because of our luck. None of us could get enough of my sister.

We started to settle into a new routine, and the prospect that things could be OK started to dawn in all of our minds. However, this peace was brutally short. On the third week, our stepfather died.

My brother and I were both asleep when my aunt came to tell us what had happened. I thought she was joking… until she told us how it happened. It turned out that our mother had gone to his room and stabbed him to death while he slept. I didn't believe it had happened until I was told our mother had done it. They were so violent towards each other that everyone had said something terrible would happen eventually, and it did. Everything good we had been building in the months before crashed around me. I hardly remember the weeks that followed. More often than not, I cried myself to sleep. I spent a lot of time trying to remember the last thing he said to me, the last time I saw him, asking myself if I could have stopped it or if it was my fault for moving out. I only saw my aunt cry once; she was on her own so we wouldn't see. She was always trying to protect us, no matter what.

That day it became apparent that we were never going back to live with our mother; we really were 'in care'. After everything that happened, the prospect of moving and being split up was not an option. Despite all the difficulties and issues, our aunt decided to take the three of us on permanently. I can't imagine how we would have coped if we had been forced to leave and live with strangers. Our aunt knew what we were going through because she was going through it too. She could understand us in a way that a foster carer never could. My stepfather's death has left all of us with scars, but it removed the walls we had built up between ourselves, and brought us together as a family. The tragedy united us.

My stepfather's death sparked a change in the way others saw and treated us. My status moved from a child with a complicated home life to a child in care. I was now the subject of formal processes such as personal education plans and regular meetings with members of school staff who I had previously had nothing to do with. My teachers expected less of me; they assumed that my background and the fact that I was in care meant I couldn't do as well. I was given excuses to leave class, to skip lessons I didn't like, to take my lessons on my own. I knew this was unnecessary; I was annoyed that suddenly I was a problem child. I took advantage. I skipped the lessons I didn't like, I sat in the nurse's office when I hadn't done my homework, waiting for someone to draw the line or tell me off, but no one ever did. I had always thought of myself as a hard worker: there were lessons in which I excelled, and I loved it when I was given the chance to show what I could do, but any challenges or extra work were taken away with everything else. I think the lowest point for me while adjusting to our new life was when I realised that even the teachers I looked up to had started to expect me to fail. It started to seem like getting good grades and going to university wasn't possible. I didn't see the point in wasting my time trying to prove myself to people who had already given up on me.

At home I had just as many issues adjusting to our new life. I thought there were a lot of professionals when we first moved in with our aunt, but it was nothing compared to the time after my stepfather's death. We all needed to know there was permanency in us all living with our aunt, so my aunt chose to go to court in the hope that the three of us would be placed under Special Guardianship Order. We were introduced to more people than I could remember. We had numerous social workers and support workers, the head of the local authority, the Children's Guardian – and I know there were even more my aunt was dealing with. Sometimes we only met a person once, even when they became deeply involved in court proceedings. Though I could deal with meeting all the new people, I had difficulty having to relive the worst aspects of my childhood every time a new person was introduced. Even though it never got easier to discuss, there was always another person that wanted to know the situation from our point of view.

One of the biggest issues we had in meetings with professionals was trying to prove that we meant the things we said. Though we would be told that we were understood and that everything was OK, we would later be sent reports that said they didn't think we were serious in our opinion. It was infuriating. The question that seemed to come up with every meeting was whether I wanted to see my mother, and although every time I was asked this I replied with 'no', it seemed impossible for everyone to accept. The Children's Guardian found it particularly difficult to believe that at 14 I was capable of making such a decision without some form of outside influence. The fact that I didn't want a relationship with a person who had emotionally abused and crippled me, who had chosen herself over her children, and who was capable of murder, didn't seem to cross anybody's mind. Although I was well within my right to choose not to have contact, my mother and the Children's Guardian decided that my aunt was forcing me to stop contact, and that for her own selfish gain she was trying to 'poison us against her'. They made my aunt's relationship with me out to be something sinister, suggesting it was built on nothing more than petty spite aimed at our mother. It hurt that the professionals that were supposed to choose the best thing for my siblings and me couldn't see how much we needed to be close to our aunt. It was hard enough to learn to trust and rely on her without our motives being questioned. It was difficult knowing we were having to fight to stay together when this was the first place we had ever felt looked after, when at home we suffered years of neglect without anyone questioning it.

In the years that followed these first six months we faced many trials as a family. We faced broken relationships, applications for orders failed, there was not always stability, and we had more than our fair share of arguments. But we survived everything and continued to move forward. I've grown from the damaged and abused 14-year-old into a 20-year-old with hopes, dreams and real prospects. I study English and music at university, while working to help improve the care system for new generations. Now six years old, my sister is growing into a beautiful and intelligent child, and she enjoys reading almost as much as I do! My brother is working full time, and is living independently.

And my aunt? My aunt is still my rock. She's my shoulder to cry on. She's cooked meals when I have too many deadlines. She's sympathy and love when I'm ill. She's the person I work to make proud. She's the person who will give me away at my wedding. She's my aunty, friend and mother all rolled into one. When I look back at everything that happened during my childhood, it's not the pain and heartbreak I think of, it's my aunt's unswerving loyalty and dedication to our family.

I find it hard to be sad when I have someone who cares for me as much as she does.

Amy's aunt, Cassie Felton, gives her own perspective:

Amy was a child who had to take on far too much for her young years. She did the best she could and she did a good job. She was a child though, and although I could never give her back that innocence I could give her back some of her childhood, even if I had to force her into it. The guilt she suffered when her stepfather died I think is probably normal despite reassurances that none of this was her fault and there was nothing she could have done. I'm glad she only saw me cry once, as she needed someone to be strong in order to help her. Amy's past will always be a part of who she is, no one can ever change that or take it away, but she has not allowed herself to be defined solely by her experiences. Instead, she is dedicated and determined to be better. I have watched her grow and flourish and have every faith she will achieve all she sets out to do. She may not be my daughter but I love her as if she was and I have a mother's fierce pride in her. She carries, and always will carry, that pride with her wherever she goes.

CHAPTER 2

What Does Family Support Involve for Parents who have Intellectual Disabilities?

Sadie Young

More than four decades have passed since the initiation of 'care in the community' and the associated government programme that brought about the progressive closure of the institutional hospitals that historically provided the prime means of support for adults with intellectual disabilities. Subsequently, UK legislation and the policy of inclusion have further helped to educate society and better integrate this sector of the society into mainstream. Approximately 2 per cent of the population in the UK have an IQ below 70 and are so are considered to have cognitive functioning within the range of learning disability. A further 7 per cent has learning difficulties, defined as having an IQ below 80. Of course, not all people with intellectual disability will become parents, but since the late 1980s the numbers have gradually increased, and parenthood is no longer the exception but a general rule for those who are able to form adult relationships.

The role of parent places demands upon anyone's coping abilities and this is especially true for a person with an intellectual disability. It is not unusual to encounter situations where concerns arise, and this has highlighted the need for significant ongoing support for these parents, although this can be difficult to secure. The adult learning disability team usually only become involved to support the individual rather than the family, and the children's social care service lacks the specialist knowledge concerning intellectual disability. To some extent this has meant that professional support in the UK continues to be reactive rather than proactive, and although specialist assessments have become more readily available in instances where child care proceedings are initiated, there is a lack of the long-term and preventative support that these families need (Tarleton, Ward and Howarth 2006). There remains a reluctance to develop specialist parenting support services and there is an expectation that the families adapt to mainstream provision, with the addition of some degree of specialist input. A support package is often put together that relies on disparate resources from adult and child services from both voluntary and state provision. This being the case it would be reassuring to believe that these parents also had access to supportive family networks on which they could rely. Extended family support is intuitively a positive option, but in practice the situation can be particularly complex for these parents.

In today's society, the definition of family is likely to produce a variety of responses that originate primarily from personal experience, with the romantic ideal being rooted in the cultural discourse of the eighteenth century. Bailey (2012) suggests that the memories of childhood and the process of describing parental qualities helped individuals to formulate their familial and personal identities in terms of social status, moral value and personal worth; they helped to develop a sense of self and self-esteem. This still holds true today in that we are all to some extent the product of our socialisation and our parental relationships, and familial ties can impact upon us throughout our lives. So how important are family ties and the associated support to someone with intellectual disability? It is helpful to begin by considering how a parent with intellectual disability copes first with the demands of wider society.

Wider social issues

Following the introduction of an educational inclusion policy it has become the norm for a person with intellectual disability to progress through a school career that emphasises and encourages independence. Legislation concerning human rights has created a positive expectation and belief that everyone should be supported to follow their chosen path in life and be given the opportunity to succeed. Consequently, young people with intellectual disability often pursue the goal of parenthood fuelled by their natural desire to start a family and to further normalise their position in society. The pathway to parenthood commonly begins shortly after leaving school or college when the young person is in their late teens or early twenties. As a rule, professionals frequently become involved during the pregnancy, and where concerns exist assessments take place. If the assessment has a positive outcome the relevant services become involved and provide the identified level of assistance; that may involve housing, practical support and education. If the assessment has a negative outcome and concerns persist, legal proceedings commence and arrangements are made for the children's long-term care to be met elsewhere. Research shows that there is a risk greater than for any other group that the children of parents with intellectual disabilities may be removed by the child welfare authorities (Booth, McConnell and Booth 2006).

It is known that due to the social status of parents with intellectual disability they are more likely than other parents to be living in socially disadvantaged circumstances (SCARE 2005). They have to encounter wider social problems such as poverty, debt and poor housing, which adversely affect their ability to parent to the best of their ability. Furthermore, due to the vulnerability of this group they are frequently exposed to paedophilia, sexual abuse and domestic violence. People with intellectual disability are often seen by perpetrators as easy victims (Beail and Warden 1995) and it is not uncommon to find that they have inappropriate social and family networks, making it impossible to consider members of their family as a means of support. In fact, in some instances the children are removed because the parents are unable to provide a protective environment for them away from their family group.

Left to their own devices it can prove difficult for someone with intellectual disability to cope with what might be considered by others as straightforward responsibilities such as attending their children's medical appointments, organising household chores or paying bills. They require prompting, guidance and someone who can help them with tasks requiring basic literacy skills. This is not always readily available and they have to rely on others much more than the average parent and this can raise anxiety and promote covert behaviour, as they are aware from the outset that their parenting is being closely scrutinised. Furthermore, because of the nature of their condition a person with intellectual disability tends to perceive their experiences in a concrete and superficial way, as they lack the insight to attain a deep understanding. This means that they can easily become confused or anxious about a situation and this is further exacerbated by their poor communication skills.

It is acknowledged that the ability to communicate is central to social functioning. The more able we are to understand others and to express ourselves the more socially successful we are likely to be, but when a person is intellectually disabled communication is seldom a strength. Communication has implications from birth and in some instances can affect the bonding between parent and child. As the child with intellectual disability develops, their spoken language is frequently delayed and their literacy skills often follow a similar path. In adulthood there may be a discrepancy between verbal skill and comprehension and this can lead others to believe the person has a greater understanding than is actually the case, or conversely that they don't understand when they actually do. The lack of ability to express emotion verbally can also have an impact on social relationships in that it can result in frustration and what might be perceived as uncooperative or antagonistic behaviour. This tendency to be misinterpreted by others can have profound effects on social relationships and can lead to the development of an inappropriate social network as a means of attempting to cope with life's problems.

Communication is also essential to learning so another core issue for this group is the acquisition of knowledge. Parents with intellectual disability, like all new parents, need to learn how to care for their child. Most young parents will gain some understanding from the way they themselves have been parented, but this can only be helpful when they have experienced good parental role models and this is not always the case for parents with intellectual disability. Although a small proportion of this population do receive good quality ongoing support from family members it is more common for them to receive no support at all. The reasons for this situation are complex so it is helpful to consider the types of familial relationships that emerge from both research and clinical experience.

No family support

The most commonly encountered situation for parents with intellectual disability is one where they have little or no support from the grandparents or other members of their extended family. Frequently, parents with intellectual disability seem to be wholly reliant on professional and voluntary support, and although it may be counter to the norm, it is not unusual to find a couple living in isolation from their families. Typically, parents with intellectual disabilities receive only limited social support from their family, friends or the community (McConnell, Llewellyn and Ferronato 2006) and given their restricted coping abilities they present as vulnerable adults within the wider society.

One reason for this may be due, in part, to their familial history as when intellectual disability occurs it may be the result of inherited cognitive deficits that present intergenerationally. This being the case many parents with intellectual disability have parents who also have some degree of intellectual disability. Behaviour-genetic studies show that general cognitive ability, typically indexed by a total score on a standardised IQ assessment, is approximately 50 per cent heritable (Plomin 1999; Simonoff, Bolton and Rutter 1996). Furthermore, low cognitive functioning together with inadequate parenting prevent the formation of strong social bonds and potential family support.

Due to their own intellectual disability the grandparents may simply be unable to offer appropriate support and this may go some way to explain why children of parents with intellectual disabilities are over-represented in child welfare proceedings, representing 15–25 per cent of all children placed by the courts away from their family home. The first national survey of adults with 'learning difficulties' in England found that 48 per cent of the parents interviewed did not have care of their children (Emerson, Malam, Davies and Spencer 2005). Additionally, where there is inadequate parenting the children are likely to spend their childhoods away from their natural parents (Booth, McConnell and Booth 2006) and are raised elsewhere, further hindering the formation of close family ties. Given this complex situation there is frequently a combination of risk to the child presented by the wider family coupled with an inability by the parents to protect their child. This can result in some instances in a need physically to avoid family members. A situation of no support can also occur when the grandparents or extended family members do not have intellectual disability themselves but find it hard to accept that their child with intellectual disability is capable of parenthood. They may feel that they are unable to offer the degree of long-term support necessary to support their child or to offer a kinship placement to their grandchildren; rather they protect themselves by choosing not to get involved. In doing so they avoid the emotional distress that they feel is inevitable, given the perceived probability that the children will ultimately be removed into care.

Regular family contact

Another dynamic that may emerge for the parent with intellectual disability is where they live separate from, but are significantly involved with, members of their extended family including grandparents, aunts, uncles and siblings who all provide a means of regular support. They rely on their wide family network to provide a readily available social resource, but this can have both positive and negative effects on their ability to parent successfully. From a positive perspective where the grandparent or family member provides a good role model they are an invaluable means of support with regular home visits, advice and child-minding. They help to develop the parent's knowledge, self-esteem and sense of security and if things do go wrong the relatives are often able and willing to step in and, if necessary, provide a potential kinship placement. However, in some instances where the extended family is willing to offer support it may not always be an appropriate source. As discussed previously where there is intergenerational intellectual disability the whole family may be vulnerable to inappropriate relationships and this can prevent it from even being considered as alternative permanent carers. If the situation raises safety concerns it can mean that the parents need to sever family ties for the sake of their children, and this can happen at a time when they are most in need of close support.

Kinship care

For the reasons that have already been discussed, kinship care is not a straightforward matter for parents with intellectual disability, but it would nevertheless seem to be an alternative that is well worth consideration. The option of remaining within a family group for a child helps to secure their identity, enhances self-esteem and provides them with a sense of belonging. Also, it should not be overlooked that despite the problems in identifying suitable kinship carers for this group, there remains a number of families where the grandparents, a close relative or family friend successfully provide care within the extended family.

From clinical experience there are two situations that are most commonly encountered where a kinship placement would be appropriate. The first type is where the parents with learning disability have lived independently with their children for several years before concerns arise about their ability to care. These concerns may have arisen for such reasons as a breakdown in their parental relationship or an increase in family size placing further pressure on their ability to cope. Where family ties have been maintained and the children are integrated a kinship placement is clearly preferable to a placement with strangers.

Another type of kinship placement that can emerge for this group is simply the continuity of an already existing domestic arrangement where all of the family share the same home and one or both parents have intellectual disability. In these cases the parents have never lived independently and have always relied upon the grandparents or other family members for support. In these instances the mother and baby, or both parents and their children, are able to live successfully with the grandparents or another extended family member. However, this type of family support is usually only sustainable in the short term as the situation can slowly deteriorate when the family grows in size and there is a need for increased space. Relationship problems are likely to emerge and there is often a blurring of household and child care responsibilities amongst the adults. It becomes increasingly likely that the parent or parents will move into their own accommodation and there is a natural assumption that the children will move with them. In such cases it would seem reasonable to take a proactive approach by considering a kinship placement for the children before the parents with intellectual disability move out into what may become an unsafe situation. Of course, it may be that once away from the grandparents' home the parents will succeed in providing adequate care for their children, but this is unlikely to happen without the appropriate support. Where an arrangement has been previously agreed it serves as an 'insurance policy' that can avoid further costly and stressful assessments of the situation, and is likely to result in far less disruption for all concerned. In instances where it becomes clear that the parents are unable to cope there can then be a smooth transition for the children from one carer to another within their family group.

Summary

Government policy and legislation since the 1970s has brought about progressive social change that has resulted in people with intellectual disabilities choosing to become parents. Unfortunately, the role of parent all too often proves to be challenging for them and this means that child protection concerns arise. As a result as many as 48 per cent of parents with intellectual disability who go through the child protection process lose the care of their children (Emerson, Malam, Davies and Spencer 2005).

One issue would appear to be that state social provision struggles to meet the long-term needs of families and child care professionals tend to adopt a reactive rather than proactive approach to support. Coupled with this, a person with intellectual disability is personally and socially disadvantaged from the outset in that they are likely to live under poor socio-economic conditions, they struggle with communication, and do not possess the basic coping skills that many of us take for granted.

It is argued that where parents with intellectual disability cannot parent their own child the extended family is best placed to offer the long-term care that would allow the children to develop a sense of belonging, self-esteem and personal identity. However, where the parent has an intellectual disability the situation is often complex and there are instances where to remain involved with the extended family could have negative effects on their ability to cope. Furthermore, there is a high probability that the grandparents, like their children, will have some degree of intellectual disability and this might raise questions concerning their suitability to provide a kinship placement. Where the whole family is socially vulnerable, consideration would need to be given to any possible links with inappropriate social networks, and they would need to be able to provide protection from the perpetrators of sexual abuse who view people with intellectual disability as easy targets.

There are many significant social and personal challenges that an adult with intellectual disability has to overcome in order to achieve parenthood, and the chances of success are more likely to be increased where they receive an appropriate level of support from the outset. This is not always readily available especially where the requirement develops into consistent and long-term support. Research shows that approximately half of those who become parents will lose their children through the care system. This figure is by any comparison excessive, but it would be naive to say that all that is needed is the right level of support. Sadly, it is the case that some parents with intellectual disability will simply be unable to cope without what equates to 24-hour supervision, and this would certainly have implications for the child's emotional development. Given these circumstances, it would seem that the better option would be to first consider the family as a potential support resource and, where appropriate, explore and promote the possibility of kinship care.

References

Bailey, J. (2012) *Parenting in England 1760–1830: Emotion, Identity and Generation.* Oxford: Oxford University Press.

Beail, N. and Warden, S. (1995) 'Sexual abuse of adults with learning disabilities.' *Journal of Intellectual Disability Research 39,* 382–7.

Booth, T., McConnell, D. and Booth, W. (2006) 'Temporal discrimination and parents with learning difficulties in the child protection system.' *British Journal of Social Work 36,* 997–1015.

Emerson, E., Malam, S., Davies, I. and Spencer, K. (2005) *Adults with Learning Difficulties in England 2003/4.* Leeds: Health and Social Care Information Centre.

McConnell, D., Llewellyn, G. and Ferronato, L. (2006) 'Context contingent decision-making in child protection practice.' *International Journal of Social Welfare 15,* 230–239.

Plomin, R. (1999) 'Genetics and general cognitive ability.' *Nature 402,* C25–C29.

SCARE (2005) *Helping Parents with Learning Disabilities in their Role as Parents.* London: Social Care Institute for Excellence.

Simonoff, E., Bolton, P. and Rutter, M. (1996) 'Mental retardation: genetic findings, clinical implications and research agenda.' *Journal of Child Psychology and Psychiatry 37,* 259–280.

Tarleton, B., Ward, L. and Howarth, J. (2006) *Finding the Right Support: A Review of Issues and Positive Practice in Supporting Parents with Learning Difficulties and their Children.* London: The Baring Foundation.

CHAPTER 3

Siblings and Kinship Care

David Pitcher, Sarah Meakings and Elaine Farmer

Sibling relationships permeate kinship care, yet they are rarely mentioned explicitly in the literature. However, as we get close to families, their importance becomes more apparent. Sibling relationships can occur in each generation in kinship care:

- A child may be cared for by an older brother or sister.

- Adult siblings may become the kin carer for a nephew or niece, that is the children of their own adult sibling.

- A child may be placed into a family in which there are already children, and so needs to develop a sibling-type relationship with the existing children, to whom he or she is already related.

- The relationships between children and their siblings have to be managed within kinship care, whether they are placed together or are apart and need contact.

In this chapter, we will attempt to look at the way in which sibling relationships shape kinship placements. We begin with an overview of the existing literature on siblings, and then look at some of the situations involving siblings that have arisen as part of a large study of children's views of growing up in informal kinship care (Selwyn, Farmer, Meakings and Vaisey 2013). We shall then see whether the literature can help us better to understand this central aspect of kinship care; and whether the particular situation of kinship care can in turn add perspective to the literature.

An overview of the literature on siblings

The sibling relationship, especially as described in the psychoanalytic literature, is one of intense yet ambivalent emotions which, within the intimacy of the family, takes on a raw and primitive quality

(Oberndorf 1929; Pfouts 1976). Alfred Adler (1938) talks of the arrival of a younger sibling as a 'dethronement'. It has also been described as a 'shock' or 'trauma' (Mitchell 2003, 2006) which can have lifelong effects, especially if not managed sensitively by the parents (Dunn and Kendrick 1982). There is no room here for sentimentality as a child faces another younger child who represents, at the deepest level, both belonging and the possibility of rejection. Jealousy and betrayal mingle with loyalty and devotion in a way that is curiously sustaining: 'those who are bound by blood and battle have close, quick bonds' (Perlman, 1967, p.148). In the early years especially, a sibling relationship can overshadow even a parental relationship and 'almost literally represents all the world to [the child]' (Oberndorf 1929, p.1014).

Perhaps the most commonly used word in describing siblings is 'rivalry'. Originally, *rivalis* means someone who shares rights to the same stream (in Latin, *rivus*). This illustrates perfectly the combination of competition for the same, perhaps scarce, resources; yet also the same shared situation, demanding cooperation. A sibling relationship is not one that has been chosen, and is one that never goes away. It may also be longer lasting than the relationship with parents, a spouse or even children. Siblings, in a way that no one else can ever be, are 'fellow inheritors of the legacy' (Silverstone 2006, p.235).

Linked with this, it is significant that unlike relationships with parents, partners or employees, there are no socially prescribed rules or rituals surrounding sibling relationships and no social expectations that they should be harmonious (Bank and Kahn 1982). Indeed, such rules as there are tend to be contradictory, such as 'Be close, but not too close…co-operative yet not dependent' (Bank and Kahn 1982, p.11). This has the effect of increasing any confusion and ambivalence within the family. Coupled with the psychological power of the sibling bond as described above, this can make for a potent combination.

Elspeth Morley (2006, p.198) uses the analogy of a staircase to describe the ways in which sibling relationships are qualitatively different from parental relationships. Just as a staircase has both a *lateral* tread and a *vertical* strut, ascending in a continuous manner, so a child's relationships are of two distinct types. 'Vertical' relationships, up the generations, are those which involve parenting, such as care and discipline. The central dilemma for 'horizontal' relationships, which include those between couples, peers and siblings, is 'we are the same but different'. A developing child needs to work this out within a 'social laboratory' (Bank and Kahn 1982, p.199) that is at once intense, ambivalent, has no clear guidance and is impossible to avoid.

When sibling relationships function well, patterns develop whereby the most negative feelings are able to be avoided. There may, for example, be a pattern of rapid shifts of status or alliance (Einstein and Moss 1967) so that no single sibling is 'on top' all the time. Or, siblings may occupy different niches (for example, develop different interests) to minimise competition. In more dysfunctional relationships, patterns of dominance and rivalry become stuck and fixed: reciprocal feelings of concern become fixed 'care-giving'; rivalry becomes aggression; loyalty comes to mean survival. In these situations, mutual feelings are likely to become more intense.

Bank and Kahn describe the sibling relationship not as one bond, but as consisting of 'multiple bonds...a fitting together of two people's identities' (Bank and Kahn 1982, p.15). Those with a number of bonds, such as sharing the same experience of parenting, the same school, similar life events, the same gender and who are close in age, can be described as 'high access' siblings (Koch 1960). This helps to differentiate levels of sibling connection, something that is important for social workers and others in considering whether siblings should be placed together if removed from home. Although arguably all sibling relationships are significant, not all sibling relationships are of equal significance. The concept of multiple bonds is also helpful in recognising that there are some sibling-like relationships (such as step-siblings or foster-siblings) whose importance is too often undervalued by adults (Pitcher 2011).

The literature (Timberlake and Hamlin 1982) suggests that those looking at sibling relationships from the outside, including parents and grandparents, tend not to see what is going on. Siblings have their own codes and rituals. There is a tendency to dismiss their significance, sometimes by lumping 'the kids' together and taking their relationship for granted. Parents can feel sentimental about sibling relationships, or they can simplify or idealise them. It may be emotionally uncomfortable to keep in mind the intensity and complexity of relationships between siblings. However, researchers have been drawn to a number of themes. These include the following:

- *The significance of ordinal position*: Earlier researchers, notably Alfred Adler (1938) was interested in the effect that age position has in determining character. For example, it was thought that the oldest child might tend to be somewhat conservative and an organiser; a middle child has to learn to cooperate and also strives to achieve; while the youngest may have the space to develop their own abilities but may be something of a complainer.

- *The extent and direction of mutual influence.* This has been subject to careful observation, and Abramovitch, Corter and Lando (1979) have shown how a younger child may influence an older child, as well as the other way round. Studies have also looked at the effect of having a disabled sibling (Stoneman and Berman 1993).

- *How sibling relationships change in the light of children's developmental stages.* This encompasses from the time before the arrival of a younger sibling to older adulthood (Cicirelli 1995). There is also a small literature looking at sibling bereavement, the significance of which is often relatively unacknowledged by others (DeVita-Raeburn 2004).

- *How the nature of sibling relationships is constructed by social processes (Edwards, Hadfield, Lucey and Mauthner 2006).* This includes such feelings as responsibility, cooperation or a younger child's sense of entitlement to protection from an older sibling.

- *How parental behaviour and attitudes may shape sibling relationships.* Parents can give subtle messages that condition the development of the relationship. A good example of this is the process described by Frances Schachter (Schachter *et al.* 1976) as 'de-identification', whereby differences are simplified and magnified, such as 'he is the sporty one, she is the studious one', and so on. The effect of being defined in comparison with a sibling can have a lasting effect on a person's self-concept.

In terms of substitute care, a valuable literature has grown up looking at issues to be considered in deciding whether siblings who are being fostered or adopted should be placed together or apart (e.g. Lord and Borthwick 2008). There is also important evidence, from the earliest research on foster care onwards, that placing a child too close in age to the siblings in a foster family (or where the foster carers' children are under five) may lead to placement breakdown (see e.g. Cautley 1980; Parker 1966). Indeed, studies continue to show that a key reason for foster care breakdowns is that the fostered child has a negative impact on the siblings already in the family (see e.g. Farmer, Moyers and Lipscombe 2004; Sinclair 2005). A less often noted finding is the obverse: older siblings in foster families are sometimes key supports for the foster carers in looking after a fostered child, for example, by acting as the child's confidante, looking out for the child in school and modelling pro-social behaviour (Farmer *et al.* 2004). However, there may be a considerable impact on 'children who foster', for example if they lose out on their parents' attention, are exposed prematurely to knowledge about child sexual abuse or need to deal with sequential loss as fostered children leave the family. There is increasing research interest in the impact that fostering has on the children of foster carers (see e.g. Part 1993; The Fostering Network 2008; Twigg 1994; Twigg and Swan 2007). No such attention has yet been paid to the children of kinship carers.

In a similar way, the literature on siblings who care for siblings is scanty. This theme brings together all the various strands of understanding as well as the difference (and possible confusion) between 'vertical' and 'horizontal' relationships. When a sibling caring for a sibling makes an appearance in the literature, it is usually in the context of young children whose parents are not wholly absent, but may be emotionally absent (Silverstone 2006), or where a busy mother delegates her caring role to a daughter. In a moving historical study of adult psychotherapy clients who had been either sibling carers and/or been cared for by an older sibling, Eunice Pollack (2002) chronicles the negative consequences for the 'little mothers' and their 'charges', of a role they had no choice but to accept. The children in this study had grown up in large working or lower middle class families between 1895 and 1940 where babies and young children were often brought up by their older sisters. Some of Pollack's findings, which confirmed those of others (Rosenbaum 1963; Welins 1964), were that:

- both the caring and cared for siblings felt that the mother was insufficiently accessible, and longed for her attention

- the 'little mothers' showed a premature sense of independence which concealed their neediness and fear

- the caring siblings showed ambivalence or hostility towards their younger siblings, swinging from extremes of benevolence to cruelty. Supposed 'discipline' often masked coercion and hostility, born of resentment of their role. They were unable to be a real parent, 'unable to give what they had never received'

- the experience of caring affected their attitude towards later parenthood, either feeling the need to become parents or else fearing having their own children. It also negatively affected the relationships between the siblings in adulthood.

The study found that the 'sibling' elements of rivalry were always present, and were in fact intensified by this pseudo-parental relationship.

Kluger (2012) sees things in a more positive light. He looks at a study of Chinese American adolescents (Juang and Cookston 2009), whose traditional patterns of family life were in contrast to norms in their new society, and suggests that in cultures in which so-called 'alloparenting' between siblings is the norm, it can serve to increase a sense of self-esteem and enable the learning of important life skills in older siblings and can protect against depression. He suggests that the Western model of family life, in which there is a clear differentiation of role between parents and children, has had a 'levelling effect on power relationships among siblings' (p.121), making it harder for siblings to become effective carers, should that become necessary.

These studies provide an important understanding, but the findings are not necessarily directly transferable to situations in which adult siblings take the decision to care for a younger sibling because of parental absence or death.

In a recent study by the Family Rights Group, *Big Bruv, Little Sis* (Roth, Lindley and Ashley 2011) interviews were conducted with 12 adult sibling carers, as well as obtaining views from the Family Rights Group's electronic discussion board. Although this was a small sample, the findings tie in with practice experience. The situations they looked at were very varied, from two brothers living together aged 16 and 22 to a family arrangement which was very close to foster care. The average age gap was 14.9 years, and the most common reason for the need for care was the death of a parent, followed by a parent's use of alcohol, parental mental illness and domestic violence. Among the most significant findings of the study were the following:

- Most had been taking a lot of responsibility for their younger siblings well before becoming their full-time carer.

- Sibling carers met with little understanding from employers or social workers. Schools tended to be more supportive.

- Housing was often cramped, financial resources limited and family relationships stressful.

- The nature of the sibling relationship had to undergo changes, for example as the need for discipline arose.

We now move from this brief survey of the literature to consider some of the contemporary situations encountered in a recent piece of research. This two phase study of informal kinship care was undertaken by the University of Bristol, in partnership with the children's charity Buttle UK, and was funded by the Big Lottery. In the first phase, restricted access micro-data from the UK Population Census were re-analysed to estimate the extent of kinship care in the UK in 2001 and to describe the characteristics of the kinship carers and children (Nandy, Selwyn, Farmer and Vaisey 2011). In the second stage, *The Poor Relations? Children and Informal Kinship Carers Speak Out* (Selwyn *et al.* 2013), 80 children aged 8 to 18 across the UK were interviewed. Using a multi-method approach, the researchers considered from the children's perspectives what it was like growing up with relatives or friends in informal kinship care and assessed the children's and carers' wellbeing on a range of measures. The views and experiences of the 80 kin carers bringing up these children were also explored. The definition of informal kinship care in this second part of the study was that the kinship carer was bringing up a child who was not a looked after child and the carer had not been approved as a kinship foster carer. This group of kinship carers was not generally in contact with children's services.

The study did not set out to look specifically at sibling relationships in kinship care but, as we have suggested, it was inevitable that sibling relationships would figure largely in the accounts of the children, young people and kinship carers who were interviewed.

Situations within kinship care involving siblings

Siblings placed together or apart

It has been argued that kinship care arrangements are beneficial in that they enable children to remain living with their siblings more often than is the case for children fostered by strangers (see e.g. Shlonsky and Berwick 2001). Indeed, children in the study who moved to kinship care accompanied by their sibling/s, said that this had made their transition easier.

However, in this study we found that many of the kinship children were in fact separated from siblings, particularly when families were large. Of the 52 children who had been living at home with brothers or sisters, more than half (54 per cent) were separated from at least one sibling at the time of the move into kinship care. Separated siblings stayed with a parent or went to live with other relatives or entered care (or a combination of these). In a few cases older siblings became independent earlier than planned. Half-siblings were sometimes separated when a family member chose to take only the child to whom they were biologically related.

The kinship children often described their difficulties in coming to terms with living apart from siblings and this was especially painful when one or more siblings had remained with a parent. Occasionally children were worried about the welfare of brothers or sisters they had left behind in the care of abusive or neglectful parents, but more often they were troubled by the preferential rejection shown by their parents (Rushton and Dance 2003). Some children wondered what it was about *them* that had led to a parent not wanting them or abandoning them and they did not know why it was that a parent could care for some of their children but not others:

Case study: Max

Max, aged 10, moved in with his aunt having been exposed to neglect and indifference by his drug using parents. He remained living in the same neighbourhood as his mother, who was bringing up his younger brother and sister. Max saw his mother every school day in the playground collecting his siblings. Sometimes she would ignore him, but at other times she would chat. Max told us that he found the situation 'hard…because I see my mum picking (siblings) up (from school) and I think why couldn't that be me?'

Children told us that they were concerned about maintaining links with siblings who lived elsewhere and some worried about the impact of the separation on their long-term relationships with them. Typical worries included:

'When William gets adopted he won't want to be my brother any more.'

'Never getting to see my brother again.'

'Are my sister and me going to be together and keep contact when older?'

Pseudo-sibling relationships

Kinship placements are distinctive because children join families where they are related to the other children. For example, the children of grandparent carers (other than the child's parent) will be aunts and uncles to a kinship child, while the children of aunt and uncle kin carers will be cousins. The arrival of a kinship child in a family requires existing members to re-negotiate their roles. The original relationship between the carer's children and the kinship child has to change to become more 'sibling' like, as they usually spend large amounts of time together and call on the shared resources of the carer. Moreover, the kinship child may take another child's position, for example by becoming the oldest child in the family.

These pseudo-sibling relationships were often apparent in the study, particularly between cousins, with some carers describing their own children and the kinship children as like brothers and sisters. However, unsurprisingly, some of these relationship were more harmonious than others and while a number of children had developed close and affectionate bonds (such as that between a kinship child and her slightly younger cousin who had '*always wanted a sister*'), other children formed more troubled relationships, occasionally characterised by resentment and jealousy.

The arrival of a child with serious emotional and/or behavioural difficulties put added strain on relationships and in these instances carers often reported that their own children resented the extra attention shown to the kinship child, especially if this had the effect of displacing the carers' children.

Case study: Joanna

Joanna moved in with her aunt and uncle after her mother, who had mental health difficulties, was unable to care for her. She was extremely violent and abusive and had no empathy or interest in other people's feelings. Her carers could only just about manage her. The impact on others in the family was huge and the carers recognised that their own children's needs had been sidelined in the course of bringing up their very troubled niece. Their children complained about the lack of attention they were shown and accused their parents of showing favouritism towards the kinship child who they referred to as 'Mum's golden girl'. The carers wondered whether the serious mental health problems one of their sons developed in early adulthood was linked to their family situation.

In a rather different way, in a few cases the parents of children in kinship care developed relationships with their children that were akin to those of older siblings, rather than parents. In one such case a father, whose son was cared for by his grandmother (the father's mother), developed a rivalrous sibling-like relationship with his own son. He was jealous if the grandmother bought anything for his son, demanding to know what she had bought for him. It was not uncommon too for children to describe contact with their mothers as being like seeing an older sister.

Caring for a sibling's child

An uncle or aunt who becomes a kinship carer is, of course, caring for the child of his or her sibling. In this study, these carers were of two types. In the first, the parent had died. Before their death some had asked a brother or sister to bring up their child. These carers often expressed a prevailing sense of sadness – they not only faced the challenge of supporting a bereaved child, but having lost their sibling, were dealing too with their own personal grief:

> I mean I have days where I cry…I'm quite honest with (the children) and I say I miss your mum…you know, she's my big sister, she was my best friend… It feels like someone's gripping my stomach and twisting it because I don't know how…I'm going to cope. (Aunt bringing up sister's children)

The second type was carers whose brother or sister had abused or neglected their own child. This situation troubled some carers so much that their relationship with their adult sibling was severely impaired:

> I've always said to hate somebody you've got to have feelings, I don't have any feelings (for my brother), there's no association there because of what he put Josie through. Hate is a strong word and

to hate someone, there has to be feelings there and I don't, I have nothing towards him. (Aunt bringing up brother's child)

The issue of maintaining boundaries with the children's parents, where necessary, could be difficult for aunt or uncle carers, who as siblings, had never been in a relationship of authority over their brothers or sisters, especially if they were younger than them. Conflict over parenting matters sometimes occurred and there were instances of carers being physically assaulted by their adult sibling. Severing contact was one way of enforcing this boundary, but could bring problems. When one sibling became the rescuer and the other the irresponsible one, their differences were further reinforced, particularly in the minds of the siblings' parents.

Siblings caring for siblings

The first part of the study which was a re-analysis of the 1991 census data 'Spotlight on Kinship Care' (Nandy, Selwyn, Farmer and Vaisey 2011), showed to our surprise that the second largest group of kinship carers in the UK are siblings (38 per cent), that is households where a sibling was the only adult in residence. It also showed that sibling carers experience particularly high levels of poverty.

In the second part of the study (Selwyn et al. 2013), in five families siblings were caring full time for younger siblings. The age difference between the sibling carer and the oldest child being cared for was from 4 to 12 years. In some instances the carer had been the 'parental child' in the family who took responsibility for their siblings because a parent was not doing so. When the parent died or deserted the children, this older sibling often felt a strong sense of duty to look after the children. In other families, when a parent died, the oldest sibling could see that he or she was in the front line to care for the younger children when no other relatives came forward to provide assistance.

All the sibling carers had made major sacrifices and lost life opportunities in order to bring up their younger siblings:

My whole life just suddenly turned upside down, I'd suddenly got this seven year old that's my responsibility. I was planning on going to university and getting a good career, and I was going to study zoology, and go off and travel the world and that's not happened. (Sibling carer bringing up sisters)

> It's just been a massive impact on me. I feel like I've missed out a lot. He's been such a huge responsibility and it has caused some of my problem by loss of confidence… A lot of my friends in sixth form they actually like stopped talking to me. I did lose a lot of friends. (Sibling carer bringing up brother)

In addition, sometimes, these young kinship carers felt they were not accorded proper respect or recognition by agencies such as the school or the local authority (see also Roth, Lindley and Ashley 2011). People who they met sometimes assumed that they were very young parents – or as one put it 'gym slip mothers' which they saw as an insult – or else that they were 'not proper parents' because of their age. One of the sibling carers responded to the challenge of parenting by embracing an authoritarian role, with clear rules and expectations written up on a board. Another managed to maintain something of her 'sisterly' relationship. All the carers were grappling with the question 'How can I be both a parent and a sibling?' and 'What kind of life is left for me?'

There was no evidence from this study of sibling rivalry, such as is described in the literature, but there was a feeling amongst some sibling carers of deep resentment about their situation. They recognised, however, that the situation that had led to the children moving in with them was not the fault of their younger siblings and that they had chosen to take on their care, in spite of the consequences for them:

> If I'm honest I didn't resent them but I resented my situation, I felt really, really trapped. And I've kind of felt like my life was over. (Sibling bringing up sister and brother)

Some sibling carers spoke movingly about their motivation to improve the life chances of their brothers or sisters and were determined that the children would have a better childhood than they had had:

> My mum was dabbling in drugs and I had a bad childhood with drugs and alcohol and witnessing all this…so when I took charge of (my sister) I was like, I'm going to give her a better life than I had, because my whole childhood was being neglected, because both my parents were too self-obsessed with drugs and themselves. And so I've always given her the best and do the best for her. (Sibling bringing up sister)

While carers wanted to ensure that the deprivations from the past and present were not felt by the siblings they were bringing up, the feeling of missing out themselves and the strains of managing on low incomes were very great. It emerged that all of the sibling carers in the study scored in the clinical range for depression on the measure we used.

Managing competing demands

There were a number of families in which perceived inequality between siblings at various points on the generational ladder caused difficulties. Tensions were particularly evident between adult siblings, when their parent was bringing up a grandchild. In one instance, for example, a grandparent caring for her daughter's son was bitterly criticised by her own adult son, who believed that his children were missing out on grandparental contact and was angry at his sister for not parenting her own child.

Discussion and ideas for practice

The data from *The Poor Relations? Children and Informal Kinship Carers Speak Out* (Selwyn *et al.* 2013) cannot be an exhaustive account of all possible permutations of sibling relationships, but it has the advantage of being up to date and in-depth. It also accords with our casework experience. What, then, can we say about sibling relationships in kinship care by bringing the literature to bear on the research material, and the research material on the literature?

First, it is clear that sibling relationships are powerful throughout the life cycle, and they work in ways that are often not immediately recognised or visible. Whether considering a new kinship placement, or working with an existing one, it is important to try to identify the various pressure points at which the influence of sibling relationships is felt. These relationships may well not be comfortable and there may be attempts to minimise difficulties; but they should be examined closely. It is true that siblings can represent a calm, reassuring presence for each other and many studies show that children have better outcomes when they enter care or return to parents with siblings. But it is too easy to lapse into comfortable or clichéd views about siblings, and to miss the element that can 'displace and dislodge a person from who and where they thought they were' (Mitchell 2003, p.205). One of the main aims of this chapter is to suggest how sibling relationships can be seen at work in every generation in a kinship placement. Despite the overuse of the word 'rival', the concept of competing and at the same time cooperating for the same resources is a meaningful one. The distinction between lateral and vertical relationships, with their separate functions, is also important, and easy to miss in some families.

Second, sibling relationships are not all the same, and it is important to identify the various strands that make up the connection. At the same time, no sibling relationship is unimportant – whether this is a biological relationship, which causes a child to worry that her sibling who is being placed for adoption 'won't want to be my brother any more' – or whether it is a fraternal or social bond that has been built up through long days spent together, where the lack of blood connection may make it invisible to others.

Third, an appreciation of sibling relationships is central in understanding and helping a family to understand the complex process of realignment that takes place when a kinship placement is made. Cousins become 'siblings'; a mother or father can become like a sibling when they are no longer the carers; a sibling can take the parental role. The distinctive sibling dynamics may then come into play. This may be compounded by shared loss, and will not take place without some resistance and resentment, even if it is not acknowledged.

Finally, it has to be stated that overall the care of children by their own siblings carries considerable additional difficulties, especially for the sibling carers who are often very poor, live in overcrowded conditions and have to forego further education and employment possibilities as well as compromised social lives. There needs to be much more assistance for them and recognition of their contribution as carers when they may be only just beyond childhood themselves.

Conclusions

This chapter is an exploratory treatment of a subject that merits much fuller research. Each of the four areas highlighted requires further qualitative studies. In particular, it would be useful to understand the following:

- How do children who are already related join to form a new sibling group, and how can this be assisted?

- What are the varied situations of siblings who care for their younger siblings and how might this vary by ethnicity (Nandy et al. 2011)? In addition, there needs to be more understanding of the psychological issues involved. The implications of a sibling's expectation to care beyond childhood – for example so-called 'post parental care' of older adults with disabilities – has also not been properly investigated (Dew, Llewellyn and Balandin 2004).

- What are the different expectations of a sibling's obligations and relatedness in some non-Western cultures? It would be interesting to see how this affects the experience of caring both within these cultures, and when it occurs within a dominant surrounding culture, such as a Western welfare system. For example, in one case in which one of the authors worked as a social worker, a young refugee was being cared for by an older male sibling who was only just into adulthood. He had promised their parents, who were possibly now dead, that he would look after his brother. The local authority found it impossible to 'approve' this sibling as a carer using its procedures, but the child would accept no other care.

Such research would have the benefit of addressing themes that are never likely to lose their relevance. Tales of love and hate between brother and brother, sister and sister, and between half or step-siblings have appeared in myth, drama and literature from the earliest times and are still front page news (see, for example, Jenkins 2010). As one sibling carer, bringing up her sister after their mother's sudden death poignantly remarked:

> I felt a little bit angry at my mum for leaving me in this situation, but I wouldn't have it any other way, I wouldn't want anyone else looking after my sister.

References

Abramovitch, R., Corter, C. and Lando, B. (1979) 'Sibling interaction in the home.' *Child Development 50*, 997–1003.

Adler, A. (1938) 'Socially Obstructive Situations and their Removal.' In *Social Interest: A Challenge to Mankind*. London: Faber and Faber.

Bank, S.P. and Kahn, M.D. (1982) *The Sibling Bond*. New York: Basic Books.

Cautley, P.W. (1980) *New Foster Parents: The First Experience*. New York: Human Services Press.

Cicirelli, V.G. (1995) *Sibling Relationships Across the Lifespan*. New York and London: Plenum Press.

DeVita-Raeburn, E. (2004) *The Empty Room: Surviving the Loss of a Brother or Sister at Any Age.* New York: Scribner.

Dew, A., Llewellyn, G. and Balandin, S. (2004) 'Post-parental care: a new generation of sibling carers.' *Journal of Intellectual and Developmental Disability 29,* 2, 176–179.

Dunn, J. and Kendrick, C. (1982) *Siblings: Love, Envy and Understanding.* Cambridge, MA: Harvard University Press.

Edwards, R., Hadfield, L., Lucey, H. and Mauthner, M. (2006) *Sibling Identity and Relationships: Sisters and Brothers.* London and New York: Routledge.

Einstein, G. and Moss, M.S. (1967) 'Some thoughts on sibling relationships.' *Social Casework* November, 549–555.

Farmer E., Moyers S. and Lipscombe J. (2004) *Fostering Adolescents.* London: Jessica Kingsley Publishers.

Jenkins, A. (2010) 'Don't be fooled when siblings talk about being friends.' *The Independent,* Saturday 25 September.

Juang, L.P. and Cookston, J.T. (2009) 'A Longitudinal Study of Family Obligation and Depressive Symptoms among Chinese American Adolescents.' *Journal of Family Psychology 25,* 3, 306–404.

Kluger, J. (2012) *The Sibling Effect: What the Bonds among Brothers and Sisters Reveal about Us.* New York: Riverhead Books.

Koch, H. (1960) 'The Relation of Certain Formal Attributes of Siblings to Attitudes Held toward each Other and toward their Parents.' *Monographs of the Society for Research in Child Development 25,* 1–124.

Lord, J. and Borthwick, S. (2008) *Together or Apart? Assessing Brothers and Sisters for Permanent Placement.* London: BAAF.

Mitchell, J. (2003) *Siblings: Sex and Violence.* Bristol: Polity Press.

Mitchell, J. (2006) 'Sibling Trauma: A Theoretical Consideration.' In P. Coles (ed.) *Sibling Relationships.* London: Karnac.

Morley, E. (2006) 'The Influence of Sibling Relationships on Couple Choice and Development.' In P. Coles (ed.) *Sibling Relationships.* London: Karnac.

Nandy, S., Selwyn, J., Farmer, E. and Vaisey, P. (2011) *Spotlight on Kinship Care: Using Census Microdata to Examine the Extent and Nature of Kinship Care in the UK at the Turn of the Twentieth Century.* Bristol: University of Bristol. Available at www. bristol. ac.uk/Hadley, accessed on 14 May 2012.

Oberndorf, C.P. (1929) 'Psychoanalysis of Siblings.' *American Journal of Psychiatry 85,* May, 1007–1020.

Parker, R. (1966) *Decisions in Child Care.* London: Allen and Unwin.

Part, D. (1993) 'Fostering as seen by the carers' children.' *Adoption and Fostering 17,* 1, 26–31.

Perlman, H.H. (1967) 'A note on siblings.' *American Journal of Orthopsychiatry 37,* January, 148.

Pfouts, J.H. (1976) 'The sibling relationship: a forgotten dimension.' *Social Work,* May, 200–204.

Pitcher, D. (2011) 'Brothers, sisters and contact.' *McKenzie: The National Magazine of Families Need Fathers 92,* Spring, 17.

Pollack, E.G. (2002) 'The childhood we have lost: when siblings were caregivers, 1900–1970.' *Journal of Social History 36*, 1, Fall, 31–61.

Rosenbaum, M. (1963) 'Psychological effects on the child raised by an older sibling.' *American Journal of Orthopsychiatry 33*, April, 515–520.

Roth, D., Lindley, B. and Ashley, C. (2011) *Big Bruv, Little Sis: Research Findings on Sibling Carers Raising their Younger Sisters and Brothers.* London: Family Rights Group.

Rushton, A. and Dance, C. (2003) 'Preferentially rejected children and their development in permanent family placements.' *Child and Family Social Work 8*, 257–267.

Schachter, F., Shore, E., Feldman-Rotman, S., Marquis, R. and Campbell, S. (1976) 'Sibling de-identification.' *Developmental Psychology 12*, 5, 418–427.

Selwyn J., Farmer E., Meakings S. and Vaisey P. (2013) *The Poor Relations? Children and Informal Kinship Carers Speak Out.* A Summary Research Report. Bristol: University of Bristol and Buttle UK.

Shlonsky, A.R. and Berrick, J.D. (2001) 'Assessing and promoting quality in kin and nonkin foster-care.' *Social Service Review* March, 60–83.

Silverstone, J. (2006) 'Siblings.' In P. Coles (ed.) *Sibling Relationships*. London: Karnac.

Sinclair, I. (2005) *Fostering Now: Messages from Research.* London: Jessica Kingsley Publishers.

Stoneman, Z. and Berman, P.W. (1993) *The Effects of Mental Retardation, Disability and Illness on Sibling Relationships.* Baltimore, CA: Paul H. Brookes Publishing Co.

The Fostering Network (2008) *Fostering Families: Supporting the Sons and Daughters of Foster Carers.* London: The Fostering Network.

Timberlake, E.M. and Hamlin, E.R.II (1982) 'The sibling group: a neglected dimension of placement.' *Child Welfare 61*, 8, 545–552.

Twigg, R. (1994) 'The unknown soldiers of foster care: foster care as a loss for the foster parents own children.' *Smith College Studies in Social Work 64*, 3, 297–313.

Twigg, R. and Swan, T. (2007) 'Inside the foster family: what research tells us about the experience of foster carers' children.' *Adoption and Fostering 31*, 4, 49–61.

Welins, E.G. (1964) 'Some effects of premature parental responsibility on the older sibling.' *Smith College Studies in Social Work 35*, 1, 28–40.

CHAPTER 4

The Position of Mothers when a Child is Placed with a Grandmother

Erica Flegg

The advocates of kinship care have put the case well for the benefits to children of remaining within the wider family if they have to be removed from their own parents' care for reasons of safety or welfare. However, this arrangement can also leave the child enmeshed in whatever negative family dynamics may have led to, or contributed to, the child being taken into care in the first place. In this chapter I would like to explore some of the issues arising in kinship care placements where a child is placed in the care of a maternal grandmother when there are child protection concerns about the mother's 'ability to protect'. It is my hope that if these issues are properly understood and anticipated by managers and case workers, plans can be made for therapeutic intervention to mitigate any negative effects. Such intervention has the potential not only to help the particular child or children deemed to be at risk but also to bring about positive change in the family system as a whole. By counteracting generational patterns that have harmed children in the past, there will be a benefit to all the children within the wider family.

I start by outlining some of the practice issues that arise, looking at the psychological processes involved for case workers, and go on to look at parent and family characteristics of the demographic groups of which they are a part (Bell 2006). I then consider the psychological processes within the family that are set off or reinforced by the kinship care arrangement, and their impact on the child. Next, I outline a method of working therapeutically with the mother and the family, and describe good practice pointers from this for caseworkers. I will be primarily looking at psychotherapeutic intervention with the mother to work for the rehabilitation of the child(ren) while they are placed in the care of the maternal grandmother. However, I also discuss issues arising in related contexts, such as when older children have been permanently placed with a grandparent, and the local authority becomes involved again when the parents have another child.

The experience on which this chapter is based is that I work as an expert risk assessor in family law cases where there are concerns about the safety and welfare of the child. I am also a psychotherapist who has developed a way of working with mothers (and sometimes both parents) to take into account the child protection concerns, in liaison with the local authority and preferably also the children's guardian. This way of working and its rationale have been described in detail elsewhere (Flegg and Bell 2008). In this chapter I will identify common themes that have arisen from my assessments and therapeutic work when working for change with the mother when her children are placed with her own mother, usually under an interim care order. Where I have undertaken the risk assessment of the mother (and sometimes both parents) I will normally have specified the necessary treatment targets in the recommendations. I have sometimes subsequently been instructed to carry out this treatment work, and this gives me a special insight into the ability of treatment intervention to improve safety in the family. It is vital that treatment is closely tied to the identified risks and that treatment progress is evaluated according to criteria agreed and understood between therapist/practitioner, social worker/referrer, and the client herself.

This is not a model of therapy that most people are used to: it is not confidential or open ended (see further below), and it is predicated on the needs of the child rather than the adult (although of course the two are closely related). This tends to be the first stumbling block in co-working cases with other professionals, as they can assume that the therapist is working for the mother and not the child. No doubt this unhelpful way of viewing the therapy is reinforced by our adversarial family law system (Waldegrave 2006) in which parents are pitted against the state and the Children's Guardian, who is the representative for the child within the legal process. Very few therapists have in fact been trained to see their role in terms of child protection when working with adults. This emerges as a particular problem when co-working cases with substance abuse agencies; for example I have heard a drugs worker argue that a mother should not have her children removed because it might drive her to suicide.

Living with uncertainty and agreeing behavioural indicators

When a local authority assesses a grandparent to care for a child, strengths and weaknesses will of course both be considered. However, in the kinship assessments I have seen in the course of my work, I notice a tendency for the authors to emphasise those aspects of a case in their reports that justify or evidence the position they have taken regarding the risk to which the child is likely to be exposed in the care of a given person (this is something we all tend to do in putting a case; but see also Calder on the dangers of workers starting with a hypothesis and then gathering evidence to support it, in his chapter on an evidence-based framework in Talbot and Calder 2006). In other words, when arguing against a kinship placement, the risks are emphasised, and when arguing in favour, the strengths. It is also fair to say that few assessors demonstrate expertise in risk assessment – in my experience, discussion of risk is often brief, superficial and imprecise, referring to problems in broad brush-strokes. This is not necessarily the fault of the assessor, who likely does not have specialist training in risk assessment methodology and who may otherwise show many insights about the family. However, this is the first likely area of weakness in the success of a kinship placement in reducing risk to the child: risk needs to be accurately assessed in the first place, and remedies carefully identified and implemented. Problems have sometimes arisen in my work where I have been brought in to undertake treatment in cases where the risk has not been subject to expert assessment; in those cases I have to develop treatment targets as I go, tailored to the emerging picture, which combine attitudes and current behaviour with 'static' factors, that is the behavioural history, which are essential for an accurate risk assessment. Often, casework is hampered by having inadequate collection of historical data, which needs to come from a number of different sources (Faust 2012; Skeem, Douglas and Lilienfield 2009).

In cases where the kinship placement has been approved, then the grandmother's role is seen positively. In the local authority's perspective, her strengths are maximised and her weaknesses minimised. The opposite tends to apply to the mother. The reason for the placement is the perceived deficit in her protectiveness, and, understandably, this tends to be the centre of the expressed child protection concern when the case is discussed. This sets up a dynamic within the case that can mirror established patterns within the family, but it also reinforces a tendency in the approach of caseworkers to try to avoid uncertainties in the management of risk (the avoidance of the anxieties aroused by uncertainty is a universal phenomenon; it is also discussed with reference to casework by Talbot and Calder 2006). Once the kinship placement has been defined as a place of safety, it allays anxieties on the part of those responsible for safety (the local authority) to see it in this perspective and to see the mother as the sole risk-poser. The alternative is to 'live with uncertainty' and take a more nuanced, shifting view (which the case might require, but which we tend to find more challenging to our need for order and reassurance). This tendency to 'split' ('good, safe kinship placement' versus 'bad, unsafe mother') becomes subject to radical reverses, whereby the kinship placement can also suddenly be perceived as 'bad' because of a development in the case, and the child may be removed into local authority foster care. Although this is a caricature, I have observed a reluctance on the part of caseworkers to consider and address risks to the child within the kinship placement once the child has been deemed to be safe enough there. I have also encountered a reluctance to take on board issues raised by the mother with the social worker regarding the welfare of the child in the placement.

Complaints by mothers about the placement (kinship or otherwise) are commonplace in my work. She feels threatened in her motherhood, she is likely to feel aggrieved about the process that led to their placement there, and she may well have hostile cognitions that contribute to this and which have also contributed to the risk to the children (because hostile people are more likely to become engaged in aggressive relationships with others, and to have a diminished social support network).

The way in which the mother communicates her complaint is likely to alienate others and make it less likely that her complaints will be heard and addressed. The hostile tendency is reinforced in the process. In my work I always encourage mothers to support the placement for the sake of the child, and also to improve her relationship with the social worker (without which cases are seldom successfully resolved; this working relationship also provides a test case of the mother's ability to improve her social and communication skills). Yet it is important that if she does raise concerning issues during the course of our work (treatment typically lasts six months of weekly sessions), she is supported to think about these in the light of her improving empathy for her child and increasing risk awareness. She then needs to be helped to demonstrate her therapeutic gains and child-centredness, as well as her new ability to communicate assertively (rather than aggressively), by raising the issues with the social worker – effective treatment evaluation means that clients need to demonstrate behavioural change that is measurable over time during the course of the therapy. When the mother does make this effort, however, I often find that she gets 'knocked back', as the social worker responds in a manner defensive of the placement, perhaps overly accustomed to the role of defending the placement from a hostile, complaining mother. Unfortunately, this reaction is antithetical to case progress and risks contributing to another process that can undermine the effectiveness of treatment, the social worker viewing the therapist as an advocate for the mother (while seeing him/herself as an advocate for the child, in line with the adversarial legal process mentioned earlier), and thereby pushing the therapist closer towards the risk of colluding with the client, as the therapist also experiences the social worker as prejudiced against the mother or not listening to her.

What I am looking for, then, when working a case, is for the social worker to be willing to live with the uncertainty about whether the mother will successfully complete the treatment, and to agree with me (and the children's guardian if possible) a list of behavioural indicators of change (specific rather than general) that the mother can work to demonstrate during the course of the treatment. Clients need encouragement and they need to know where the 'goalposts' are. They need to be able to fail and try again, learning in the process; they need positive reinforcement when they get it right. Sometimes, however, it emerges that other professionals do not genuinely believe that treatment has any real prospect of success (local authorities apparently sometimes pay for or contribute to the treatment for the sake of appearances in the family justice system: the mother has to be seen to be given 'a chance'). Such cases are easily spotted when the therapist asks: 'What does the mother need to show over the next six months to prove that she can keep her child safe at home? How can she do this?' to which the other professionals are unable to respond (or even say there is nothing she can do). Where the social worker does wish the treatment well, then, he or she can show this by taking seriously child protection issues raised by the mother about the child's safety and welfare in the placement.

Common generational factors in the failure to protect

A reason to be mindful of potential problems in a kinship placement where there are concerns about the mother's ability to protect is that such a parenting deficit is often generationally transmitted (Bell 2006, 2013). In my experience, many mothers whose children are removed because of safety concerns about domestic violence were themselves exposed to domestic violence as children. Quite often, they are the oldest daughter in a family where the maternal grandmother was herself a teenage mother in an abusive relationship (but who did better with her later children) or they are the least favoured child, or in some other way the 'black sheep' of the family. Family of origin factors are included in the risk indicators for compromised ability to protect in mothers (Bell 2013). A mother is at raised risk of failing to protect if she has a history of:

- attachment problems (parental separation; poor relationship with either parent, particularly her mother; loss of contact with a parent; poor relationship with a step-parent; being threatened with being put in care; being looked after; suffering from parental favouritism to siblings)

- maltreatment (including neglect; harsh parenting; physical, emotional or sexual abuse; bullying by siblings or at school/in the community)

- exposure to domestic violence

- conduct and/or adjustment problems (including school failure, truanting, bedwetting, emotional and behavioural problems, offending); sometimes these are more towards the offending end of the spectrum (raising risk of the mother being defiant and aggressive in later life) and sometimes more towards the poor adjustment end (raising risk of her lacking assertiveness and becoming a victim).

Because of her adverse experiences, the lack of parental empathy at the time and lack of help within or outside the family, a girl with such a history is more likely to present with behavioural problems both within the family and in the community, including at school. This means that her own mother will find her a less rewarding child, and may well, partly because of her own likely deficits as a parent because of the lack of nurturance she herself received as a child, blame her daughter for being 'difficult' (a common characteristic of families involved in the child protection process is a 'blaming' inter-personal way of relating and an externalising way of responding to problems: 'it's not my fault so it must be your fault'). When the girl's mother has a further child or children, this tendency is likely to be reinforced as maternal attention is diverted to the baby, the girl feels further deprived of understanding and support, and the younger sibling, having a better experience of maternal nurturance from a more mature mother, presents in a more rewarding manner and becomes a more favoured child. Both the older girl and her mother then become stuck in a 'vicious circle' of reproducing their own and each other's behaviour. Another possibility, based on my observations, is that the girl may be the product of a particularly unhappy and conflictual liaison with the father in a family where the children have different fathers, and this is reflected in the mother's less approving relationship with that child.

Developmental difficulties such as these can lead to a girl manifesting conduct problems such as opposing authority, getting into trouble at school, truanting, fighting and leaving school early with poor results (which itself leads to many negative outcomes and raises the risk of victimisation in later life). She is more likely to have sex early and to become pregnant, owing to a poor ability to take care of herself combined with a risk-taking attitude (and the lack of guidance from a supportive relationship with her mother). The 'assortative mating process' means that she may well be inclined to be attracted to a male with similar anti-authority and aggressive attitudes and behaviour, and to prefer 'bad boys' as more exciting (Feiring and Furman 2000). The tendency of the girl's mother and her family of origin to disapprove of her relationship will of course likely drive her further into it. This tendency is then reinforced when statutory authority becomes involved, and it may become a matter of pride for the young mother to resist the pressure to admit she made a mistake in partner choice and that this has put her child at risk. Where the young mother is also drawn into substance abuse, particularly of narcotics (becoming an 'addict') these problems are compounded because of the social opprobrium that attaches to drug addiction (Oetting and Donnermeyer 1998; Room 2005).

The impact of stigma and humiliation

In the communities in which child protection intervention is most prevalent, despite widespread negative attitudes to social services, great stigma attaches to mothers whose children are placed in care, even if this is a kinship placement. Professionals – to whom it is important not to disrespect the mother despite her shortcomings as a parent, which may after all be largely attributable to her life experience – should bear in mind that however liberal their own attitudes, the mother is likely to suffer humiliation in her family and community. Some hardened mothers are willing to say that this is the 'wake-up call' or 'kick up the backside' that they required, but in my experience they more often are undermined by this. A very judgemental tone can characterise the maternal grandmother's relationship to her daughter, and this is exacerbated where the grandmother also blames her daughter for engaging in drug abuse. Such attitudes tend to be reinforced by the power of the state behind the placement and the relative lack of accountability of the grandmother. The mother understandably feels infantilised by the process (Birch 1992; Hoffnung 1995; O'Reilly and Morrison 1993), and in addition to the pain of losing the care of her child often has to suffer the additional pain of watching her child experiencing a more nurturing love and care from the grandmother than the mother herself had as a child (Pitcher 2002).

An additional problem, especially from the point of view of promoting the prospects of a successful rehabilitation at the end of therapy, is that the child in the kinship placement will pick up the familial attitudes to their mother (O'Reilley and Morrison 1993), and will likely learn to disrespect her (which may already be a problem especially with male children whose father was abusive to his mother). Mothers are very sensitive to these slights and it is important not to load this any further through the way the case is handled. For mothers whose self-respect is already low, this is particularly important.

For these reasons, when working therapeutically with the mother, it can greatly assist the work if the maternal grandmother can be included in the therapy, even if only for a few reparative sessions. As the mother deepens her own understanding of the lack of nurture that she herself experienced, she needs to find a non-destructive way of communicating her hurt to her own mother and to be helped to find comfort. The grandmother often will have little understanding of her alienated daughter, and sessions in which she develops her understanding can bring very beneficial change to the family as a whole. Since such sessions are seldom organised, the focus being only on the mother, a useful exercise instead can be to help the mother write a letter to her mother expressing these feelings. Such a letter will usually require many drafts to move away from an angry blaming mode (which always tends to alienate the reader) to a deeper form of communication that helps the grandmother to see things from her daughter's perspective. Being able to help with this in the form of role play, for instance, will help the therapist to show the mother that she or he understands how the mother feels, and enable feedback to show when understanding needs to be improved. This process deepens the therapy and may help the mother to move out of her initial position of seeing the therapist as yet another professional who is judging her and putting her down. Once the mother has achieved this task, she can move on to the more advanced task of writing a letter of reparation to her own child. Mothers typically start by telling the child how they didn't mean to hurt them and it will never happen again. They need therapeutic help to stay with the child's experience rather than their own, and avoid trying to assuage their own guilt.

A confusing predicament for some children

In one case I worked, a mother had had several older children placed permanently with her own mother, the younger ones being by the same father as the baby now in their care. The parents had made many changes and had abstained from drug abuse before entering therapy. The grandmother had a very judgmental attitude to the parents and in particular seemed unable to accept changes in the father, which seemed to me to be unhelpful to his children as well as to the mother, since children's services had left the new baby in their care. A different social worker had been responsible for overseeing the placement and she was now inactive on the case. I had no opportunity to meet with the grandmother or have any significant input to that placement. The parents had contact with the children (although one of the older children declined to see her stepfather at the time) but were not allowed to take them out unsupervised. This situation seemed very unhelpful in view of the fact that the baby was allowed to live with the parents – what sense could the family make of this in terms of risk assessment? With the agreement of the social worker, the parents offered the children the chance to put in writing, via the social worker, what questions they would like to ask their parents, and to say anything they wanted the parents to think about or work on in therapy. The children made good use of this, but one question they asked was 'Why are you allowed to keep the baby when you can't have us?' Indeed. The system doesn't help children with this and the law shows that the guiding principles are unclear: is biological parenthood the trump? Or continuity? Or best parenting? Under British law, a parent can apply to vary or discharge a Special Guardianship Order if she or he can show 'a significant change of circumstances'; but the direction of current case law is in the direction of preserving an existing placement. Such applications have a double hurdle built in, as a parent must first apply for leave to apply, and such leave is commonly refused.[1]

The punishment and shaming of the vulnerable

In another case, a young and very immature mother who had children by two different partners (being unlucky enough, in view of her scarce resources, to have twins the second time) had them removed from her care and placed with her mother after one of the younger ones was injured by her partner (not the father) while in his care. This was a very vulnerable, passive mother with low self-esteem. She had moreover been subjected to a criminal trial and found guilty of failing to protect her child partly because she had initially been untruthful in trying to offer an alibi for her partner. When she came home to live alone after the destruction of her family, she found her walls daubed with abuse by neighbours because of the guilty verdict. It was a case in which I found it very difficult to find any public interest in the prosecution and criminalisation of this vulnerable young woman: her self-esteem could not have been any lower when she came to me for therapy, and the verdict did nothing to help a therapist enhance her protectiveness to her children (who after a lengthy process were finally rehabilitated to her care despite this). This mother was so passive that she barely had any language with which to express herself. It would have been easy for any case worker to bully her endlessly with exhortatory lectures. Being bullied was after all the main thing she knew from life (and unfortunately the most common feature of the cases I have worked is that the mothers all feel bullied by the child protection system much in

---

1   See, for example, U and BTU [2011] EWCA Civ 1526.

the same way as they previously felt bullied by harsh parents or partners: the experience is of arbitrary power, judgment and punishment).

This young mother – let us call her Kayleigh – had been raped as a teenager in her mother's home. Because she had not been supposed to have a boyfriend in the house when her mother was out, she was afraid to disclose and had never told her mother. Thus began her career with men. The history speaks to her lack of confidence in her mother's nurturing care, but this aspect of the case was very much sidelined. Because of her passivity and the crushing impact of the criminal verdict, her shame was complete and my task was to bring out the silenced person within and help her find her own voice, connecting her own experiences of victimisation to her difficulty in recognising abusiveness in a partner, and being able to stand up for herself and her children. With the best of intentions, the social worker and her mother tended to exhort Kayleigh to do better, while her mother tended to 'take over' with the children, rather than help her to emerge as a person. This could do little to counteract the impact of the shame this mother felt.

In working with non-protective mothers, one of the first things I do is talk to them about contraception and ask them to demonstrate that they are protected against further pregnancy. We discuss why it is important to their existing children for them to focus on their needs and not risk depleting their limited resources further by having another child. Many mothers are already pregnant again by the time they are referred for treatment; their own mothers do not seem to help protect them in this way, and it seems that many caseworkers feel inhibited in talking directly about sex, although the mothers themselves seldom do, in my experience. Unfortunately the child protection system tends to penalise those mothers who take this on board: one mother who wanted to work with me was denied the opportunity because while fighting unsuccessfully for the rehabilitation of her children, she had an abortion; her children were placed outside the family, and because she was no longer pregnant, she was dropped by the system. Predictably, she appeared again a few years later.

The pitfalls of paternal kin placements

Cases I have worked where a child has been placed with the paternal kin have thrown up even greater problems. One young mother – a 'black sheep' of her family who had been cast out by her mother to live with her abusive grandfather, and who had then had children with a 'bad boy' – became embroiled in a long-term abusive relationship that had many separations and reconciliations (itself a risk indicator). Despite the fact that the paternal grandfather was a bully who had produced two 'tearaway', violent sons, the young couple's eldest son was placed in the care of him and his wife, apparently on the grounds that they could offer better care than the maternal family (bullies often give an impression of being relatively 'together') and kinship care was what the child needed for his sense of identity. This fatally tied the mother to the father's family and meant that she would never be able completely to separate. Despite some gains in treatment, the decision contributed to events that led to the adoption of the two younger children outside the family. Despite the fact that this outcome was predictable, the kinship placement was never put in question.

Kinship placements of children with the families of perpetrators of domestic violence, maltreatment and even family murder are surprisingly common. In one case I worked, the mother's older child was placed with the paternal grandmother when the father killed the baby, the child's full sibling. No maternal kin were available for the role. This decision presented me with a very difficult task and gave the mother, in my view, a very confusing message about risk. The grandmother, who disputed her son's guilt, was supported by all authorities involved in taking the child to see the father in prison. Although the child was finally rehabilitated to the mother, the decision trapped the family in ongoing contact with the perpetrator's family, challenging the child's perception of reality. The paternal grandmother seemed to take every opportunity available to her to use her position as kinship carer to discredit the mother in the eyes of the authorities (she blamed the mother for what had happened). When the mother expressed her frustration and complained, the two women were depicted as 'as bad as each other', although the grandmother was always praised for her so-called generosity in taking in her grandchild. It seemed the mother was hardly ever praised, and when she raised questions about contact, this was not seen as protective. A family therapist was engaged to try to help the two women to improve their relationship, although the fact that the son of the one woman had killed the son of the other was explicitly 'off limits' in the therapy. This provides an example in my view of how kinship placements can exacerbate the child's difficulties. In this case, it seems to me, if there were sufficient risk concerns to remove the child from the sole care of the mother (perhaps debatable) this might have been better done by putting them together in a placement where the mother's parenting could have been monitored until doubts were reassured. However, kinship placements have even been approved with the families of men who killed the child's mother (Lennings 2009).

In the case just discussed, the mother was blamed for having doubted the father's guilt at the outset. The fact that she changed her position utterly during the course of the therapy won her no points, and merely led to speculation about her inconsistency or reliability. The fact that the grandmother actively supported her son's campaign that he had been wrongfully convicted did not attract any adverse comment and was seen as a mother's understandable loyalty. This blatant double standard in terms of protectiveness and unfair treatment of mothers in child protection cases is characteristic, unfortunately, of my case load and the system itself. For instance, at the time of writing I have assessed a case in which a mother has been criticised for failing to protect her older children from harsh parenting by her partner, the father of younger siblings. All this mother's children were permanently removed. The younger siblings were however placed with the same father who maltreated the older children (who were placed outside the families). Apart from anything else, this message to the mother about risk is very confusing and makes the therapeutic intervention much more difficult.

The persecution of the 'bad mother' still goes on

In another case, a mother also lost all her children and her gains in therapy were overruled. She was criticised for not separating from her partner who was found to have sexually molested his niece. When she did decisively separate from him in the course of the therapy, she won no points for this, and her decision was doubted. When her choice finally proved to be genuine, the 'goalposts' shifted and she was given feedback that she would not be considered on her own. Her partner would now be considered, because he was 'low risk' whereas she had a history of neglect (during a time when she had been very depressed). In addition, this mother was said to have a history of associating with sex offenders. The history turned out to have some false and misleading information: one of the men named had been convicted of a non-sexual Schedule One offence; the mother had never left the children in the care of this man, lived with him, or taken them to see him; but the information was nevertheless recycled many times, even after these errors were brought to light. At the same time, the family court had awarded this man residence of his child. The mother, then, was required to have a higher standard of protectiveness than the family court – in my view an absurd proposition, but in any case very confusing for her. She became so demoralised that after her baby was permanently removed she was unable to find the will to return to see me – understandably, given the long distance she had to travel and the effort she had expended to no avail. This appeared to be a case in which prejudice against the mother was so entrenched that therapy, and even objective risk assessment, was a futile endeavour. This would appear to be the case more often in instances where the mother has a history of neglect, which seems to arouse more negative perceptions in case workers than almost anything else.

Opportunities to work with the wider family can be creative

On a more positive note, my experience shows that in a context in which treatment is adequately funded, kinship placements of the children with the maternal grandmother can offer the opportunity for productive and creative practice in cases where there is a good working relationship between agencies, and there is opportunity to bring in the wider family to the mother's sessions.

In conclusion, I offer some pointers for practice where therapy is undertaken with a mother whose children have been placed with her mother after a generational failure to protect:

- There is a need for accurate risk assessment.

- Treatment targets need to be derived from assessed risk and be child protection focused.

- There needs to be an agreed list of indicators of behavioural change.

- The social worker must be willing to live with uncertainty and to evaluate the change process.

- The mother must be able to raise valid concerns about the placement.

- The grandmother must be drawn into the therapeutic process, making reparation to the mother possible.

- Reparation to the mother enhances her ability to make reparation to her own children.

Broader questions include: when, if ever, should special guardianship orders be reviewed? Should kinship care be viewed so uncritically, especially when it might trap a mother to a perpetrator's family? Why do we so often give mixed messages to mothers about protectiveness and still apply double standards to them?

References

Bell, C. (2006) 'Towards an Empirical Basis for Domestic Violence Risk Assessment.' In C. Talbot and M.C. Calder (eds) *Assessment in Kinship Care.* Lyme Regis: Russell House Publishing.

Bell, C. (2013) *The Domestic Violence Risk Assessment Framework (DVRAF).* Copyright © 2003–2013. Email: calvinbell@ahimsa-saferfamilies.co.uk

Birch, D. (1992) *Are You My Sister, Mummy?*, 2nd edn. London: Youth Support.

Faust, D. (2012) *Coping with Psychiatric and Psychological Testimony*, 6th edn. Oxford: Oxford University Press.

Feiring, C. and Furman, W.C. (2000) 'When love is just a four letter word: victimisation and romantic relationships in adolescence.' *Child Maltreatment 5*, 293–298.

Flegg, E. and Bell, C. (2008) 'Working with Parents for Family Safety where Domestic Violence is a Child Protection Concern.' In M.C. Calder (ed.) *The Carrot or the Stick? Towards Effective Practice with Involuntary Clients in Safeguarding Children Work.* Lyme Regis: Russell House Publishing.

Hoffnung, M. (1995) 'Motherhood: Contemporary Conflict for Women.' In J. Freeman (ed.) *Women: A Feminist Perspective*, 5th edn. Mountain View, CA: Mayfield Publishing.

Lennings, C.J. (2009) 'Uxoricide: when daddy kills mummy, what happens to the children?' *Child Law News, The Children's Court of New South Wales 4*, 1.

Oetting, E.R. and Donnermeyer, J.F. (1998) 'Primary socialisation theory: the etiology of drug use and deviance.' *Substance Use and Misuse 33*, 4, 995–1026.

O'Reilly, E. and Morrison, M.L. (1993) 'Grandparent-headed families: new therapeutic challenges.' *Child Psychiatry and Human Development 23*, 3, 147–159.

Pitcher, D. (2002) 'Is Mummy Coming Today? Managing Contact Arrangements in Kinship Placements.' In H. Argent (ed.) *Staying Connected: Managing Contact Arrangements in Adoption.* London: BAAF.

Room, R. (2005) 'Stigma, social inequality and alcohol and drug use.' *Drugs and Alcohol Review 24*, 2, 143–155.

Skeem, J.L., Douglas, K.S. and Lilienfield, S.O. (eds) (2009) *Psychological Science in the Courtroom.* London: The Guilford Press.

Talbot, C. and Calder, M. (eds) (2006) *Assessment in Kinship Care.* Lyme Regis: Russell House Publishing.

Waldegrave, C. (2006) 'Contrasting national jurisdictional and welfare responses to violence to children.' *Social Policy Journal of New Zealand 27.* Available at www.familycentre.org.nz/Publications/index.html, accessed 30 March 2013.

CHAPTER 5

The Wider Family Context of Kinship Care

Jeanne Ziminski

Introduction

When I was asked to write this chapter I reflected again on how complicated it is to pin down that flexible word 'family', never mind the 'wider family'. There are multiple stories about 'family', a word that seems infinitely pliable and to have great rhetorical power, as seen in the use in the London 2012 Olympics of the phrase 'the Olympic family' of athletes and officials. When families where there is kinship care are involved in state interventions, professionals are understandably focused on the triangle of child, carer and birth parents, against which they are aware to a greater or lesser extent of the wider kinship carer family.

This chapter aims to shift the perspective in order to foreground the wider family and to consider how relationships in the family of origin of the carer and the child impact on the care that is given in the kinship care situation. My starting point is that descriptions of 'family' are not mutually exclusive, but are descriptions that depend on context. Coming from a social constructionist frame (see Gergen and Gergen 1992) and seeing systemic family therapy as a form of conversation constructed from and feeding into broader stories of our society, I see the use of 'family' as changing to fit the situation. It could be said that kinship care is itself a statement of a family's belief in a wider concept of family beyond the nuclear unit of parents and children. This chapter goes beyond O'Brien's (1999, 2001) typology of diamonds of inclusion and exclusion to consider the whole family history that brought the kinship care relationships into being.

In exploring this aspect of the wider family, I have been influenced by Nixon, who, in discussion on Family Group Meetings, talks of relatives and friends as natural support systems:

if wider families are ignored or overlooked in decision-making processes affecting children, a lack of engagement and commitment to the plans made by professionals is likely. This can form a cycle of mistrust and misunderstanding, which has a corrosive effect on relationships between families and professionals. (Nixon 2001, p.97)

For Nixon, family can be a powerful form of collective responsibility, actively excluding dangerous individuals.

Some of what follows is based on my doctoral research where I interviewed 16 kinship carers (see Ziminski 2007a and 2007b for further details): the voice of other parts of the family is therefore meditated through their lens as it is the carers' story of the wider family, with their perspectives of other family members' views. In addition to my research, the stories of family members I have met through clinical encounters as a family therapist, and through personal discussions with own family members, inform my ideas. This chapter thus considers how kinship carers see the wider family, and the beliefs and stories that are important to them, as they negotiate their day-to-day lives. I then go on to unpick what I see as some of the specific challenges and opportunities for the wider family as part of their involvement in the kinship care situation.

The importance of the wider family

There are a number of studies showing the importance of the wider family in children's lives (Brannen 2000; Dench and Ogg 2002; Griggs, Tan and Buchanan 2010). Brannen's survey of 941 10- and 11-year-old schoolchildren in the general population indicated the importance to children of wider family relationships. Three quarters of the survey children saw aunts and uncles at least monthly, and several children included as relatives persons not related by blood or marriage.

Grandparents in Brannen's study were 'part and parcel of the everyday worlds of many grandchildren and constituted a key source of instrumental and expressive support' (2000, p.137). Dench and Ogg's (2002) study of over 2000 families, undertaken through the British Social Attitudes Survey 1998, is particularly interesting as it looks at grandparenting in Britain from three perspectives – that of the grandparents, of 'linking' parents, and of teenage or adult grandchildren. An interesting finding from Dench was of a polarisation in closeness following family separation, grandparents becoming either more heavily involved with their grandchildren or losing contact.

Having noted this, in my research no one I interviewed, from whatever cultural background, *expected* to be taking on the full time care of these children. It was not part of their story of their identity in day-to-day life in Britain. They were taking on an unusual task. Tanya, an African-Caribbean paternal grandmother of 56, contrasted her own position with that of her elderly mother in the Caribbean. Her mother had taken on the care of her first grandchild in a social context in which a grandmother might make the choice to care, rather than necessarily doing so because the parent had failed in his or her care. For her mother, it was accepted by family and community as an ordinary thing to do: 'Mum cared for her from when she was born. She took her off my sister although my sister was a married woman. The first granny and oh the first grandchild stays at home. That was it…that's the norm.' Rather, all the grandparents I interviewed saw themselves as providing a safety net. They expected to provide care for their grandchildren in the absence or failure of parents, but they did not expect, in the ordinary run of things, that they would be obliged to take on their full time care. Several grandparents drew on this 'safety net' discourse as an obvious obligation to act (see also Griggs *et al.* 2010).

Defining 'the wider family'

The use of the language of 'family' as a rhetorical discourse brings with it positive associations of warmth and connection, 'cultural capital' (Holstein and Gubrium 1994, p.248) upon which many kinds of relationship can draw – for example a work group or organisation. Family discourse is used by people to advocate particular meanings about their attachments and responsibilities towards each other. It is called on when such relationships are called into question, in order to provide 'affectional, custodial and durational grounds' for the existence of these relationships (p.238).

In my research with kinship carers it became clear when interviewing the carers that they felt comfortable holding different and sometimes contradictory views of 'family' depending on context, as this comment from Bob, a 24-year-old white British young man caring for his ten-year-old brother, shows: 'Whatever, but those five people and that's it. That's my family but to me, that's my family, close family, but my family that's the people who live in this house now… You see…this is just me and Jim.' Thus family is a word that contains ideas of people boundaried by household, by biological connection, and also by more amorphous ideas of mutual closeness and caring. When questioned, carers in my research made a distinction between, and use of at different times, an interpretation of 'family' as inclusive, which promoted a story of group support for carer and child, and a more restrictive interpretation of 'family' limited usually by household or lineage, with the aim of excluding certain people. For both Bob and Jim, the addition of the small word 'my' appeared to change their meaning of 'family' from a general concept to a much more restricted term. In some circumstances, particularly in the confusion that can arise through the kinship care situation, confusion about terms and a resultant lack of a joint understanding could lead to problems. For example, one kinship carer, a grandmother, described how the children she was caring for were not defined as 'immediate family' and so were not invited to her sister's wedding. She was calling on an inclusive discourse of family, but her sister was resisting this and holding on to a much more restrictive definition.

Carers described a dynamic construction of 'family': the effect of the experience of kinship care on that construction was to drive a change of meaning, but it could be in the direction of either greater inclusion or restriction. Depending on the circumstances, the taken-for-granted image of 'family' as a place of safety could be promoted more strongly or completely overturned. Clare had experienced a contraction of the view of 'family' following intra-familial abuse, which had rocked her previously positive image:

> Well, now I talk about family, and my family is my husband my son and my two grandchildren. And that's my family now. But before it was my Mum, my Dad, my brothers, my sisters, their families, and their families and you know the whole, anybody that was linked up with me that was family, it was family to me.

Children's own constructions of the meaning of 'family' draw on a mixture of personal experience and normative expectations, according to O'Brien, Alldred and Jones (1996). In their drawings, children expressed uncertainty about the request to draw their family, 'all your family or just your house?' (O'Brien et al. 1996, p.95). This indicates again that the definition of family is more than co-residence, and that different constructions of family can co-exist.

For some respondents, links to blood/biological relationships were not privileged above those 'aunties', friends of family or other forms of constructed relationships such as godparents. Isolated carers appeared to relate their experience to a cultural story about 'how families should be'. Cultural differences in the meaning of 'family' were pointed out by ethnic minority participants. For example, Anila, an Indian paternal grandmother, explained:

> Well after the immediate family, meaning brothers and sisters and all that? Well, your cousins and uncles and even in India I would say that sometimes you consider your really good friends' parents and all that as family as well...even at my age I would call somebody else's mother 'aunt'.

Following this construction of the importance of family, and because of the lack of accessible family in Britain, Anila had promoted her son's and then her granddaughter's relationships with English godparents, though recognising it to be still a different kind of family relationship than would have been possible in India.

Weeks, Donovan and Heaphy (1999) study of gay and lesbian relationships has shown that people do make choices about this. Those who feel excluded and unsupported by their kin group create 'families of choice' who take over the practices associated with kin. The transfer of the language of 'family' implies a transfer of constructs and meaning from kinship relationships into these other social friendship networks.

Talking family: how carers talk about wider family involvement and support

Stories of 'family closeness'

In addition to stories of interpersonal attachment and bonding, carers drew on accounts of closeness and belonging in terms of a family script-meanings held by family members jointly. A number of carers drew on 'family closeness' as a defining characteristic of their family, summed up in accounts of 'being there'. Family closeness was drawn on, not necessarily as a reason for kinship care, but as a support to the task which made carers more able to cope. It appeared to engender feelings of safety and security for carers at times of potential conflict and stress. Carers gave several descriptions of successful shared care such as was described by Kath and Len, older maternal grandparents.

They felt well supported by their several adult children who all lived locally, and regularly involved the child, their nephew, in activities with their own children. In so doing, they also gave some respite to their parents. Both white British and ethnic minority carers spoke about this as a natural support built on images of close family, and for Diana (a white British maternal aunt) this closeness of family was an important part of her decision to take over the care of her niece and nephew.

Family closeness was also noted in its absence for a few women whose access to support was limited by, for example, migration or intra-familial abuse. Friends could then 'stand in' for family. Change in the meanings of 'family closeness' could depend on the outcome of particular events in the family which either reinforce or undermine the family story about closeness, while at the same time, a family script about closeness could drive the wish for contact and interaction between family members.

Another approach is to see emotional connection between particular children and adults within a family as the consequence of the practices of emotional and physical caring, which lead to the subjective experience of greater closeness to individuals. This was the experience of Diane, a maternal aunt: 'It's maybe brought us back to…you know, focusing back on actually how the wider family is important now, I think that you know we have moved away from that a lot.'

Finch and Mason (1993) found that as people build up commitments of caring they become tied into a series of expectations. Because responsibilities are the result of interactions between individuals over time, parental commitments are the most intense. In this analysis, it is not intrinsic bonding or affection that form the tie, but rather 'practices of care'. Following this argument kinship carers can also be expected to develop high levels of emotional commitment and great sense of obligation.

Stories of 'family belonging'

A number of carers also drew on stories of family belonging, of family identity through knowledge of one's family history, which supported a push for family connection even in acrimonious family situations. It may be that this is a story that in many families is taken for granted and unvoiced unless there are threats to a family's or child's identity such as through abuse, the absence of family members or discrimination.

Shared care or 'passing the parcel'?

Farmer and Moyers (2008) noted that 17 per cent of children placed in kinship care had previously been with other kin. It seems to me it is important to differentiate between situations such as Diane's where the children had two long placements with different aunts, and Anila's where no one person in the maternal family had claimed Cora before she came forward. Cora had moved around different members of her maternal family like 'pass the parcel'. The importance of her granddaughter feeling she belonged within a family was commented on by Anila as one of the reasons for her deciding to take on the care of ten-year-old Cora despite initial reservations due to her own age, and at a time when she did not have a strong pre-existing bond with her.

> And yet I've only got to know her since she's been staying with me…because of this parcelling around and all that and because she came to me I realised that for the child it was so important that she had a family, that she could call someone 'grandma', yes?

Anila thus appeared to use family belonging as a way of standing in for the absence of a personal relationship between herself and her granddaughter before taking on her care.

Challenges and opportunities: kinship care and the wider family

In order to understand the context of family relationships within which kinship care arises, we need to expand and unpick the sometimes undifferentiated concept of 'the family'. This can be seen in the kinship care literature (e.g. 'relatives' used by O'Brien 2001). Greeff begins this process in exploring the importance of family dynamics, current and historical roles, power relationships and behaviours involved in the process of day-to-day caring for kin, noting alliances that can offer support or may undermine the situation (Greeff 2001, p.51).

My thinking about kinship care has been particularly informed by Finch and Mason's studies (Finch 1989; Finch and Mason 1993) into family obligations and negotiating family responsibilities. Their study was of a two part nature: first looking at publicly professed 'norms' regarding kinship responsibilities between adults elicited through a survey using case vignettes; and second ascertaining actual family practice through semi-structured qualitative interviews, with multiple members of a small number of kin groups in the north of England. Although Finch specifically excludes relationships between parents and minor children, she does discuss children's participation in terms of adult kin's negotiations over their childcare needs – sometimes a particularly thorny area of kinship care.

In their survey of public beliefs, Finch and Mason (1993) found that the concept of reciprocity between individual family members was a potent idea. In practice, their qualitative data showed that getting the balance right between dependence and independence and not allowing loss of control in a relationship was important, and was a central part in negotiating responsibilities. This was not just about instrumental exchange: 'People are also negotiating about their position within the network of kin relationships and the form that their specific relationships with each individual will take' (Finch and Mason 1993, p.58). The central issue therefore seemed to be the *negotiation* of the exchange and the dimensions of the moral commitment between people.

Intergenerational patterns of family relationships

Old wounds surface at a time when there are difficult decisions in families, as is often seen when adult children and their parents are having to make decisions about the care of parents when they are very elderly. Diane was caring for her niece and nephew following the breakdown of the placement with another sister which took place following the death of the children's mother. She described her views of why her sister took on the children as being due to her guilt at feeling resentment for being displaced as their father's favourite by the children's mother:

> Cathy was quite obsessed about having them, which was interesting really… I think that my sister's decision to have the children is, was actually linked to her relationship with their mother… There was this ten year gap and then along came this other child [the children's mother]…and I think my sister felt dislodged really by her…

The particular family therapy approach of Boszormenyi-Nagy's Contextual Therapy (Boszormenyi-Nagy, Grunebaum and Ulrich 1991) offers useful ideas for working with kinship care families. This involves an intergenerational focus, analysing generational and current loyalties between family members (Marchand and Meulenbergs 1999):

the aim is to track how intergenerational rules limit behavioural options in the present and how 'invisible loyalties' represent an unresolved issue from generation to generation. This can be apparent when working with families where there are old grievances relating, for example, to relationships between the birth parent of a child in kinship care and the parent's siblings when they were children. This can impact on the present, and can cause resentment that a favoured child is once again begin treated differently. The special treatment that a kinship care grandparent is offering a child by caring for them is resented either directly, or through complaints about grandparental neglect of their other grandchildren in comparison with the kinship care child. (Barratt and Granville 2006 also comment on this process).

This feeling of resentment can in turn be exacerbated by the carer feeling that the cared for child has extra needs due to experience of abuse, rejection or loss. Such a symmetrical escalation of resentment and distancing can be tackled through therapeutic conversations that enable each party to hear, understand and respond to the other's position and feelings, opening up the possibility of a greater level of support from a grandparent's other adult children.

Intergenerational patterns of kinship care

Accounts of intergenerational patterns in parenting and kinship care were rarely given spontaneously in the interviews, though when they appeared they seemed to have powerful meanings for the narrator. Carers assumed their own parents would have reacted in a particular way to the kinship care situation, which led them to understand their own caring as either copying or reacting against the parenting styles of their parents.

John Byng-Hall (1995) writes extensively about families using replicative or corrective family scripts as they bring up their children, compared with how parents were themselves brought up. Replicative scripts occur when previous positive experiences of family life and being parented are copied by succeeding generations, offering a template or an expectation of how to act. Carers can be consciously positioning themselves as replaying the story. For example, Bob drew heavily on a positive discourse of his grandfather's parenting to find a way to look after his brother successfully in the absence of any personal experience of child-rearing:

...because Mum and Dad split up when I was young, and the person that brought me up was my grandfather. Cos I was living with him since I was six. So I classed him as my father figure...and the way I see it is that I class my grandfather as my friend as well as my grandfather...so I just want to be like well what my grandfather was, what I'm like, what I want to be with, like what my grandfather was with me.

Bob's childhood experience was the only one of the interviews in which childhood patterns were replicated to the extent of carers having themselves been cared for full time and for a long period in kinship care, although Linda, another sibling carer, had also had experience of shared care in Nigeria between her parents and aunts and uncles. For Bob, this was clearly a profound influence on how he thought about and behaved towards his brother, Jim.

In addition, Della, a maternal grandmother, had been herself in the position of a birth parent with a child in kinship care, and was now caring for her grandson, Joe:

My mum did the same you see, because I had Tim when I was very young...out of wedlock...which in those days was absolutely a complete disgrace...and she brought Tim up so in actual fact I am doing what my mum did. So history is repeating itself in a way, under very different circumstances but...it boils down to the same thing, bringing up a child doesn't it?

Della explained she had made no explicit link with this she had decided to look after her grandson but in the reflective space of the research interview recognised her and her mother's actions as similar, though in a very different cultural context. Unmarried motherhood no longer had the social stigma; rather her daughter's difficulties were with drink and a violent partner.

Carers' generational position in wider family

Relationships between child, carer and wider family are also mediated by the carer's generational position. Grandparents had the advantage of being experienced parents themselves, as well as generally holding a position of authority which seemed particularly important where there were safeguarding issues and a need to protect from abusive birth parents. This seemed a harder line to hold for the aunt who had concerns about her substance misusing sister. Interestingly, both the sibling carers, Bob and Linda, were caring after the death of the child's mother and with the agreement of the wider family and professional network, as well having appreciable levels of support from them. They did not have to manage any major conflict over the care they were providing.

Parenting adult children

Whereas some carers were continuing to hold a powerful parental voice with their adult children – one grandmother told how all her children brought her grandchildren to her for them to be chastised – others were aiming to negotiate different relationships with the children's birth parents, as well as aunts and uncles. Gower, Dowling and Gersch (2005) challenge the dominant life cycle narrative of adult children gaining independence and separation from their parents, rather pointing out parent–adult child connection and the task of parenting adult children as a lifelong commitment. In their research they found that adult-children and their parents placed a high value on *negotiation* about beliefs, behaviours and expectations in the changing relationship: concerns about communication, how to let go and yet remain connected, and how to communicate with each other. In the sometimes highly emotional circumstances of the kinship care situation, it is therefore unsurprising that clarifying roles, expectations and behaviour between adult family members can be complicated and potentially fraught. For example, maternal grandmother, Kath, spoke about her 30-year-old son's reaction to her and her husband who were caring for his sister's son:

> ...for selfish reasons [laughs]...because I think he thought he wasn't going to get quite as much attention... I think he would rather I hadn't done it. He said, 'Oh I think it's too much for you Mum,' I mean that was his reason for it, but I think it was selfish really.

Sibing (sister) relationships

Another aspect promoting family relationships was that of the importance of the support of adult sisters for some female carers. Linda, a young Nigerian/British woman caring for her younger sister Rose and brother David, talked about the different kinds of support her other adult sisters gave her:

Jennifer…if I want a sensible ear you know somebody who is going to point out you know 'what about this or what about that', then I'll speak to Jennifer. If I'm really fuming and I want to scream and shout at somebody then I go to Noreen.

This story of sisterhood was also vividly described by both the maternal aunts in the research, and seemed to have some importance in the impetus towards kinship care, in the absence of any shared social expectations about the relationship between an aunt and a niece or nephew. This was also in contrast to the absence of any substantial cultural expectations of support from brothers, and lends credence to the argument relating to the feminisation of kinship care alongside broader social scripts of women as carers.

Maternal/paternal family relationships

The differentiation of relationships between paternal and maternal relatives, often described as 'the two halves of the family', is an important one. Thompson found that, whereas children tended to lose contact with the grandparents on the non-custodial parent's side after divorce, the intensity of the relationship with the grandparents on the custodial side often increased, with grandparents (more than aunts or uncles) becoming 'emotional intermediaries' (Thompson 1999, p.479) between children and their parents at a time of parental stress.

Depending on carers' constructions of family, they could take very different positions about a child keeping contact with each half. Maternal grandmother Clare, who was estranged from her daughter and son-in-law, had regular contact with her granddaughters' paternal aunt, who had produced a full paternal family tree at Clare's request.

I'm a big believer in knowing your family. We always say, 'You can choose your friends, but you can't choose your family', and I think as time goes on it's going to be very important to the girls to know where they belong, where they belong [sic]… As much as I like to blank their side of the family out, she's still got that side of the family.

In contrast, for Anila, as she spoke with a therapist, her granddaughter's Cora's identity was constructed through the account of Cora as her son's daughter, physically and emotionally similar to him. She privileged her connection to Cora at the expense of Cora's mother and aunt, not appearing to respond to the therapist or Cora's account of joint connection.

My research looking at therapy sessions with kinship care families explored several dilemmas that could arise where definitions of 'family' diverged, for example between paternal and maternal sections of the wider family, in such a way that one part of the family wanted to write off another part as having no or negative importance in a child's life. Professional views about heritage and identity may be challenged by a family's construction of the need for closeness and connection with one part of family rather than another, pushing for the account of 'family belonging' to outweigh the complexities of a child's individual identity as stemming from both parts of the family. The dilemma for carers and child becomes one of how to achieve a joint construction of 'family' that can allow them to form a cohesive enough family unit.

Conclusions

Kinship care can only really be considered properly alongside a conceptualisation of family in its widest sense. In order to promote a successful experience of care for child and family, it is important to look beyond the triangle of birth parent, carer and child to understand the network of wider family relationships, its history, its tensions and its resources.

One way for professionals working with kinship care families to access this resource and understanding can be to make use of Family Group Meetings so that wider family members can be part of the process, express their views and offer support where possible (Marsh and Crow 1998). The importance of preparation for such a meeting cannot be underestimated, so that the coordinator has some understanding of the relationships of power, authority, alliances and resulting loyalties within which the family group meeting is taking place. Such preparation is particularly necessary in a child protection context where dynamics of family secrets, distrust and deceit may be operating (see also Freeman and Ingham 2006).

One goal for therapeutic intervention, alongside looking at the dilemmas in family negotiation which caring for kin brings, is to achieve a joint definition of 'family' with consequent expectations about obligations, connections, attachment and contact (Ziminski 2007b).

This chapter is mainly built from the voices of carers and I am very grateful for them allowing me to learn a little of their family life. A fruitful future direction for research would be to build on this experience by seeking out the views and stories of the wider family network.

References

Barratt, S. and Granville, J. (2006) 'Kinship Care: Family Stories, Loyalties and Binds.' In J. Kenrick, C. Lindsey and L. Tollemache (eds) *Creating New Families: Therapeutic Approaches to Fostering, Adoption, and Kinship Care.* London: Karnac. Tavistock Clinic Series.

Boszormenyi-Nagy, I., Grunebaum, J. and Ulrich, D. (1991) 'Contextual Therapy.' In A.S. Gurman and D.P Knistern (eds) *Handbook of Family Therapy*, Vol II. New York: Brunner-Mazel.

Brannen, J. (2000) *Connecting Children.* London and New York: Routledge.

Byng-Hall, J. (1995) *Rewriting Family Scripts.* New York: The Guilford Press.

Dench, G. and Ogg, J. (2002) *Grandparenting in Britain: A Baseline Study.* London: Institute of Community Studies.

Farmer, E. and Moyers, S. (2008) *Kinship Care: Fostering Effective Family and Friends Placements.* London: Jessica Kingsley Publishers.

Finch, J. (1989) *Family Obligations and Social Change.* Oxford: Blackwell.

Finch, J. and Mason, J. (1993) *Negotiating Family Responsibilities.* London and New York: Routledge.

Freeman, P. and Ingham, J. (2006) 'Multiple Child Abuse That Involves Wider Kin and Family Friends Within Intergenerational Networks: A Theoretical Model.' In C. Talbot and M.C. Calder (eds) *Assessment in Kinship Care.* Lyme Regis: Russell House Publishing.

Gergen, K. and Gergen, M. (1992) 'Toward Reflexive Methodologies.' In S. McNamee and K.J. Gergen (eds) *Therapy as Social Construction.* London: Sage.

Gower, M., Dowling, E. and Gersch, I. (2005) 'Parenting Adult Children.' In A. Vetere and E. Dowling (eds) *Narrative Therapies with Children and their Families.* London and New York: Routledge.

Greeff, R. (2001) 'Family Dynamics in Kinship Foster Care.' In R. Broad (ed.) *Kinship Care: The Placement Choice for Children and Young People.* Lyme Regis: Russell House Publishing.

Griggs, J., Tan, J.P. and Buchanan, A. (2010) '"They've always been there for me": grandparental involvement and child well-being.' *Children and Society 24*, 200–214.

Holstein, J.A. and Gubrium, J.F. (1994) 'Constructing Family: Descriptive Practice and Domestic Order'. In T. Sarbin and J.I. Kitsuse (eds) *Constructing the Social.* London: Sage.

Marchand, H. and Meulenbergs, W. (1999) 'Working with Family Complexity – Supporting the Network.' In R. Greeff (ed.) *Fostering Kinship: An International Perspective on Kinship Foster Care.* Aldershot: Ashgate.

Marsh, P. and Crow, G. (1998) *Family Group Conferences in Child Welfare.* Oxford: Blackwell Science.

Nixon, P. (2001) 'Making Kinship Partnerships Work: Examining Family Group Conferences.' In R. Broad (ed.) *Kinship Care: The Placement Choice for Children and Young People.* Lyme Regis: Russell House Publishing.

O'Brien, M., Alldred, P. and Jones, D. (1996) 'Children's Constructions of Family and Kinship.' In J. Brannen and M. O'Brien (eds) *Children in Families: Research and Policy.* London: Falmer Press.

O'Brien, V. (1999) 'Evolving Networks in Relative Care: Alliance and Exclusion.' In R. Greeff (ed.) *Fostering Kinship: An International Perspective on Kinship Foster Care.* Aldershot: Ashgate.

O'Brien, V. (2001) 'Contributions from an Irish Study: Understanding and Managing Relative Care.' In R. Broad (ed.) *Kinship Care: The Placement Choice for Children and Young People.* Lyme Regis: Russell House Publishing.

Thompson, P. (1999) 'The role of grandparents when parents part or die: some reflections on the mythical decline of the extended family.' *Ageing and Society 19,* 471–503.

Weeks, J., Donovan, C. and Heaphy, B. (1999) 'Everyday Experiments: Narratives of Non-Heterosexual Relationships.' In E.B. Silva and C. Smart (eds) *The New Family?* London: Sage.

Ziminski, J. (2007a) 'Systemic practice with kinship care families.' *Journal of Social Work Practice 21,* 2, 239–250.

Ziminski, J. (2007b) 'Dilemmas in kinship care: negotiating entitlements in therapy.' *Journal of Family Therapy 29,* 438–453.

PART 2

Intervention and Support

CHAPTER 6

"It Takes a Village"

Placing Grandparents and Extended Family at the Center of Safeguarding Vulnerable Children

Andrew Turnell and Susie Essex

Many of the problems of safeguarding[1] work arise from a lack of vision about what constructive practice looks in sufficient detail to address the challenges practitioners face in everyday practice. While almost every professional will affirm the commonly heard saying "it takes a village to raise a child" and the importance of involving kin when children's services intervene in a vulnerable child's immediate family life, all sorts of practical challenges and anxieties tend to follow when considering placing grandparents and others at the center of the practice. These include the following:

- The case almost inevitably becomes more complex and requires extra time for the responsible professionals because involving extended family members brings significant others into play who inevitably have strong views about the immediate family, the children, what should happen and the perspective of safeguarding authorities.

- When considering kinship placements there are always challenges regarding assessing the suitability of the prospective carers and statutory practitioners will almost always worry that the problematic parents will have ready access to the children in a kinship placement.

---

1 The UK typically uses the terms "safeguarding" and "safeguarding services" to refer to what most other English-speaking countries call child protection and child protection services. Given this chapter draws on international examples and will have an international readership we will use the terms interchangeably.

- Professionals tend to worry that the relatives of parents who have abused or neglected children will also be problematic.

- Parents themselves, when caught up in child protection matters, are often wary of involving relatives because of the problems, judgements and shame that they feel will follow.

If kinship care and responsibility when social services get involved are to become more widely embraced in practice and not just as an aspiration it is vital that practitioners are offered tools and skills that help them address these challenges and complexities. Our chapter sets out to serve that purpose. The ideas we present here come from the direct clinical practice of Susie and her close colleagues, Margaret Hiles and Colin Luger and from Andrew's consulting work with child protection agencies throughout Europe, Japan, Australia and North America (Essex, Gumbleton and Luger 1996; Hiles and Luger 2006; Hiles, Essex, Fox and Luger 2008; Turnell and Edwards 1999; Turnell and Essex 2006). The chapter offers practice based evidence (Ferguson 2011; Jones, Cooper and Ferguson 2007) in its best sense, since all the ideas have been used extensively in many cases by treatment and frontline statutory professionals in the UK and internationally.

The ideas and tools we will present here are:

- the Family Safety Circles tool and questioning skills to build a naturally occurring network around the children and parents

- the Signs of Safety assessment or mapping process

- the Three Houses tool for engaging children in assessment and planning

- the Words and Pictures method for explaining the child protection concerns to the children and all members of the network

- a safety plan method for creating everyday safety for the children.

To bring these ideas to life we will use a fictitious, composite case example based on many cases from work covering over 20 years. The case concerns the children "Germaine", aged six years, and "Kestie", aged three. They are dual heritage children, with a white UK mother and African Caribbean father (see Figure 6.1).

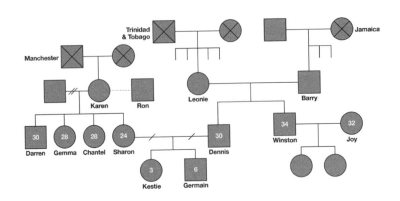

FIGURE 6.1 GERMAINE AND KESTIE'S FAMILY GENOGRAM

Germaine and Kestie live with their mother Sharon, 24, and see their father Dennis, a truck driver, when they visit their paternal grandmother Leonie twice a week after school. Leonie is a district nurse in the local area. Sharon's mother, Karen, also lives locally as do Sharon's two sisters and her brother. Sharon's father left when she was 12 years old and there has been no contact since that time. Sharon has struggled over the years with alcohol abuse and children's services believe there are times when she often smokes large amounts of cannabis. Family members and children's services say Sharon's home is often very messy since Dennis left two years ago. Prior to the most recent incident that led to the removal of the children, Sharon went through a "depressed" period where she often slept and didn't want to get out of bed and the children were frequently late or absent from school and nursery. During this period both grandmothers were worried. Karen would visit to try and help but she and Sharon would often end up fighting as Sharon felt like her mother was constantly telling her off like a naughty child. When the children visited Leonie, she would make sure they ate as much as she could get them into them and would put treats in their backpacks. During this period, because of a report from the school, a children services' social worker became involved with the family. The worker found Kestie a nursery place and arranged after-school care for Germaine three days a week. He closed the case as Sharon had got her life back together and because school and nursery said the children were doing well and were mostly dropped off and picked up on time. Sharon was seeing her GP to get help with her alcohol problems.

The case came back into the safeguarding system following police being called to Sharon's house during a noisy late night party when they found the children out on the street on their own. At the police station Sharon was disorientated and confused. The social worker from the out-of-hours team was called to find a place the children could stay. When asked about extended family Sharon told the police and social worker that the children must not go to stay with her mother because she did not think that her mother's new partner, Ron was okay and seemed embarrassed and vague about the possibility of the children going to stay with Dennis's family. This Saturday evening was a very busy night for the out-of-hours team so the worker organized for the children to go to emergency accommodation and made a referral for the case to be reopened for a new assessment and ongoing work.

There are many challenges for a child protection system in using kinship care quickly in child protection cases; while some jurisdictions are set up to place children with kin when emergencies such as this arise many, probably most, are not. The agencies we are aware of that routinely place children with extended family from the outset have paid particular attention to putting in place a clear expectation and strategies that make this happen and a separate chapter could be written on the work involved in creating such a culture and practice shift. Strategies can be as simple as always asking the parents who they would want the children to go to, through to making sure multiple workers are available when children are to be removed from their parents so one can focus on the parents and another on the children. Agencies that habitually use kinship placements quickly have in our experience also adopted a proactive "risk-sensible" (Munro 2011) approach to involving extended family members of whom they often have limited knowledge.

While kinship care is a crucial part of involving the naturally occurring network around the immediate family this is only part of the picture. We want to offer here a trajectory for intervening in families that provides professionals with a means of bringing extended family into the middle of the child protection throughout assessment, safety planning and reunification.

Weaving a shared vision of what's needed: skillful use of authority and utilizing every scintilla of what's working well

The culture and practice of children's services has many default settings that tend to overlook extended family and friendship networks and instead prioritize professionally driven interventions (Farmer and Moyers 2008). Placing a naturally occurring network of extended family and friends at the center of the assessment and planning requires:

- a clear vision of constructively involving family and friends throughout the life of the case

- the statutory professionals to place their authority behind the active participation of a naturally occurring network

- a rigorous forensic acuity to identifying and honoring everything that is going well in the immediate and extended family and friendship network, particularly in the care of the children.

Assessment in child protection is almost always a professional undertaking completed in professionalized language for a professional audience. If the immediate and extended family are to take significant responsibility for addressing the safeguarding concerns the assessment and planning process must be undertaken in ways that family can understand and participate in. The Signs of Safety risk assessment and planning process (and all of the methods and tools described in the chapter) designed to be undertaken together with family members, including the children. The approach is based on the logic that for professionals to get out of the case it is family members that are the most important people to think through the situation and to take action. The Signs of Safety assessment process (Turnell and Edwards 1999; Turnell 2012) focuses the assessment and planning on four straightforward questions (see Figure 6.2):

1. What are we worried about?

2. What's working well?

3. What needs to happen?

4. Where are we on a scale of 0 to 10 where 10 means there is enough safety for child protection authorities to close the case and 0 means it is certain that the child will be (re) abused (judgement)?

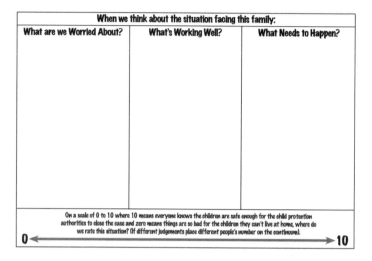

FIGURE 6.2 SIGNS OF SAFETY ASSESSMENT AND PLANNING FORM
SOURCE: ANDREW TURNELL 2011

Child protection professionals get involved in families' lives because of serious problems for children and the professionals therefore quite naturally tend to focus their attention on concerns. The engine room of all the methods and the overall approach we are proposing in this chapter is for the professionals always to inquire and listen with an ear for the doubleness of things – the positives present even in the face of problems. These positives are drawn upon, not in any way to minimize the seriousness of the concerns, but to create energy to explore these concerns with more intelligence and depth. This is purposive, conscious work to resist the more usual "problem-saturation" (White and Epston 1990) that characterizes child protection practice (Dale 2004; Farmer and Owen 1995; Maiter, Palmer and Manji 2006). Susie calls this attitude and approach "cross-stitching", meaning the more difficult a subject is to explore, the more the professionals need to honor the family and network members to create the energy to enable them to engage with the complexity of the issues. To enact this cross-stitching process, professionals need to be proactively thinking of questions they can use to animate conversations that focus on the children and also build hope and engagement. This is precisely the process that underpins the Signs of Safety risk assessment. Here we present questions that balance exploring worries with what's working:

What most worried you about tonight? What do you think most worried the children? What do you think most worried the police?

What worries you about involving _____? (Grandma, Nan, Pop, Dennis)

What most worries you about Sharon's care of the kids?

Sharon, what most upsets you about how your Mum talks to you about what you do with the kids? What's the worst example of your Mum getting into you about your parenting?

What do you most love about your kids?

What are the best times you have with your kids?

What would the kids say are the best times they have with you?

Who in your extended family do they spend time with that they enjoy and that is good for them?

Who helps you most with the kids?

Of the things your Mum says to you that make you feel like she's telling you off are there any things she says that you think you should listen to?

What do your kids like most about Granma?

What does _____ do that helps you most with the kids?

What most impresses you about Sharon's care of the kids?

What do the kids most like about their Mum?

What will the kids miss the most being away from their Mum?

When workers can engage with and cross-stitch between concerns and positives families report they feel a sense of balance is brought to their experience (Skrypek, Idzelis and Pecora 2012), the more depth will be built into a shared assessment, and the more likely family will take responsibility to build solutions. For example, Sharon almost inevitably will to some extent resist involving her mother because she feels ashamed that the police and social services have removed her children and she already feels blamed and criticized by her mother. Leading Sharon in a cross-stitching conversation between Sharon's frustration with her mother and what her Mum does that is helpful from Sharon and the children's perspective will create a greater chance of involving Sharon's mum, together with Sharon, in what happens for the children. When professionals can ground their work in an inquiring rather than expert stance, prioritizing family members' thinking about the opportunities and struggles their relationships and connections pose for each other, the more likely it is that they will be able to play an active role in thinking through and addressing the child protection concerns.

Parallel to this participatory assessment questioning process with the adults naturally connected to the children, it is vital the professionals move quickly to involve the children in describing their experience and what they want. Nicky Weld and Maggie Greening from New Zealand have created a practical tool called the Three Houses (Turnell 2011; Weld 2008, 2009) that uses the same core domains and questioning stance as Signs of Safety and has assisted workers all over the world to quickly involve children in child protection cases. The tool involves interviewing children by sketching with them the outline of three houses, a house of worries, good things and dreams. The worker then asks the children questions within these domains which they can draw pictorial or word based answers alongside, to which the worker usually adds any exact additional verbal description the children offer about their experience (see Figure 6.3).

'Three Houses' Child Protection Risk Assessment Tool to use with Children and Young People

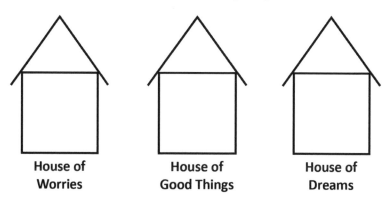

House of
Worries

House of
Good Things

House of
Dreams

FIGURE 6.3 "THREE HOUSES" CHILD PROTECTION RISK ASSESSMENT
TOOL TO USE WITH CHILDREN AND YOUNG PEOPLE
SOURCE:TURNELL 2011

The tool provides a focused shared physical activity to discuss the child's experience that avoids simply focusing on what's wrong, which many children will naturally resist. To use the tool most effectively it is usually best to prepare a range of questions in advance and we encourage workers to focus particularly on questions for the houses of good things and dreams rather than worries with lots emphasis on questions about extended family and friends such as:

What are the best things about your life?

What are the best times for you at home?

Who are your favourite people you like being with?

What are your favourite things to do with Mummy?

What do you like most about seeing grandma (Daddy, Pop and Nan)?

What are the best times you have with Mummy and grandma (Daddy, Pop and Nan)?

If you could have things just the way you would like them at home and all the problems were solved what would be happening?

What would you all do?

Who would visit?

Who would help Mummy if there were problems?

While we help Mummy get her problems sorted out who would you most like to live with?

In the case of Germaine and Kestie it would likely make best sense to interview them together. Most likely Germaine would provide the more detailed responses but involving Kestie often encourages an older child like Germaine to take the questions more seriously. The sorts of questions described above tend to draw answers about favourite family times like reading at night, playing and having a meal together when Granma comes over and family get-togethers and the like. While it is easy to dismiss such experiences this information is actually the gold that enables professionals to honor Sharon and the other adults in the extended family and to create a relationship where they will more likely bring forward their best efforts in resolving the problems. The children's answers in the house of good things will provide detail about what is going well in their lives and will inevitably also point to and usually deepen the exploration of the problems. For example, the children may draw a picture and describe the nice food and eating all they want when visiting Nan and Pop: this points to and usually leads to talking about being hungry with their mother. This is a key reason we ask workers to pay more attention to questions for the houses of good things and dreams as these consistently lead to exploring the children's experience of what they are worried about quite naturally. Children's services practitioners experienced in using the Three Houses tool report that exploring the house of dreams leads to the child offering a vision of what they want but it also regularly leads easily into discussing what the children are worried about.

At the beginning of a house of dreams exploration children will almost always talk about wanting particular toys or games and these sorts of answers should be recorded seriously, they are important to the child and when the Three Houses words and drawings are later shown to the parents and kin it is hoped they recognize these answers as their child's thinking. A child like Germaine will then often say things like "I want mummy to have enough money so we always have food", "I don't want to be in the dark again" (power cut off), "I don't want mummy to have the parties at our home and I don't want her to have Brant and Shelly to come over", "I want Mummy to always wake up and help me and Kestie in the morning", "I want Mummy and Gran to get on better and Gran not to yell at Mummy", "I want to see Daddy more".

While we don't have space to address many questions practitioners will have about this work these are addressed elsewhere (Turnell 2011). The whole purpose of the Three Houses process is not to create a professional assessment of the child's world but rather to document the child's experience using the child's exact drawings and words to then bring these back to the adults the children belong to. Time and again we have seen that while parents and extended family might be wary of professional assessments and views, when they see the child's own words and pictures describing their experience this creates a significant breakthrough where the adults put aside their own shame, blame and differences and will more readily work together for the children.

Using the Signs of Safety assessment to bring forward the professionals concerns and goals

The Signs of Safety assessment and planning process is a participatory process where everything written in the framework needs to be in straightforward understandable language. A central part of the assessment and planning requires the professionals to clearly identify the core issues they see need to be addressed (danger statements) and what it is they need to see to be satisfied the children will be safe in the future (safety goals). The earlier these can be created and negotiated with all family members in the life of the case, the more quickly a purposive direction can be created. The aim here is to distil the core concerns but also do this together with clear statements of what is needed to deal with the problems, thus making it more likely the family can engage with the seriousness of the problems. The safety goals are used to set clear expectations from the statutory agency placing their authority behind the requirement of involving extended family and friends for the agency to be willing to reunite Sharon and the children and close the case. In the case we are considering we would expect the danger statement (there can certainly be more than one but there is only one in this case) and safety goals to look something like this:

Danger statement: Holly and Shaddy, Hellingford Children's Services, are worried Sharon will feel so sad and alone she'll keep using drugs and drinking so much she will lose focus on Kestie and Germaine and keep doing things like sleep late into the day or party like she did on July 5th when the police found the children out on the street at night. If these things keep happening Holly and Shaddy are worried Kestie and Germaine will get very scared and even hurt when they are unsupervised and alone and that they won't get looked after, get to school and nursery like they should and rather than just being kids they'll end up worrying all the time about Sharon.

Safety Goals: Holly and Shaddy, Hellingford Children's Services, know how much Sharon loves the kids and how much the kids want to be with her and *want* Kestie and Germaine *to be with Sharon. For this to happen they need:*

- Sharon to work with Holly and Shaddy and one or two people who are close to her to create a simple and honest explanation for Kestie and Germaine about Sharon's problems with drugs and alcohol and feeling alone and why the kids can't live with Sharon right now.

- Sharon to discuss and create an honest, detailed plan made with her family and friends that shows everyone that when Sharon does get overwhelmed and sad what she will do to get herself back on track for the kids. If Sharon can't do this the plan will spell out who in Germaine and Kestie's safety network will help with the kids so Kestie and Germaine always get the attention, get played with, talked to, cuddled like they need however sad or overwhelmed Sharon feels.

- Sharon to discuss and create a detailed plan with her family and friends that shows everyone she won't use drugs or drink or if Sharon does drink or use everyone knows what the plan is to make sure the kids are with someone that is drug/alcohol free until Sharon is sober and clean.

When social services intervene in cases like this one they tend to use their authority to prescribe professional services so it would be typical in this case that Sharon would be sent to drug and alcohol rehabilitation, counseling and/or mental health treatment for depression and possibly a parenting evaluation and subsequent course. In the approach we are proposing we are focused on the statutory agency using its authority to prioritize involving the kin and friendship network alongside Sharon to get them involved to think through together the problems and what action is needed. The aim is to place responsibility back with the people that have primary and lasting connection to the children and for professionals to use their statutory authority and skillfulness to act as facilitators in this endeavor.

Family Safety Circles tool

With social services requiring the involvement of a family and friendship network around the parents and children it is important to explore not only who it may be possible to involve but also to explore the issues that involving each person might bring into play. Professionals can tend to view dynamics – such as problems family members have with one another – as a hindrance or even a complete road block to involving kin and friends. Our view is that since these are likely the very dynamics that have got in the way of the family and friendship network working together for the benefit of the children, children's services involvement provides a perfect opportunity to explore and unravel these dynamics and tensions. The sorts of questions and foci we have described in using the Signs of Safety and Three Houses assessment and planning processes should already have begun to build this picture. To take this further many children's services workers find it very useful to use a simple tool Susie created called Family Safety Circles that assists them to explore with parents and children who they can involve and the issues that might be involved around those people.

To begin this process it is often useful to brainstorm and list with the parents everyone they know: friends, extended family, workmates, neighbors, people they know from religious communities, clubs and activities they participate in, people that are involved with their children's lives including teachers, carers and coaches. To use the Family Safety Circles process the practitioner then draws three concentric circles on a whiteboard or flipchart and invites the parents to think about a key question and put these people's names in the concentric circle that fits best. Figure 6.4 shows five typical questions we use the circles process to address.

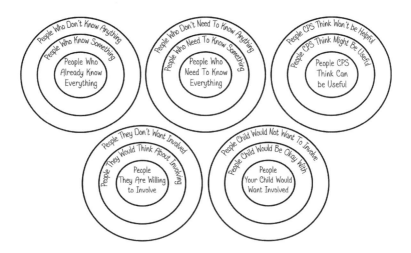

FIGURE 6.4 FAMILY SAFETY CIRCLES WITH TYPICAL KEY QUESTIONS

Professionals often fall into the trap of pre-judging and seeking to exclude certain friends and extended family members around parents. We are looking for professionals to restrain their own judgement process and use something like the Family Safety Circles method to ask the parents to think through who can be most helpful and what issues might crop up with the people that are naturally connected to the parents and children. The purpose again is not to deliver expert answers but to use professional expertise to question and make the adults around the children think through with who and how they can best work to demonstrate the children will be safe and well cared for.

Words and Pictures explanation for the children (and everyone else!)

Child psychiatrist Tilman Furniss (1991, p.22) made the observation that, "child abuse is a syndrome of secrecy". All family and friendship networks can create dynamics where difficult issues are avoided to keep the peace and because it is very difficult to find words to talk about embarrassing issues. When the issues are circumstances where children could be or are hurt, the difficulties typically compound. Extended family members are often very concerned but not knowing how to speak openly anxiety builds. The way these matters often do get an airing is when someone in the family "confronts" the parent(s), exactly as Sharon's mother does in the case we are following, or when family members find themselves in a fight. These sorts of "discussions", however well intentioned, are usually counter-productive feeding more shame, recrimination, silence and isolation. While it is easy for professionals to pathologize these sorts of family dynamics we think it is vital instead to bring compassion, recognizing that almost all families struggle to be open about difficult issues.

We also know from a considerable body of research that children caught up in child protection matters and those who have come into care consistently don't understand why social services intervened in their lives (Farmer and Moyers 2008; Rose and Philpot 2005).

For family members to work together to make sure the children are safe everyone must understand the child protection concerns and be able to consider and discuss them in a constructive manner. Our way of breaking the secrecy Furniss speaks of and to create openness involves enlisting the parents and extended family in creating an explanation for the children about the concerns. The method we have created for doing this is called the Words and Pictures explanation. While the professionals facilitate the process, the most critical aspect of the Words and Pictures explanation is that it is created together with the parents and extended family. Since it is their story they must own and be happy with it before the children are given the explanation. This distinguishes the Words and Pictures process from Life Story Book work (Rose and Philpot 2005; Ryan and Walker 2007).

Creating a Words and Pictures explanation in cases like that of Sharon, Dennis and the extended family usually takes three or four carefully focused sessions. Professionals wishing to utilize this method can find the detail of the process elsewhere (Devlin 2012; Hiles, Essex, Fox and Luger 2008; Turnell and Essex 2006). In summary, we always begin by showing family members an example of a Words and Picture explanation used in a similar situation. We then explore with all the family members questions like:

- What do the children already know about why they can't stay with Sharon?

- What questions are they asking?

- What explanations have they overheard?

- What do they need to know?

The professionals then draft an explanation for the family members to consider and over a number of sessions refine the story with the parents and network. As the story is refined with the family it is also important to make sure the story captures the professional perspective about the seriousness of the concerns. Finally, as the explanation evolves in discussion with all parties, simple age-appropriate drawings are prepared to accompany each aspect of the explanation. With this method it is easy to become "product focused", concentrating exclusively on producing the explanation for the children. While creating an explanation is the shared purpose it is the process of working with the parents and extended family over an extended period focused on what to tell the children that builds the family's capacity for constructive openness. The explanation is most definitely important but the main prize is to help everyone in the extended family to think more deeply, intelligently, compassionately and openly about the problems since this is what will create lasting safety for the children.

Once the explanation has been created and everyone agrees with it, all members of the extended family are invited to a meeting where the explanation is presented to the children. It is important to go through the explanation slowly with the children so they and everyone present can process the significance of the story. To assist in this the children are invited to contribute to the drawings. Figure 6.5 shows the sort of Words and Pictures explanation we would expect for Kestie and Germaine.

In leading many Words and Pictures explanations with many extended families we are continually struck by the power of this process. Many aunts, uncles and grandparents have expressed the sentiment one grandmother stated "I have listened to social services complaints about my daughter for many years but it wasn't until we created this story that I really understood what they were on about."

1. There was a big meeting called a Child Protection Case Conference.

"WE ARE VERY WORRIED"

2. They were worried because the Police found Germaine and Kestie on their own, on the road, late at night. Everyone said they are too young to be on their own in the road.

3. The Police went to Mummy Sharon's house.
They don't know what had happened at Mummy's house
before they arrived. Mummy seemed confused and there were
a lot of empty bottles everywhere. They were worried.

4. The Social Workers said to Mummy that they realise she has lots
of problems at the moment, and they were worried she has a big
problem with alcohol. Mummy says she has had problems but that
she doesn't agree with all the Social Workers concerns.

The Social Workers have told Mummy that she mustn't look after
children whilst she has a big problem with alcohol.

5. Whilst Mummy is sorting all this out, she has said to the Social
Workers that she will agree that you (Germaine and Kestie) should
stay with Granny Lorraine and Granddad Barry. Mummy wants you
both home as sonn as she can show people things are okay.

6. Mummy has said she will work with Tom (her Social Worker) and a doctor called Dr. Kieran Jones to sort out some of the problems.

Everyone has said, "We all want to help to make things safe for Germaine and Kestie".

Signed ....

Date ....

FIGURE 6.5 WORDS AND PICTURES STORYBOARD FOR GERMAINE AND KESTIE SO THAT THEY KNOW WHY THEY ARE STAYING WITH GRANNY LEONIE AND GRANDAD BARRY

Safety plan

Possibly the most difficult question for any children's services professional to answer in any given case is: *what do you need to see to satisfy you the children will be safe and you can close the case?* This is confirmed by the fact that when parents who have had involvement with child protection services are studied they consistently say they didn't know what professionals wanted them to do (Dale 2004; Dumbrill 2006; Teoh, Laffer, Parton and Turnell 2003). Child protection professionals and courts tend to send parents and families to services, therapy, treatment and educative programs as a proxy for child safety. In reality, children are made safe through specific behaviors and actions taken by adults in their everyday interactions with the children, most particularly at moments of difficulty and danger. In our experience when professionals can focus their work on building safety as everyday lived actions and behavior this creates a more straightforward and understandable context making working together with and within extended families much easier.

In this way a safety plan ceases to be confused with a service plan and instead can be seen as the specific arrangements the immediate and extended family will put in place so that the children will always be safe and well cared for, paying particular attention to past circumstances that have put the children in harm's way. The exploration of the problems in a straightforward manner undertaken through the Signs of Safety assessment (the adults thinking about the situation) and Three Houses assessment (the children's experience of the situation for the adults) and the Words and Pictures explanation (the adults' description of the problems for the children) all of which are designed to bring everyone to a place where they have the understanding and acuity to actively participate in creating a specific, everyday safety plan. Since the safety plan is all about the children and will directly affect their interactions with their parents and their extended family the safety plan should be expressed as straightforward rules that the children can understand.

The most important aspect of safety planning is that the plan is co-created with the family and an informed safety network. Since it is a plan that the family must live out it must be completely owned by them. As with the Words and Pictures work, while it is easy to focus on the final product of the written plan the most important part is the process of getting everyone in the family network to think and plan together how they can make sure the children are safe and looked after no matter what happens. The key role for the professionals is not to deliver answers but to ask sharper and sharper questions that raise the hard issues the family needs to consider to make all the family and friendship network members think through and find answers that will work in their situation. The sorts of questions that we would expect to be addressed in Kestie and Germaine's situation include:

- When has Sharon been sad/felt alone and was still able to do what she needed to do for the children?

- Who helps Sharon when she is struggling?

- What are the first signs that Sharon is not coping and might need help?

- What's the best way to offer help for Sharon and the kids? Who should do this and how?

- What if these things happen would most worry Kestie and Germaine?

In a process that mirrors the creation and presentation of the Words and Pictures explanation we are looking for the parents and the safety network to create a Words and Pictures style safety plan that is then presented to the children with all the adults present. In this way, the parents, extended family members and friends involved in the safety network are thinking through and making commitments to each other and to the children that have far more significance than commitments made to professionals. In the case of Kestie and Germaine we would anticipate a safety plan that looks something like that shown in Figure 6.6.

The drawings connected to the plan are important as they enable a "picture-tells-a-thousand-words" engagement with the commitments that goes beyond the written words. The professionals and the family members think through and create the drawings together before the presentation to the children and this deepens family members' thinking. When the plan is presented to the children, the drawings both deepen their understanding and also provide the opportunity for their active participation. For example, children can be asked if they think the drawings are good likenesses of their kin and can be encouraged to add details to the drawings. We also often use two drawings in relation to a particular rule such as the first set of drawings connected to rule one. With the two different drawings the children are asked to tick the drawing that corresponds to the rule and place a cross on (or through) the picture that breaks the rule.

PLEASE KEEP SOMEWHERE SAFE.
Family Safety Plan for Germaine and Kestie and all their family

1. This is a plan for Germaine and Kestie to return home to live with
   Mummy Sharon. And to show the Social Workers that everyone
   will work together to make sure Germaine and Kestie are safe.

2. Mummy Sharon has told the Social Workers and everyone she
   will not drink alcohol when Kestie and Germaine are in the house,
   and she will not have other people drinking alcohol in her house.

3. If Mummy drinks alcohol, e.g. a family wedding, she will want a
   network person there to help look after Kestie and Germaine.

4. Mummy Sharon will get Germaine and Kestie ready for school. Granddad Barry has said he will help Mummy, and come to take Germaine and Kestie to school and nursery.

5. Mummy will collect Germaine and Kestie from school and nursery on Tuesday and Thursday. Granny Leonie will collect them on Wednesday, when they will see Daddy Dennis for tea. On Friday and Monday they will still go to after school club as Mummy goes to College now Monday, Wednesday and Friday.

6. Mummy will need some time at the weekends to do some college work. Granny Karen, Auntie Jemma and Uncle Darren will have Germaine and Kestie for the days on Saturday, to take them out on their scooters and to Soft Play at the Community Centre.

7. If Mummy is having a difficult time, or has a big worry (like a big gas bill), she will ring Auntie Gemma or her key worker Jenny from the "Emile Blanch Unit" (the Hospital where they help people who have had problems with alcohol).

8. If Germaine or Kestie are worried about school, friends or anything they can talk to Mummy, Granny Leonie, Granny Karen, Granddad Barry, Auntie Gemma, their teacher.

9. Mummy, Granny Leonie, Granny Karen and everyone will all check at least once a week, to make sure Germaine and Kestie are not worried. Germaine has a stone whale (family safety object), which he will move off the draweres in the bathroom if he wants to talk to someone. His teacher will also ask him how the whale is from toome to time

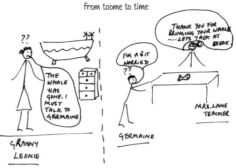

FIGURE 6.6 FAMILY SAFETY PLAN FOR GERMAINE
AND KESTIE, AND ALL THEIR FAMILY

Reunification

While the safety plan presented here is the sort of final plan that we would expect to see that would provide confidence for everyone that the children will be safe in reunifying with Sharon, for the plan to be meaningful and effective it must evolve over time. Reunification is a purposive journey that needs to start on the first day of removal and is best accomplished when professionals create a clear, timetabled trajectory with Sharon and the extended family. A clear, timetabled trajectory makes a huge difference for parents and family members since it gives them hope through clear steps and goals but is usually very challenging for professionals who are worried about whether parents and kin will succeed and what should happen if there are setbacks. While we do not have space to go into detail here we would expect the reunification process to involve creating shared assessment with the family members through the Signs of Safety and Three Houses frameworks, involving extended family quickly and placing the children in a kinship placement as soon as possible. We would then move on from here promptly and purposively into creating a Words and Pictures explanation for the children and then into safety planning. We would expect the whole process in a case like this to take four to six months with successively increasing contact between Sharon and the children following the completion of the Words and Pictures explanation. Once the immediate family is reunified we would hope that social services would continue to monitor the case for three or four months, fully handing over the monitoring and support to the friendship and kinship network at closure.

Conclusion

While most professionals would fully endorse the sentiment "it takes a village to raise a child", the reality within western children's services since Freud is that we have built a professional-centric culture where the business of raising a child seems to be located with a mother and a therapist. Placing extended family back in the center of child care for vulnerable children caught up in child protection concerns is a significant culture shift for children's social services. In the end, this culture shift has to be enacted by practitioners and for them to deliver on the promise of kinship care and active kin participation in safeguarding matters requires equipping practitioners with specific ideas, tools and methods to achieve this aim. In this chapter we have sought to offer a range of practical methods and an overarching trajectory that we have seen work well in many social services cases in many countries that maximizes the chance for the naturally occurring network to step forward around vulnerable children and their parents.

References

Dale, P. (2004) '"Like a fish in a bowl": parents' perceptions of child protection services.' *Child Abuse Review 13*, 137–157.

Devlin, J. (2012) 'Telling a child's story: creating a words and pictures story book to tell children why they are in care.' *Social Work Now 49*, 13–20.

Dumbrill, G. (2006) 'Parental experiences of child protection intervention: a qualitative study.' *Child Abuse and Neglect 30*, 27–37.

Essex, S., Gumbleton, J. and Luger, C. (1996) 'Resolutions: working with families where responsibility for abuse is denied.' *Child Abuse Review 5*, 191–202.

Farmer, E. and Moyers, S. (2008) *Kinship Care: Fostering Effective Family and Friends Placements.* London: Jessica Kingsley Publishers.

Farmer, E. and Owen, M. (1995) *Child Protection Practice: Private Risks and Public Remedies.* London: Department of Health.

Ferguson, H. (2011) *Child Protection.* London: Palgrave.

Furniss, T. (1991) *The Multi-professional Handbook of Child Sexual Abuse: Integrated Management, Therapy and Legal Intervention.* London: Routledge.

Hiles, M., Essex, S., Fox, A. and Luger, C. (2008) 'The words and pictures storyboard: making sense for children and families.' *Context 97*, 13–19.

Hiles, M. and Luger, C. (2006) 'The resolutions approach: working with denial in child protection cases.' *Journal of Systemic Therapies 25*, 24–37.

Jones, K., Cooper, B. and Ferguson, H. (2007) *Best Practice in Social Work: Critical Perspectives.* London: Palgrave.

Maiter, S., Palmer, S. and Manji, S. (2006) 'Strengthening worker-client relationships in child protective services.' *Qualitative Social Work 5*, 2, 167–186.

Munro, E. (2011) *Munro Review of Child Protection, Final Report: A Child-centred system.* London: Department for Education. Available at https://www.gov.uk/government/publications/munro-review-of-child-protection-find-report-a-child-centred-system, accessed on 9 September 2013.

Rose, R. and Philpot, T. (2005) *The Child's Own Story: Life Story Work with Traumatized Children.* London: Jessica Kingsley Publishers.

Ryan, T. and Walker, R. (2007) *Life Story Work: A Practical Guide to Helping Children Understand Their Past.* London: BAAF.

Skrypek, M., Idzelis, M. and Pecora, P.J. (2012) *Signs of Safety in Minnesota: Parent Perceptions of a Signs of Safety Child Protection Experience.* St. Paul, MN: Wilder Research.

Teoh, A.H., Laffer, J., Parton, N. and Turnell, A. (2003) 'Trafficking in Meaning: Constructive Social Work in Child Protection Practice.' In C. Hall, K. Juhila, N. Parton and T. Pösö (eds) *Client as Practice.* London: Jessica Kingsley Publishers.

Turnell, A. (2011) *Of Houses, Wizards and Fairies: Involving Children in Child Protection Casework.* Perth: Resolutions Consultancy. Available at www.signsofsafety.net, accessed on 4 June 2013.

Turnell, A. (2012) *Signs of Safety: Comprehensive Briefing Paper.* Perth: Resolutions Consultancy. Available at www.signsofsafety.net, accessed on 4 June 2013.

Turnell, A. and Edwards, S. (1999) *Signs of Safety: A Solution and Safety Oriented Approach to Child Protection Casework.* New York: Norton.

Turnell, A. and Essex, S. (2006) *Working with Situations of 'Denied' Child Abuse: The Resolutions Approach.* Buckingham: Open University Press.

Weld, N. (2008) 'The Three Houses Tool: Building Safety and Positive Change.' In M. Calder (ed.) *Contemporary Risk Assessment in Safeguarding Children.* Lyme Regis: Russell House Publishing.

Weld, N. (2009) *Making Sure Children Get 'HELD': Ideas and Resources to Help Workers Place Hope, Empathy, Love and Dignity at the Heart of Child Protection and Support.* Lyme Regis: Russell House Publishing.

White, M. and Epston, D. (1990) *Narrative Means to Therapeutic Ends.* New York: Norton.

CHAPTER 7

Undertaking an Expert Assessment for the Court

Anna Gough

Introduction

> Kinship care is a practical expression of the pattern of relationships within the extended family: in most cases it will express the warmth and commitment between family members, a sense of solidarity and mutual support, and a shared sense of care and responsibility for the child. In some other families, by contrast, the offer to care for a child may be resonant of competition, criticism, condemnation or of dutiful obligation within the extended family. (Greeff 2001, p.47)

This chapter provides a personal account of my work as a clinical psychologist in the family courts. It will focus on the specific issues that can arise in kinship assessments, as reflected in the above quote. I will provide an overview of the different scenarios that have prompted the court to instruct an expert. I will then reflect on the vital components of a robust assessment, before identifying the gaps in the research field. For a more general overview of the work of an expert witness in the family courts, please refer to Bond, Solon and Harper (1999) and the Family Procedure Rules 2010 Part 25 (Ministry of Justice 2012).

Why instruct a psychologist?

Social workers, Children's Guardians and other professionals are competent to complete assessments of kinship placements, and advise the court about the capacity of the carers to meet the child's need for stable and permanent care and promote a coherent sense of identity. The vast majority of cases are determined without the need of a psychological assessment. However, there are other cases where issues are more complex, or where adult positions appear entrenched.

In the event that I am instructed to provide a psychological opinion to the court, I have found that the assessment of kinship placements is more challenging than other assessments (e.g. cognitive assessments, parenting assessments). There are many reasons for this. Kinship assessments typically involve a number of interviews with key family members (e.g. parents, grandparents). Individual narratives tend to contain multiple beliefs and associated emotions – about each other, the past and the future. This can include a parent's anger at a grandparent for putting themselves forward as an alternative carer (e.g. 'They are in competition with me'), or a grandparent's frustration with their own child (e.g. 'How did they let this situation happen?'). Unresolved feelings often emerge about historical events that continue to shape current interactions and family relationships ('They have always thought I'm not good enough', 'They have always wanted to take my child from me'). A psychological assessment must explore all these beliefs and emotions, as they are likely to re-emerge in the future and impact on placement stability. The task is to monitor the presence of emotions and the multiplicity of perspectives, tolerate the intensity in the room and then weave them together through open dialogue with all parties wherever possible.

There can be challenges for an expert when the local authority is actively promoting a placement within the birth family, and yet the assessment raises concerns about the long-term emotional welfare of the child. While it is in a child's best interests to remain with their birth family or friends (as opposed to entry into the care system), kinship placements are not risk free. Assessments have to focus beyond the physical care that can be offered to a child, and explore the stability of family relationships that will continue post-placement. One of the most complex issues is contact between kinship carer and the birth parent(s). I have found that some kinship placements are excellent in isolation. However, the level of conflict between different family members then merely replicates the emotional harm from which a local authority has sought to protect a child. It is often helpful to create a 'balance sheet' of advantages and disadvantages for the child and share these with the family and all involved professionals, in order to find potential solutions in the course of an assessment.

The request for an expert assessment can arise at different stages of a child's placement with relatives or friends. An early assessment was sought for an unborn child, Baby M:

Case study: Baby M (unborn child)

A mother was found to have a history of concealing the pregnancies, births and deaths of two babies over a four-year period. Professionals became aware that the mother had presented at her doctor's surgery. She was found to be 28 weeks pregnant. Serious concerns were raised about the mother's ability to care for Baby M. The maternal grandmother and step-grandfather put themselves forward as alternative carers. The court ordered an assessment of the mother and the grandparents, to identify the nature of family relationships, the grandparents' understanding of the previous concealed pregnancies, their motivation to offer a home to Baby M and their ability to promote her sense of identity. At the end of the assessment, I concluded that the grandparents were unable to provide an explanation for their daughter's actions in the past, and were unable to attune emotionally to this. Further exploration revealed that they were aware of the previous pregnancies, but their inability to raise concerns masked a long history of avoidant patterns within the family system. Joint meetings with the mother and the grandparents indicated that the family system would still regard the mother as the Baby M's main carer, with the grandparents on hand to offer support, as and when needed. Therefore, the reality was very different from the proposal of a permanent placement for Baby M with her grandparents.

Another reason for instructing a psychologist can arise when a parent alleges that the prospective future carers – often the grandparent(s) – have been abusive or non-protective in their own childhood. Farmer and Moyers (2008) describe these future carers as 'high risk relatives'. A psychological assessment has to consider the safety of the child, as well as his or her welfare. It needs to explore the perspectives of the parent and prospective carers, identify significant events from the past, the adults' current understanding and perception of these events, and the impact on the stability of family relationships over time. The following case study illustrates this scenario and the interventions that can follow to promote stability:

Case study: Ben (4) and Rory (7)

Ben and Rory were placed with their maternal grandmother on an interim basis, after concerns were raised by the social worker about the mother's relationship with a violent partner who had previously harmed a child in his care. The mother agreed to this placement, but sought the eventual return of the children. She cited a long history of physical and emotional abuse from the maternal grandmother, as well as a failure to protect her from sexual abuse from a former partner during her adolescence. The maternal grandmother vehemently denied these allegations, citing her daughter's mental instability as the reason. A psychological assessment was ordered by the court to explore the dynamics between the mother and the grandmother, in order to provide an opinion about placement stability and sustainability of contact arrangements over time. In this case, the most significant risk to Ben and Rory was emotional harm as a result of repeated exposure to the strained relationship between their mother and grandmother, the two adults who they loved the most in their lives. An extended assessment allowed for joint sessions to enable the mother and grandmother to identify the issues. They were signposted to a local private counselling organisation who offered reduced fees with trainees. This consolidated the work over a four-month period. Ben and Rory then returned to their mother's care with mutual agreement between the parties, with regular staying contact with their grandmother.

I have also been instructed when children have been living in a kinship placement for some years. This typically arises when there is either opposition to a significant change in contact arrangements (e.g. an increase in contact or a move from supervised to unsupervised) or where the contact agreements are fraught with difficulty. While kinship placements result in more contact between the child and birth parents, the stability of these arrangements depends on the adults' ability to manage the change in family dynamics and the roles in relation to the child. Wheal suggested that 'the parent(s) who cannot bring up their child must feel jealousy towards the carers' (2001, p.27). This situation is often compounded by less access to resources and professional support once a child has been placed with a relative. All too often contact disputes continue for months, and in some cases years, with the consistent theme of strained adult relationships, high levels of expressed emotion and low levels of communication. A psychological assessment can help the adults to recognise this process. It cannot, in all instances, arrive at an agreed way forward, as illustrated in the case of James and Molly:

Case study: James (8) and Molly (6)

In 2008 James and Molly were placed with their paternal grandparents under a Special Guardianship Order. They were four and two years old at the time. The Children's Guardian recommended regular contact between the children and their mother. This was particularly important as the family lived in the same town, and in close proximity. The children started to express their wishes to have more contact with their mother, who had had a baby with her new partner. However the paternal grandparents would not permit the mother to visit the children in their home. They continued to supervise the contact in a neutral venue. The grandparents felt unable to agree to the mother's request for the children to have contact in her home. A psychological assessment was required to update the court about the mother's psychological state, explore the grandparents' fears, and recommend a plan for sustainable contact. In the course of my assessment, I found that the mother had made significant progress which was underpinned by reflection and an incremental increase in insight over time. Sadly, the grandparents were unable to recognise or validate this, fearful that the children would 'vote with their feet' and return to their mother. The court's intervention was needed to support the recommendation of four sessions of supervised contact within the mother's home by a family support worker, with a plan for regular contact once a week in the natural environment. While the assessment did not result in agreement, the court was provided with a clear analysis of the underlying obstacles to contact.

The psychological assessment

I have identified three essential components of an expert assessment – the psychologist as a reflective practitioner, the psychologist as a therapeutic assessor, and the psychologist as a scientist practitioner. All three refer to a specific role, but also to a value system that underpins the whole focus of assessment.

The psychologist as a reflective practitioner

Reflective practice is the foundation for ethical and robust clinical practice, in a number of different professions (Cartwright 2011; Davies 2012). This is emphasised throughout clinical psychology training programmes, and should continue into professional careers. As a psychologist in the family courts, I am often faced with emotive and challenging scenarios, which can lead to strong judgements and opinions – from families as well as professionals. I have learnt that it is essential to remain aware of my own thoughts, feelings and reactions, as well as my position in terms of professional status, gender, class and ethnicity. Maintaining a reflective stance facilitates a meta-awareness of the complex process of assessment as it unfolds.

Before commencing a kinship assessment, it is important to recognise the self in the assessment. This naturally leads to identification of my own thoughts, emotions and values about family life and the systems in which children are placed, as well as the specific circumstances of a case. Internal questions stem from my personal experiences of care within one particular family, and in a particular socio-cultural context. Owning one's perspective is necessary in order to reflect upon it. Typical questions include: What constitutes 'a family'? What do I think about these grandparents caring for this child? Are these thoughts influenced by hidden values or judgements? Reflective practice also involves meta-cognitive awareness – the awareness of other people's thoughts, and their reactions to your thoughts. In kinship assessments, open and shared reflections provide the catalyst for honest discussions that can broach perceptions of differences (e.g. in age, life experiences). Overall, I have found that reflective practice strengthens the 'internal supervisor' (Casement 1985) and moderates the risk of a kinship assessment influenced by subconscious judgments.

The psychologist as a therapeutic assessor

The majority of people who find themselves the subject of an expert assessment have never seen a psychologist before. This is particularly the case when assessing grandparents as kinship carers. From the very beginning, the task is to form a bond with the family in order to create a working relationship towards a shared goal – the best interests of the particular child. In direct clinical work, the therapeutic alliance is the primary vehicle for change. In expert assessments, the similarity is that the working relationship with the family facilitates and enhances the assessment process.

The working relationship is created as a result of many different factors drawn from my clinical work with adults, in both NHS and private settings. I have found that kinship carers benefit from clear explanations about the reasons for the assessment, and my role as a psychologist specifically in the court proceedings. This eliminates the possibility of misperceptions or assumptions, and facilitates shared language from the outset. Therapeutic conditions of warmth and respect are essential, with clear communication so that implicit fears or assumptions are made explicit. Just as in medical humanities where active listening increases the accuracy of diagnosis, close attention to a person's narrative increases the accuracy of assessment. There should be a clear identification of strengths, as well as challenges and deficits. Finally, there is an emphasis on validation. This refers to verbal and nonverbal patterns of communication that convey to the person that his or her responses make sense, and are real and true for them. I have found that these vital components to an assessment will strengthen the alliance with a family, and enable the assessment to become as therapeutic as possible. That is, I have observed real change throughout the process of an assessment – in a person's thoughts, behaviours and eventual decisions about whether or not to put themselves forward as a permanent carer for a child.

It is also important to structure the assessment in a therapeutic manner. Assessments are more accurate and effective if all steps are actively taken to reduce the level of anxiety that families inevitably feel. Anxiety impacts on performance in test situations, because disturbance in the area of the brain responsible for emotional processing inhibits higher-order cognitive tasks such as reasoning and reflection (Perry 2008). The assessment itself presents an opportunity to teach low-level anxiety management strategies, which are especially useful when families have never benefited from psychological interventions. On a practical level, I rarely meet a person for a one-off assessment. My preferred assessment method is to meet with prospective carers, on a number of occasions, in a variety of settings. Interviews take place over a longer period of time. In this way, anxiety as a negative contributory factor can be significantly reduced, if not eliminated.

The psychologist as a scientist practitioner

An expert assessment requires a psychologist to work as a scientist practitioner, gathering information from a variety of sources in order to make sense of the emerging clinical picture. As well as conducting in-depth interviews, it can be useful to administer standardised psychometric measures. These tend to be specialist tools that should only be used by qualified psychologists, and it is important to be confident about administering them. Psychometric measures are not 'stand-alone' items; rather, the results must be woven into the information gleaned throughout the assessment process. When used correctly, I have found that they can be enormously helpful. Adults sometimes disclose information on a questionnaire that they have not been able to share openly. Issues that are highlighted on the test, known as endorsed items, can be compared with self-report (i.e. a validity check), and can also guide the focus of the assessment.

To illustrate, the *Wechsler Adult Intelligence Scale – Fourth Edition* (WAIS-IV; Wechsler 2008) is useful to clarify an individual's understanding of the case before the court, and advise family members and professionals about the most helpful method of communication. The *Paulhus Deception Scales* (PDS; Paulhus 1999) can identify the presence of rigid beliefs or over-confidence, which are likely to impact significantly on interpersonal relationships, both now and in the future. A person might endorse items that pertain to severe depression and/or suicidal thoughts (e.g. General Health Questionnaire 28; Goldberg and Hillier 1979). I am then able to explain about the impact of mood states on cognitive functioning (e.g. comprehension, accurate recall, memory), and ensure appropriate professional support.

Another vital source of information comes from other professionals. Unlike direct clinical work where the therapist aligns themselves to their client, the expert assessor has to check constantly and verify (as much as possible) the person's account. Questions are often asked about the adults' presentation in other situations, the stability of their commitment to the child, the nature of family relationships and the consistency of their narrative over time.

After gathering information from a variety of sources, a psychologist has to reflect upon the often vast range of data, analyse it, and then arrive at a clinical formulation. This refers to a psychological explanation that weaves together evidence-based theories and clinical experience (Johnstone and Dallos 2006). It leads on to an opinion about the nature of relationships between adults, the ability of the family system to meet the needs of the particular child, and the interventions that might be needed to support the placement.

I have found two theories to be particularly useful in illuminating these issues. First, *attachment theory* has stood the test of time and across cultures (Bowlby 1969). It has clarified the primacy of a child's need for nurture, and mapped out the psychological consequences of safe and responsive parental care, versus parental care that is inconsistent or harmful. Securely attached children are confident that their carer will respond in a timely, sensitive and effective manner in the face of distress or anxiety. As a result, these children have a stable sense of self, others are perceived as emotionally available, and the environment feels safe or at least manageable. They have benefited from explicit and implicit modelling of emotion regulation; that is, children learn how to label, describe, tolerate and reduce distress. From this foundation of security, children are able to regulate their behaviour and therefore engage in relationships that are based on reciprocity. In contrast, children who are insecurely attached or exhibit signs of a disorganised attachment bond find it very difficult to reach a point of psychological homeostasis, and therefore relationship instability and conflict in adulthood is more common. Most of the research has emanated from the Minnesota Longitudinal Study of Parents and Children which commenced in 1975. Stroufe, Egeland, Carlson and Collins (2005) concluded that with regard to global pathology at 17½ years, the strongest single predictor from the first six years of life was disorganised attachment.

In proposed kinship placements with grandparents, one of the key questions is the transmission of attachment patterns across the generations (Benoit and Parker 1994). Research studies usually involve administering the Adult Attachment Interview (AAI) to parents, and then assessing the attachment status of the child. In my clinical practice, I ask key questions to elicit the adult's perception of emotionally available and responsive carers in childhood (e.g. 'Please describe your

Mum/Dad', 'Who did you turn to when upset?', 'What did they do?', 'How did you feel afterwards?'). It is also important to explore the resolution of attachment insecurity over time because a consistent research finding is that an adult's reflective capacity predicts the attachment status of the child. Resolution can come about as a result of self-reflection, more stable social circumstances, and formal therapy or counselling. As Music concluded, 'It is not the kind of childhood the adults have that is predictive, but rather the ability to reflect on it' (2011, p.65). A psychological assessment must therefore explore the parents' perception of care, and the grandparents' reflections about this. These narratives will reflect internalised models of care, attunement (Stern 1985) and the process of mutual regulation (Tronick 1989). All these factors underpin the stability of family relationships, and ultimately the child's secure place within the system.

Second, I have found that it has been extremely useful to draw on *family systems theory*, which looks at both the micro and macro systems that can impact on a child. The focus of the psychological assessment is to explore what these are, how these have come about, and the factors that have predisposed, precipitated and perpetuated the multitude of adult responses. It takes into account the social inequalities that exist in our society, such as poverty, unemployment and isolation, as families do not exist in a vacuum. This approach emphasises the uniqueness of each person's narrative, which is the co-construction of their understanding and perceptions of the events in their lives. Finally, it can identify the strengths as well as the weaknesses within the family system, which lead to recommendations for change.

The final case study illustrates the process of an assessment using these two approaches:

Case study: Lucy

Lucy (age 18 months) was removed from her mother's care after suffering a non-accidental injury, and placed in foster care. Concerns were raised about the mother's ability to protect, in light of her long history of substance misuse. Lucy's grandmother put herself forward as an alternative carer. An expert assessment was ordered. This explored the mother's attachment history, the grandmother's attachment history, the adults' reflective capacities and the mother's ability to accept a kinship placement. It also focused on the grandmother's capacity to protect Lucy and promote her attachment security as well as her sense of identity within the family system. While the psychological assessment identified areas of strength and resilience, it recommended that the grandmother engaged in a defined number of therapy sessions with an experienced clinical psychologist, to enable her to increase her reflective capacity about her emotional responses. These sessions enabled the grandmother to identify a tendency to avoid difficult issues and emotions (which had arisen from her own childhood), which had impacted on her ability to express concerns about her daughter's substance misuse in the past. In a therapeutic and non-judgemental setting, the grandmother felt able to recognise that she had unwittingly placed her daughter over and above her grandchild. She was able to identify both internal and external resources to successfully manage these psychological conflicts in the future. The work was successfully undertaken, and Lucy was placed with her grandmother.

Concluding comments

Clinical assessments should evolve through a process of supervision, feedback and research. This is particularly vital in this specific field. Expert opinion forms a key piece of the overall evidence that is placed before the court, which ultimately makes a decision about a child's future. It is essential that the psychologist makes a commitment to engage in robust systems of external supervision and support, in order to ensure personal and professional wellbeing. In addition, seeking feedback from professionals should be part of routine clinical practice. In reality, this can be difficult as there is often little contact between the expert and the professional network once a child has been placed (either within or outside of the family). Social workers rarely need to contact the psychologist unless this has been expressly directed by the court. While this is understandable, it leads to a break in the feedback loop. I have found that maintaining robust working relationships with social workers, Children's Guardians and solicitors can moderate this potential problem.

More research is needed to evaluate the robustness of expert assessments in kinship placements. Qualitative research methods would be particularly suited to this topic. To illustrate, using a Biographic-Narrative Inducing Method (Wengraf 2001), participants could be asked a single question to elicit a free-flowing narrative, and then two further interviews would explore the emerging themes. The systematic analysis of interviews with three to six families would lay the basis for theorisation and, most importantly, provide practical pointers for expert assessments. Finally, longitudinal studies would provide more information about the correlation between expert recommendations, and the stability of kinship placements over time. In practice, this would need to arise from joint research projects between social workers and experts in order to provide a multi-faceted analysis of processes and outcomes.

In this chapter, I have sought to provide a first-hand account of my work as an expert witness to illustrate the contribution of clinical psychology in the assessment of kinship placements. The case studies have described the complex issues that can arise within families seeking to care for a child. Finally, I have suggested that experts need to ensure that robust systems of support and supervision are in place to cope with the emotional demands of this work, and to actively seek feedback to improve clinical practice.

References

Benoit, D. and Parker, K.C.H. (1994) 'Stability and transmission of attachment across three generations.' *Child Development 65*, 5, 1444–1456.

Bond, C., Solon, M. and Harper, P. (1999) *The Expert Witness in Court.* Crayford: Shaw & Sons.

Bowlby, J. (1969) *Attachment and Loss Volume 1: Attachment.* London: Pimlico.

Cartwright, C. (2011) 'Transference, countertransference and reflective practice in cognitive therapy.' *Clinical Psychology 15*, 3, 112–120.

Casement, P. (1985) *Learning from the Patient.* London: Routledge.

Davies, S. (2012) 'Embracing reflective practice.' *Education in Primary Care 23*, 9–12.

Farmer, E. and Moyers, S. (2008) *Kinship Care: Fostering Effective Family and Friends Placements.* London: Jessica Kingsley Publishers.

Goldberg, D.P. and Hillier, V.F. (1979) 'A scaled version of the General Health Questionnaire.' *Psychological Medicine 9*, 139–145.

Greeff, R. (2001) 'Family Dynamics in Kinship Foster Care.' In B. Broad (ed.) *Kinship Care: The Placement Choice for Children and Young People.* Lyme Regis: Russell House Publishing.

Johnstone, L. and Dallos, R. (2006) *Formulation in Psychology and Psychotherapy: Making Sense of People's Problems.* London: Routledge.

Ministry of Justice (2012) *Family Procedure (Amendment) (No. 4) Rules 2012*. London: MoJ. Available at www.justice.gov.uk/courts/procedure-rules/family, accessed on 20 May 2012.

Music, G. (2011) *Nurturing Natures: Attachment and Children's Emotional, Sociocultural and Brain Development*. Hove: Psychology Press.

Paulhus, D.L. (1999) *Paulhus Deception Scales (PDS): The Balanced Inventory of Desirable Responding-7*. Toronto, Canada: Mental Health Systems Inc.

Perry, B. (2008) 'The Traumatised Child: Healing Mind, Body and Brain'. Lecture at the Child Centre for Mental Health, Islington, 14 June.

Stern, D.N. (1985) 'Affect Attunement.' In J.D. Call, E. Galenson, and R.L. Tyson (eds) *Frontiers of Infant Psychiatry: Vol. 2*. New York: Basic Books.

Stroufe, A., Egeland, B., Carlson, E. and Collins, A. (2005) *The Development of the Person: The Minnesota Study of Risk and Adaptation from Birth to Adulthood*. London: Guilford Press.

Tronick, E.Z. (1989) 'Emotions and emotional communication in infants.' *American Psychologist 44*, 2, 112–119.

Wechsler, D. (2008) *Wechsler Adult Intelligence Scale, Fourth Edition (WAIS-IV)*. London: Pearson.

Wengraf, T. (2001) *Qualitative Research Interviewing*. London: Sage.

Wheal, A. (2001) 'Family and Friends Who are Carers: A Framework for Success.' In B. Broad (ed.) *Kinship Care: The Placement Choice for Children and Young People*. Lyme Regis: Russell House Publishing.

CHAPTER 8

Permanence Planning for Children in Family and Friends Care

Establishing a Secure Base in the Re-ordering of Family Relationships

John Simmonds

Ask most people about their instinctive response if a family member finds themselves in serious difficulty that impacts on their capacity to care for a child and they would say 'I will help out'. So grandma steps in, or aunt or uncle or an older sibling to offer their spare bed for the night which may then turn into two or three nights or weeks or years. In one very important sense this is what family membership and commitment means – 'We are family. You are one of us.' Loyalty forged through the blood tie is a powerfully established feature of human nature. It is only broken in extreme circumstances. The idea of the state stepping in as an alternative preferred provider of care for children in these circumstances is something that would result in most families recoiling in horror. The state may be needed to provide universal services such as education, health and practical and financial support but that is quite different to the core of a family's life marked out and sustained by history, heritage, custom, feeling and identity. However, for some families the state has to step in on a temporary or longer-term basis because these core fundamentals are not strong enough or indeed present at all. This is so for a very small proportion of families, estimated to be about five per cent of all those where children are cared for in-family by people other than the child's parents (Nandy, Selwyn, Farmer and Vaisey 2011).

Where the state does step in, a very important concept drives the operation of the system – that of permanence and permanency planning. The concept has its roots in the writings of a number of social work practitioners in both the USA and the UK. Epstein and Heymann (1967) report on the experience and outcomes of proactively clarifying with the parents the importance of their child securing a permanent family life either through the resolution of their problems or placement in an adoptive home. The 'Oregon Project' further developed this idea because of the presence of significant 'drift' in stranger foster care resulting from the complete absence of any clear plan that identified the child's future family membership whether this was with the parents or through adoption (Emlen 1981). Similar developments took place in the UK following the publication of *Children Who Wait* (Rowe and Lambert 1973) with a very clear policy and practice framework (Fitzgerald, Murcer and Murcer 1982) that was intended to address this issue of drift. Primary in establishing and developing the concept of permanency was a powerful belief that children do not just need the experience of family life – after all that is what foster care is – but that there are qualities of family life that go beyond its mere day-to-day presence. These qualities include a sense of commitment, stability, determination and belief that family life is intended to last, come what may. As noted above, family life means history, heritage, custom, feeling and identity. In its early development, permanence was identified as a core part of child and adolescent development (Goldstein, Freud and Solnit 1973, 1980) reinforced then by the development of the concept of attachment (Bowlby 1980). Children were seen not only to need permanence to secure their full development but as a fundamental right as a human being.

Permanence in the current context of policy and practice

Permanence as a concept is now firmly embedded in policy and practice. Volume 2 of the Children Act 1989 Guidance states:

> Permanence is the framework of emotional permanence (attachment), physical permanence (stability) and legal permanence (the carer has parental responsibility for the child) which gives a child a sense of security, continuity, commitment and identity. The objective of planning for permanence is therefore to ensure that children have a secure, stable and loving family to support them through childhood and beyond. Permanence provides an underpinning framework for all social work with children and families from family support through to adoption. (Chapter 2.3)

The Guidance goes on to establish that the care plan for the child should be driven by the requirement to establish permanence for the child and that there should be an explicit plan about how to deliver this by the time of the second care plan review – four months after the child enters care. Where it is not consistent with the child's welfare to be placed with the parents or those with parental responsibility for the child, then section 22C(7)(a) places a duty on local authorities to give preference to placing the child with a relative, friend or other connected person (6)(a) where they are an approved foster carer. However, the overriding duty is to ensure that it is the child's welfare that drives placement planning. The Guidance notes that: 'most children benefit by being placed with relatives or friends or others connected with them; near their own homes; continuing to attend the same school; living with their siblings and in accommodation which is appropriate for any special needs' (Chapter 3.10).

But there is also recognition that those responsible for identifying and planning placements will often be faced by weighing up multiple factors in the child's needs where prioritising any particular issue will result in other issues having lesser importance. This is of course the challenge of child placement and why it takes considerable knowledge and skill to do it well. But there is no doubting that in statute, regulations and guidance there is a hierarchy of placement choice which prioritises return home to parents and then placement with relatives and friends. This can really be of little surprise when the question is put as outlined in the opening section of this chapter. The instinctive pull of family, kinship and community is powerful. It is where children belong and the state makes for a poor second best in most people's minds.

Given this, it is somewhat surprising that permanency has often been strongly associated with adoption by strangers and certainly in England, the coalition government's child placement policy appears to have a very strong if not dominant adoption focus. Indeed when the Department for Education castigated local authorities for the decreasing numbers of adoption placements through to 2011, the combined figures for children leaving care through adoption and special guardianship for that year was the largest ever at 4780, considerably more than at the height of the adoption figures in 2005 when they were 3800. It is important to note that the greater majority of those Special Guardianship Orders will have been made to family and friends carers (Wade, Dixon and Richards 2010). Given it was an explicit policy objective in Tony

Blair's adoption reforms to introduce a new legal order that would work as an alternative legal route out of the care system, that might have been expected to be hailed as something of a policy triumph. Indeed given the combined figures are continuing to rise with 5570 in 2012, there is significant progress being made in providing children with an exit from the care system through permanent placements with family and friends placements playing an important part in that. Although the policy emphasis seems to focus on adoption and there are explicit developments and investments in this area, the importance of family and friends placements is clearly identified in statute as identified above. There is clear guidance about this from the beginning of local authority involvement identified in the pre-proceedings phase of the Public Law Outline (Department of Children, Schools and Families 2008) through to placement and support provisions identified in statutory guidance issued on Family and Friends Care (Department for Education 2011). However, despite the fact that the current framework places such a strong emphasis on family and friends care, in many ways it does not appear on either the professional or the public agenda with that degree of prominence.

Permanence and the challenge of change and transitions

The concept of permanence in itself is a strange one. Generally in life there is very little that is permanent. Child, adolescent and adult development is an interaction between those factors that become stable and those factors which continue to exert change. Human beings are continuously in a state of development. On an everyday level we are making transitions from one context to another – home to school, work to play, being awake to falling asleep. Each one of these has an effect on bodily function and emotional and social readiness and adaptability. Over the course of time, there are more significant transitions – from a life centred on parents and immediate family to one that incorporates school life, friendships, learning, adolescence, leaving home, romantic relationships and intimacy and work and career. Managing these transitions well depends partly on what has gone on before, the nature of the demand at the point of transition and the availability of resources and support. There are frequently chance issues that enhance or challenge how a transition might be responded to. Despite the significance of change in the human developmental agenda, the place of permanence is hugely significant when it means a secure base from which the child, adolescent or adult ventures out and for most people their secure base means their family.

Creating a secure base is strongly associated with the concept of attachment as noted above. The early development of the attachment concept focused strongly on the mother's role with the attributes of maternal sensitivity core to understanding how attachment develops. Over time it has become clear that attachment is not a gender specific attribute nor is it one that is specific to birth parents. It arises out of a primary instinctual need for the human infant to maintain proximity to another person, usually an adult, who can keep them safe from danger. Bowlby placed considerable emphasis on the evolutionary nature of attachment with its origins in the 'hunter-gatherer' orientation of human beings with survival in such circumstances depending on the presence of a strong, protective adult to ward off predators. Although human beings have evolved considerably over millennia, the image is not so distant; the deeply embedded protective instinct of parents is very easy to observe and indeed to experience. The observation of the powerful cries and distress of infants and the immediacy of response indicates the power of the underlying system. The child's experience of and response to separation from their primary carer became the standard for understanding attachment with the 'strange situation procedure' (Ainsworth 1978) a gold standard test. In particular, observations of the child's behaviour following a series of brief separations (of three minutes or so) and reunions under laboratory conditions enabled psychologists to formulate three patterns of attachment called 'secure' (Group B), 'insecure-avoidant' (Group A) and 'insecure-resistant/ambivalent' (Group C). Further work in subsequent years added a further pattern, 'disorganised/disorientated' (Group D) (Main and Solomon 1986). A child classified as secure was likely to make immediate and appropriate physical contact with their primary carer, to allow themselves to be comforted and reassured and in the process to be calmed from any upset or distress they displayed during the brief separation. Within a short time, they would be observed to begin playing and exploring the room where the observation was taking place. The child's attachment system was returning to a state of quiescence and other emotional and behavioural systems that support exploration and curiosity came to the fore. A child classified as Insecure-avoidant on the other hand shows less upset during the separation and does not seek proximity during the reunion and where they do they may avoid making eye contact or physical contact that is comforting. Their attachment system does not become fully deactivated. This may show itself, for example, in outbursts of anger. For a child classified as insecure-resistant/ ambivalent, they will show much more distress at the separation and on reunion may make very strong approaches to their carer but mingled with resistance to the comfort being offered. It will take longer for them to be comforted. Lastly, the disorganised group are difficult to classify because their behaviour was not consistently patterned and their reactions to separation and reunion was a mixture of approach and avoidance mingled with unusual behaviours that include freezing, fear, appearing dazed or confused. In a study by Main and Cassidy (1988) of children age six, two particularly important sub groups of children were identified, those who were controlling and punitive of the parent and those that were controlling and caring of the parent. Both involve a role reversal of the usual parent–child relationship and indicate just how children might adjust and adapt to a parent where the qualities associated with being a primary carer are not sufficiently available to them at a time when this matters.

Permanence and attachment

There are a number of issues arising from the development of the attachment framework which are important in understanding the notion of permanency as it might apply to family and friends care. While the 'strange situation procedure' emphasises behavioural observation, Bowlby introduced the concept of 'internal working models of the self in relationships' as a psychological construct. His view was that the repeated experience of carer sensitivity, attunement and responsiveness as they develop in the early months and years of a child's life become represented in the child's mind as a predictive picture of the way that the relational world works. For the 'secure child', their world is experienced as safe, and is expected to be so. Where anxiety and new experiences come along, there is always an active and available person that the child can turn to for comfort and reassurance. The child's model then extends to what can be expected from other relationships. Where this is not so there will be corresponding negative expectations of self and others.

Although the focus in many studies and indeed in practice is on classifying the child's attachment status, the direction of effect is from the parent to the child. In an important study (Fonagy, Steele and Steele 1991) of 100 women who were expecting their first baby, their attachment classification was determined by using the Adult Attachment Interview pre-birth. They were then followed up after the birth of the baby when the infants were 12 months old using the strange situation procedure. Of the 96 women and infants in the follow-up, 75 per cent of the infant's attachment classification was predicted from the mother's adult attachment classification. Similar predictive issues have been identified with fathers in the same study (Steele, Steele and Fonagy 1996). While attachment is often described in terms of the child, it is the adults in the child's life that create the conditions that facilitate the development of attachment. Sensitivity is one feature of this and over time this has been further elaborated in the development of concepts such as reflective functioning (Fonagy, Target, Steele and Steele 1998) and mind-mindedness (Meins 1997).

The distribution of attachment patterns (van Ijzendoorn, Schuengel and Bakermans-Kranenburg 1999) of children in their early years shows distributions for non-clinical populations in the USA of 62 per cent secure, 15 per cent insecure-avoidant, 9 per cent insecure-resistant/ ambivalent and 15 per cent disorganised. It is important to note that insecure classifications are not in themselves disturbances but potential vulnerabilities. They may increase the stress in families where there is heightened emotion and behaviour such as crying or anger and make it more of a struggle to calm and reassure. This may make transitions such as starting school or making new friends or illness more difficult, but they are not in themselves disturbances. Disorganisation is somewhat different and this has been linked to evidence of frightening or frightened behaviour by the child's attachment figure. Given the attachment figure is required to be a source of comfort and reassurance this can set up a significant and unresolvable conflict for the child in needing to approach them but at the same time needing to maintain distance or even escape (Lyons-Ruth and Jacobvitz 1999). Child maltreatment is clearly implicated in such patterns but not exclusively so.

Although attachment explains a core part of child development and parenting, it is by no means a complete explanation. There are many other important issues such as setting clear boundaries for the child, providing stimulation and opportunity for play, supporting learning and cognitive development, supporting the child to resolve conflicts, celebrating and recognising important aspects of ethnic identity, culture and religion, exploring gender roles and sexuality. Many of these issues may be incorporated into the child's internal models of self in relationships and it is not difficult to see how a sensitive, attuned and mind-mindedness orientation would play a part in all of these different domains but at the same time it is important not to see attachment as the explanation for everything that happens in the course of a child's development.

Permanency and family and friends care

What are the implications of this for the concept of permanency in relation to family and friends care? Most of the children where the local authority becomes involved because of concern about abuse and neglect will be vulnerable and it is likely that their development will have been seriously compromised as a result. The idea of a secure base is likely to have been disturbed by the influence of factors such as drug and alcohol abuse, serious mental health difficulties and domestic violence. The consequences of these are various but very likely will include lack of daily routines, poor hygiene, inadequate food, health care and appropriate stimulation, and exposure to varying degrees of frightening or frightened behaviour. Characterising the circumstances of such households is difficult because there are so many individual issues at play but any notion of permanence is likely to be absent when that means a secure emotional, social and physical base and the presence of at least one adult to whom the child can return when their attachment system gives them a warning sign of danger. Where any of these adverse circumstances have been present for a child, it is likely to impact on the child's development. Children will adapt to adverse circumstances because that is what human beings are programmed to do. But the form that adaptation will take is likely to be opposite of a representation in their internal working model of the self in relationships that says 'I am loving and lovable', 'I can find comfort and reassurance from the people that I know and care for me when I encounter problems in the world as I explore' and 'The people I meet are likely to be interesting and stimulating and may welcome me into their world as I get to know them.' Children develop internal narrative accounts that directly capture their experiences of their relational world starting with their attachment figures and, as they grow, with other people – both adults and other children. These narrative accounts can be captured in well-developed techniques such as story stems

(Buchsbaum, Toth, Clyman, Cicchetti and Emde 1992; Hodges, Steele, Hillman, Henderson and Kaniuk 2003).

When family members step in to take care of the child in these very difficult circumstances, they will be faced with numerous if not an overwhelming set of issues. There will be the immediate issues of understanding what has happened, for example to their adult son or daughter or niece or nephew and what has happened to the child or children. There will be the immediate issues in attending to the children's needs and making significant adjustments in their own lives to enable that to happen. There will also be many issues resulting from the involvement of social workers and others. There may have been little sense of permanency in the often unpredictable and chaotic events leading up to the actual placement of the children with family or friends but even so the placement itself is a major transition involving loss and change, anxiety, fear and uncertainty. If there were ever a need for a secure base this would be it. If there were ever a challenge to establishing a secure base then this is likely to be it as well. Resilience and resourcefulness in the family and friends carers are what is needed and particularly the ability to focus on the experiences of the children in their distress, when they most need to feel that they have a secure base. And an important part of that would be drawing on current internal models of self in relationships. This may be one of the very great strengths of family and friends carers when the children may well have grown to know and love their grandparents, aunts or uncles or older siblings. Family commitment and loyalty embedded in existing relationships often holds the significant advantage over 'stranger' foster care. Whether these relationships have the quality of attachment relationships is a more complex question but they may share all the advantages that come from extended family relationships that work well.

Whether the placement is to be temporary, longer lasting or even permanent is likely to take some time to work itself out. The significant question in relation to the child is what do they do during the wait? And the next question for the child will be quite what to think once the plan is finally decided. These are important questions especially when attachment theory has focused on the importance of selective attachments which endure over time and which are established in the first few years of the child's life. What do these powerful experience expectant systems do inside the child as the adults work their way through to finding a solution to the problem of permanency? The most important answer to the first question is that children do not wait. They are programmed to search for adults that will care for them and they will do so in so far as they can selectively. If they are frustrated in their efforts because an adult does not or cannot provide the sensitive, attuned, mind-mindedness qualities that are needed, then they will adapt in their search and this may result in the insecure or disorganised patterns described above. The consequences of this are that the child could develop a pattern of relating that as they grow older could be recognised as compulsive self-reliance, compulsive care-giving or compulsive care-seeking. Rather than be able to depend readily on their primary attachment figures to provide safety and comfort, they have to develop their own strategies for managing separation and loss, uncertainty and anxiety. Heard and Lake (2009) contrast two forms of relating. The first they term supportive-companionable which they define as:

> A protective, explanatory and exploratory form of relating... It is warm, unanxious and is accompanied by appropriate constructive misattunements...by an unanxious acknowledgement of ignorance and an interested preparedness to extend knowledge. Conflict, when it arises, is handled by the recognition of the other's point of view and resolved by negotiation and compromise. (p.34)

The second they term as a dominating and submissive and as a form of relating it:

> forces others to follow the decisions of a controlling leader. It can appear not to be damaging when it carries the stance of a protective and even indulgent dictator. But those who do not accept a submissive and obedient stance face coercion in various forms, including being shamed and humiliated. (p.35)

It is not difficult to see how the dominating/submissive dynamic pattern comes to explain many aspects of the emotional and behavioural challenge when children do not have a secure base, and this can be a pattern from a very young age through to adolescence and into adult intimate relationships and relationships with their own children when they are parents themselves. It is also not difficult to see that at times of stress, threat and change, a supportive and companionable approach is most likely to provide solutions in a way that is reassuring and helpful, and that a dominating/submissive dynamic will do quite the opposite.

Children need to find solutions to the poor care they have experienced, and particularly to experiences of maltreatment whatever the specific manifestations of maltreatment may be. They will inevitably have been unable to do so during the period that led up to the placement with family and friends carers and then that is likely to show itself in the placement itself because it has become the child's adaptive solution to what they anticipate the relational world is likely to offer them.

Permanence and permanency planning are crucial in ensuring that the conditions that best promote a child's development become established where the child cannot return home to their parents. But it is planning in circumstances where family history leading up to the need for a plan, the planning process itself and the actual plan are marked by considerable uncertainty, separation, loss, change and trauma. For the child, the prospective carers and the parents, the issues are powerful and painful. While family 'stepping in' is something that most of us would identify with, the issues that we are likely to be confronted with are of some enormity. For carers to maintain a supportive-companionable perspective is likely to be very difficult when they are also trying to process their protective feelings towards the child, their concern for and feelings about the child's parents and their own circumstances and their concerns for and feelings about coping in the present and planning for the future. From the child's perspective, who to turn to, who might be safe, what response they might get and how long any of it might last are equally big questions. And if any of this can be settled, new issues will emerge as time goes by. All of this indicates just why social workers are important in providing information, guidance and expertise. It also suggests that their approach in such circumstances should be informed by a supportive-companionable dynamic in exercising their position of authority as professionals. It reinforces the importance of relationships and relating being at the centre of social work practice and the capacity and competence to engage with distressed, anxious, frightened or angry people and to sustain that engagement over time. In a Canadian study (Gladstone, Fitzgerald and Brown 2012) of social workers' work with grandparents, an exploration of the use of power highlighted three domains. The first focused on the allocation and distribution of resources to grandparents, a commonly identified theme of considerable feeling in many reports from family and friends carers beyond this study. The second focused on the way social workers used the power in their role to manage the work with the grandparents – sometimes in ways that were perceived to be helpful and sometimes not so. Last, the study explored how social workers negotiated agreements with the grandparents. There is strong emphasis throughout of the complex, intense and challenging nature of interactions between the parties that resulted in a mixture of helpful and unhelpful outcomes. These extend from day-to-day matters such as the storage of medication, through to contact arrangements, responding to children's needs and the status of the placement. The study concludes by identifying the unequal but inevitable distribution of power and responsibilities between social workers and grandparents. However, opportunities continually present themselves for a meaningful exchange of perspectives when issues are negotiated, differences acknowledged, assumptions are questioned and 'not knowing' is an accepted and important part of the relationship.

Permanence and the re-ordering of family relationships

Permanency planning often conveys a sense of purposeful control, decision-making and the pursuit of certainty. The creation of a sustaining and sustained secure base for a child in a family setting is the objective but the road is likely to be hazardous and marked by uncertainty, loss and change. There will be particularly challenging issues in the re-ordering of family relationships where the intention is to establish that secure base with family members other than the parents. In order to do this those family member/carers will need to feel they are entitled to claim the child (Dozier and Lindhiem 2006). The act of claiming is a psychological and social issue of some significance because it establishes the basis of who manages the child's care and development day to day and in the longer term. It requires considerable investment of resources but some significant subjective re-orientation to thinking and feeling that 'What I do above all else matters for *my* child'. Establishing this perspective is a challenge to the entitlement of the parents who will think and expect that that claim is theirs even if it is modified by relief that their child is with a family member and the immediate pressure of having to provide care to the child has been removed. There is little in research that establishes just how families negotiate these rearrangements. Some of this will depend on the quality of the relationship between the child's parent and the family member carer. If that is a parent–child relationship, then there will be a long history that may well have embedded within it all the thoughts and feelings that both parties will have that led up to the fact that the parent cannot care for the child. This may combine empathetic features or disappointment, anger and a sense of betrayal or, most likely, there will be a combination of both. When the risk to the child is such that the local authority have become involved then this is likely to involve heightened feelings of anxiety, guilt and betrayal. While a supportive-companionable form of relating may be a much-needed dynamic within the family to manage this well, the risks are that family history and narrative bring the dominant-submissive to the fore. Accusations, anger, withdrawal and passivity are the likely manifestations of this dynamic. The re-formation of a new family grouping around the child that changes who is in control and who is in charge, who claims the child and who becomes the child's secure base is highly likely to stir up reciprocal feelings of losing place, face and control. The reconstruction of family boundaries is a part of placement planning and decision-making. The displacement of family members is as important though as placement. It is very likely that the family will need considerable help with this to ensure above all that the child is the focus and their needs override whatever else the adults think and feel about their own position. There cannot be any underestimating just how important this is but also just how very difficult this is to achieve.

Therefore while permanency must be the objective for the child, in the context of complex family relationships it is unlikely that the term accurately conveys the reality of what permanency creates. As family members adjust to their new roles and relationships maybe with the affirming status of approved foster carer or Special Guardianship status, the child in some form will be adjusting their allegiance and identifications. But there is likely to be considerable feeling and memory associated with this with a mixture of relief at being settled and feeling perturbed at what is to come. Contact with parents may play a significant part in re-wakening feelings and memories, giving rise to hopes for reunification and fears for further disruption. The experience of a secure base may be crucial to the child's development but this is no simple matter when the child experiences conflicted feelings about their parents and their new substitute parents who are family members. A secure base for the child needs to provide them with opportunities to put these difficult thoughts and feelings into words or other appropriate child centred forms of communication. Emotional and behavioural difficulties are commonly recognised as an important risk factor in children who become looked after whatever their placement type. What are less often identified are the dynamics behind these difficulties as children are required to realign their relationships often on the basis of being poorly prepared psychologically through earlier developmental experiences, especially those associated with the concept of attachment. Many of these issues are captured in a study by Farmer (2010) of four local authorities with a sample of 270 children in family and friends and stranger foster care. Information was collected from local authority case files and a smaller number of direct interviews. Researcher evaluation of placement quality was established and placements that ended in an unplanned way (disruptions) were also identified. The factors that influenced outcome prior to placement were related to particular local authorities, to the status of the carers – with grandparents rather than other relatives being a positive feature – to the age of the child at placement and to parental drug misuse. The child's behaviour and the number of adversities they had experienced, placement with siblings or placement as a lone child were also significant. Further analysis of factors during placement identified poor school attendance and educational development, the continuation or emergence of behavioural difficulties, the carer's commitment to the child and the strain on them of maintaining this. Last, evidence was identified about the role of children's services including the approval of carers as foster carers, the availability of support and the supervision of contact. A logistic regression analysis of those family and friends placements that disrupted identified the combination of older age at placement, the absence of carer commitment, unsupervised contact and the child being out of control as highly significant ($p<0.001$). A similar analysis in relation to placement quality identified four factors – child truanting before placement, low carer commitment, a struggle to cope and being in a particular one of the four local authorities studied ($p<0.001$). Despite these important issues, the study identifies the advantageous nature of kinship care, in particular with grandparents, the benefits to children in terms of longer-term outcomes and the likelihood of placements lasting when compared to stranger foster care.

These are important messages and a parallel study by Hunt, Waterhouse and Lutman (2008) identifies similar advantages and messages. A Cochrane review presents the international evidence on the effectiveness and outcomes from family and friends care (Winokur,

Holtan and Valentine 2009). All of these studies reinforce the importance of high quality social work practice and the availability of timely and appropriate services. Family and friends carers face a significant ongoing challenge, as do the children whatever the well-established advantages and outcomes of this form of placement are.

Conclusions

It is difficult to overestimate the value of family as the core of human existence. Family life embodies individual development from birth to the grave in a way that the state, as important as it can be, can never replicate. The commitment, determination and resourcefulness of family extend beyond anything that can be replicated by state processes although the state can create the conditions whereby an alternative family life can emerge. This is the essence of planning for permanence. But at the centre of this overarching principle is a complex set of questions about uncertainty, loss, change and transition. The secure base and the concept of attachment have become embedded as a part of the evidence base for practice. But they are the means by which loss and change are negotiated not the means by which they are avoided. Family and friends placement requires family members to re-order and re-negotiate their relationships in the best interests of children. The basis on which they do so and the support they need in the process cannot and should not be underestimated.

References

Ainsworth, M.D.S. (1978) *Patterns of Attachment: A Psychological Study of the Strange Situation.* New Jersey, New York, London: Wiley.

Bowlby, J. (1980) *Attachment and Loss.* London: Hogarth Press.

Buchsbaum, H.K., Toth, S.L., Clyman, R.B., Cicchetti, D. and Emde, R.N. (1992) 'The use of a narrative story stem technique with maltreated children: implications for theory and practice.' *Development and Psychopathology 4,* 4, 603–625.

Department of Children, Schools and Families (2008) *The Children Act 1989: Guidance and Regulations; Court Orders* (Vol. 1). Norwich: The Stationary Office.

Department for Education (2011) *Family and Friends Care: Statutory Guidance for Local Authorities.* London: Her Majesty's Stationary Office.

Dozier, M. and Lindhiem, O. (2006) 'This is my child: differences among foster parents in commitment to their young children.' *Child Maltreatment 11,* 4, 338–345.

Emlen, A. (1981) 'Development of the Permanency Planning Concept.' In S. Downs, L. Bayles, A. Dreyer, M. Emlen, L. *et al.* (eds) *Foster Care Reform in the 1970s: Final Report of the Permanency Planning Dissemination Project.* Portland, OR: Regional Research Institute for Human Services, Portland State University.

Epstein, L. and Heymann, I. (1967) 'Some decisive processes in adoption plannng for older children.' *Child Welfare 46,* 1, 5–9.

Farmer, E. (2010) 'What factors relate to good placement outcomes in kinship care?' *British Journal of Social Work 40,* 2, 426–444.

Fitzgerald, J., Murcer, B. and Murcer, B. (1982) *Building New Families: Through Adoption and Fostering.* Oxford: Basil Blackwell.

Fonagy, P., Steele, H. and Steele, M. (1991) 'Maternal representations of attachment during pregnancy predict the organization of infant-mother attachment at one year of age.' *Child Development 62,* 5, 891–905.

Fonagy, P., Target, M., Steele, H. and Steele, M. (1998) *Refective Functioning Manual, Version 5.0, for Application to Adult Attachment Interviews.* London: University College, London.

Gladstone, J.W., Fitzgerald, K.-A.J. and Brown, R.A. (2012) 'Social workers' use of power in relationships with grandparents in child welfare settings.' *British Journal of Social Work.*

Goldstein, J., Freud, A. and Solnit, A.J. (1973) *Beyond the Best Interests of the Child.* New York: Free Press.

Goldstein, J., Freud, A. and Solnit, A.J. (1980) *Before the Best Interests of the Child.* London: Burnett Books.

Heard, D. and Lake, B. (2009) *The Challenge of Attachment for Caregiving.* London: Karnac Books.

Hodges, J., Steele, M., Hillman, S., Henderson, K. and Kaniuk, J. (2003) 'Changes in attachment representations over the first year of adoptive placement: narratives of maltreated children.' *Clinical Child Psychology and Psychiatry 8,* 3, 351–367.

Hunt, J., Waterhouse, S. and Lutman, E. (2008) *Keeping them in the Family: Outcomes for Children Placed in Kinship Care through Care Proceedings.* London: British Association for Adoption & Fostering.

Lyons-Ruth, K. and Jacobvitz, D. (1999) 'Attachment Disorganisation: Unresolved Loss, Relational Violence and Lapses in Behavioural and Attentional Strategies.' In J. Cassidy and P. Shaver (eds) *Handbook of Attachment: Theory, Research and Clinical Applications.* New York: Guilford Press.

Main, M. and Cassidy, J. (1988) 'Categories of response to reunion with the parent at age six: predictable from attachment classifications and stable over a 1 month period.' *Developmental Psychology 24,* 415–426.

Main, M. and Solomon, J. (1986) 'Discovery of an Insecure-Disorganised/Disorientated Pattern.' In T. Brazelton and Y. Yogman (eds) *Affective Development in Infancy.* Norwood, NJ: Ablex.

Meins, E. (1997) *Security of Attachment and the Social Development of Cognition.* Hove: Psychology Press.

Nandy, S., Selwyn, J., Farmer, E. and Vaisey, P. (2011) *Spotlight on Kinship Care: Using Census Microdata to Examine the Extent and Nature of Kinship Care in the UK at the Turn of the Twentieth Century.* doi:www.bristol.ac.uk/sps/research/projects/completed/2011/rj5314/finalkinship.pdf, accessed on 4 June 2013.

Rowe, J. and Lambert, L. (1973) *Children who Wait: A Study of Children Needing Substitute Families.* London: Association of British Adoption Agencies.

Steele, H., Steele, M. and Fonagy, P. (1996) 'Associations among attachment classifications of mothers, fathers, and their infants.' *Child Development 67,* 2, 541–555.

van Ijzendoorn, M., Schuengel, C. and Bakermans-Kranenburg, M.J. (1999) 'Disorganised attachment in early childhood: meta-analysis of precursors, concomitants and sequelae.' *Development and Psychopathology 11,* 225–249.

Wade, J., Dixon, J. and Richards, A. (2010) *Special Guardianship in Practice.* London: BAAF.

Winokur, M., Holtan, A. and Valentine, D. (2009) 'Kinship care for the safety, permanency, and well-being of children removed from the home for maltreatment.' *Cochrane Database of Systematic Reviews.* http://onlinelibrary.wiley.com/

CHAPTER 9

'Get Them Out of Here!'

An Exploration of Kinship Placement Breakdown

Tom Hawkins

Introduction

This chapter aims to raise awareness of the impact upon relationships where a kinship care placement is experiencing difficulties or breaks down. This will be achieved by exploring the complexities involved when placing children in kinship care. To assist in this, I will introduce two case studies, from cases I either previously worked, or have detailed knowledge of, involving younger children with differing difficulties and issues, making sure to use pseudonyms in order to maintain confidentiality (Health and Care Professions Council 2012). The use of these case studies will enable the exploration of differences and similarities. My reasoning for choosing to use younger children is because, in the normally accepted view, placement breakdowns are the result of a young person pushing boundaries, so causing the placement to come to an end (Hill-Tout, Pithouse and Lowe 2003). This is not necessarily the 'norm' as there are many differing placements. Where placements involving younger children and babies break down, it is not the child's behaviour that is the cause.

In seeking to analyse and gain some kind of perspective around placement breakdown, I will begin by placing kinship care into context, before going on to analyse the differing conflicting loyalties and pressures that are brought to the fore when professionals and courts reach decisions that result in children being removed from their birth parents. This exploration will enable me to reach some conclusions about the successful placement of children within kinship care.

Background

Research on the outcomes of 'looked after' children suggests that children placed in the care of their local authority are less likely than their peers to achieve their full potential (Social Services Improvements Agency 2007). To compound this, research also shows that this same group of children, on becoming adults, tend to be over-represented in many, if not all, areas of social need (Social Services Improvement Agency 2007). In an attempt to counter these statistics, consecutive governments have sought to introduce an ever increasing quantity of legislation (Brayne and Carr 2010) in an attempt to rectify this situation for those children receiving corporate parenting (Department for Education and Schools 2006).

It was these concerns that brought about the Children Act 1989 (HM General Acts 1989), a landmark piece of legislation which changed how children and families were to be seen by the courts and public services. It included a recognition that children were better placed within their families (Department of Health 2001). Despite this, there was no explicit 'duty' placed upon social workers to take an active role in seeking alternative placement within the child's family.

As well as bringing in a new era in adoption law, the Adoption and Children Act 2002 (HM General Acts 2002) also introduced a number of significant changes to the Children Act 1989, one of which was the introduction of a duty requiring local authorities and the judiciary actively to seek out potential kinship care placements as a more positive measure towards preventing those children from entering the care system (Brayne and Carr 2010). Identifying these placements was no longer the sole responsibility of parents and relatives.

While the introduction of these practices was based on research that clearly demonstrated that children living within their families had better outcomes than those living in foster care or residential care (Farmer 2009; Lutman, Hunt and Waterhouse 2009), the reality seemed to be that these placements were seen not only as cheaper, but also as easier to manage, especially in regards to long-term resource commitment (Barnardos 2011). For the social worker, this meant a requirement to undertake more assessments, often some distance away. It was also not necessarily easy to find family members willing to care for these children.

Once a placement is identified, a child can be placed through formal processes, such as by a court order. However, in many cases, these placements are established through informal arrangements, often put into place through negotiation between the social worker and the family, even in circumstances where the prospective carer didn't necessarily agree with the proposed placement or didn't fully understand the reasons behind the placement being proposed (Sinclair and Wilson 2003).

While the establishment of such an informal placement can prevent the escalation of conflict, it can also result in none of the child, the carer or the parent(s) having the appropriate level of protection, stability or sense of permanency (Harden 2004). Even where formal arrangements have been provided through the granting of a Residence Order, or other such orders (HM General Acts 1989, sections 8 and 14A), this does not guarantee that these placements will be any more successful.

At the time I rarely considered the complexities involved in kinship care as I tended to focus more on resource provision, placement shortages, placement breakdowns and government set performance targets.

Since moving away from statutory practice and into independent practice and academic teaching, my thinking about the encouragement of Residence Orders, and other orders, has changed as I have seen that evidence suggests that carers who were unable to become approved foster carers were sometimes encouraged to seek a Residence Order, and those who were approved as foster carers were, at a later date, urged to return to court to seek a Residence Order despite the need for ongoing social work support (Farmer and Moyers 2008, quoted in Stein 2009, p.138).

The re-emergence of some of my previous cases also contributed towards my improved knowledge of kinship care placements as I saw them coming back before the courts, this time as private law cases, due to recurring issues and challenges to previously made decisions.

My experiences have led me to reflect on, and critically analyse, the complexities involved when placing a child. Differing circumstances and variables, all of which need to be considered, may lead placements to experience difficulties and or to break down. These may be generated either by the parents or by the child.

Exploring placement difficulty and breakdown

On starting to explore kinship care placement breakdown and difficulties, two fundamental questions come to mind:

1. What does the term 'kinship care' actually mean?

2. How can family relationships be affected following the placement of a child into kinship care?

This leads to the question: Can kinship care provide 'stability' and 'permanence'?

What does the term kinship care actually mean?

It is important to provide a definition of kinship care for the purposes of this analysis. The Kinship Care UK website defines kinship care as 'A type of care and living arrangement for a child who has to live away from his or her parental home, and is cared for full-time by a member of the child's extended family or a friend' (Kinship Care UK 2012). The British Association for Adoption and Fostering (BAAF) defines kinship care as meaning:

> Relatives or friends looking after children who cannot live with their parents...[that]...may include people who are not related to the child but who are still in the child's social network. For example, someone the child knows well and trusts...sometimes this type of care is called Family and Friends Care because this more accurately describes what it is... Kinship Care can be a private arrangement or formalised through a Legal Order. (BAAF 2012)

How can family relationships be affected following the placement of a child into kinship care?

Having established a definition for kinship care, we now need to ask why difficulties exist, and why these can cause placements to breakdown.

I will be using the following two case studies:

Case study 1: Chelsea

Chelsea, aged eight months, is the second child of Sharon and the first child of Darren. Sharon's previous child, born 15 months before Chelsea, was placed in the care of the local authority shortly after being born, after concerns were raised. The case subsequently progressed into care proceedings and following a period of assessment with Sharon it was felt that she was not able to meet her baby's needs. This was due, in part, to her drug use. And so, in the best interests of the child, the baby was placed for adoption.

In the period since the adoption, Sharon had entered into a new relationship with Darren, Chelsea's father. Like Sharon, Darren was a drug user who is also known to deal Class A drugs; he also has a history of unpredictable aggressive and violent behaviour, including reports of severe incidents of domestic violence.

Due to this history, child protection concerns had been raised during Sharon's pregnancy, resulting in the local authority applying to the courts for a Care Order as soon as it was notified of the birth.

Subsequently, Chelsea and Sharon were placed in a mother and baby foster placement. Unfortunately this broke down within a short period of time. After further assessments it was established that neither Sharon nor Darren, either together or apart, would be able to meet Chelsea's needs, requiring the local authority to seek alternative permanency plans. After a period of exploration and assessment, within Darren's extended family, it was felt that a paternal aunt would be able to take on the care of Chelsea under kinship care arrangements. While initially this placement presented as successful, over the coming months this changed.

Unfortunately, despite additional support, Chelsea's aunt concluded that she was not able to care for Chelsea. This resulted in the placement breaking down and Chelsea being placed for adoption.

Case study 2: Katy and Paige

Katy, age four, and Paige, aged two, are the daughters of Karen and Brian who had separated three months prior to the children becoming known to the local authority, ending a five-year relationship. Almost immediately after her relationship with Brian had ended, Karen began a new relationship with John, who quickly moved into the property with Karen and her two daughters.

The local authority became involved after receiving a referral from Paige's GP, following Karen having presented her daughter with unexplained bleeding that had been found in Paige's nappy. Despite Karen being advised to take Paige directly to the hospital Karen delayed doing this for a number of hours.

At the hospital investigations into the possible cause of the bleeding were explored with it being concluded that Paige's injuries could not have been caused by an accident. Despite this being clearly stated to Karen she was not able to give an explanation for the injuries, and neither could John or Brian.

As Karen had clearly stated that she was not going to leave John, despite it being shown that, in all likelihood, John had been responsible for the injuries, Katy and Paige were placed with their paternal grandmother and her partner. This option was preferred by Brian as he wasn't in a position to take on the care of his daughters. Assessments had deemed placement with the paternal grandmother as being in the girls' best interests.

While it is generally acknowledged that the promotion of placement stability is one of the key responsibilities of every local authority, with this being one of the eight performance indicators (Ofsted 2012), if we consider the case studies in turn we will find that both experienced instability.

In the case of Chelsea, although a baby, her placement was not immune to breakdown! This was caused through previously unexplored, complex family relationships combined with previously unconsidered, unpredictable threatening behaviours on the part of Chelsea's father.

What happened in this case was the following:

- The paternal aunt, despite having distanced herself from her brother some years earlier, still had some sporadic contact with her mother.

- Following the placement of Chelsea with her aunt, Chelsea's father exerted pressure upon his mother in order to obtain contact details for his sister, which resulted in Chelsea's aunt receiving a number of threatening and aggressive telephone calls. This resulted in the paternal aunt being fearful for Chelsea's and her own safety.

- In addition, due to the circumstances surrounding the establishment of the kinship care placement, additional pressures had been placed upon the family: first, by the local authority being over-zealous in seeking the placement; and second, through the requirement upon the paternal aunt to sever all links with Chelsea's parents and with her own mother. This resulted in the kinship carer and Chelsea becoming isolated, combined with the fact that the aunt had felt pressured into taking on Chelsea's care. This all placed additional pressures and stress on what was already a stressful situation, causing the placement to come to an end prematurely.

In this case, was the placement breakdown inevitable and why?

On looking at the relationships within the family, we find that prior to the placement being sought there was already evidence of relationship difficulties, particularly with Chelsea's parents. Added to this, taking on of the care of Chelsea only served to increase the complex feelings that were experienced (Barratt and Granville 2006; Winnicott 1984). Barratt and Granville found that: 'What often emerges…are issues about the relationship with the birth parent[s], and changes in the relationships within the family, often as a consequence of the placement' (Barratt and Granville 2006, p.165). It could be said that it was almost inevitable that this relationship was going to worsen, given the behavioural history of Chelsea's father. His actions could have been predicted.

In addition, if the aunt's relationship with her mother had been taken into consideration, this reciprocal relationship would have been seen to be preventing the aunt from becoming isolated from her family. With this denied her, Chelsea and her aunt very quickly became isolated removing any support networks that had previously been present, which added to the level of fear experienced.

These events support the statement made by Mike Stein suggesting 'that councils find it far easier to influence decisions than they do to influence the children's day-to-day relationships' (Stein 2009, p.42). In the case of Katy and her sister Paige, although their placement did not result in a breakdown, the placement had difficulties which, if handled differently, could have caused its end in the same way that Chelsea's placement did.

After the placement of the two children with their paternal grandmother and her partner, their mother's behaviour was not overtly aggressive, but she was what I would describe as passive-aggressive. She would undermine the carers, give her two daughters false hope in returning to live with her and turn up at school when she was not meant to be there. In addition, despite the placement being supported by a Special Guardianship Order to both the grandmother and her partner, Karen returned the case to Court on several occasions, seeking to vary the provisions for contact so that she could have more contact, including overnight stays, with her daughters.

In addition, prior to the relationship between Karen and John ending, Karen gave birth to her third daughter, Alice, who was subsequently placed with the maternal grandmother, also under a Special Guardianship Order. This meant that while Alice was perceived as being safe, the nature of the relationship between Karen and her mother meant that the suspicion of collusion was high.

In this case, while there was no placement breakdown, there were a number of placement difficulties, which were further compounded by having to return to court to justify why orders should not be altered. This also included on one occasion the demand for a further, in-depth, assessment on Karen in relation to her ability to meet her children's needs.

While relationships with parents and other extended family members were not severed (Jackson 1999), relationships were tested. However the family support networks, combined with appropriate local authority support, enabled Katy and Paige to maintain relationships with all of their paternal and maternal families (Lutman *et al.* 2009).

Analysis: what was going on?

In analysing placement difficulties and breakdowns, so as to establish stability and permanence, it is important to define what is meant by each of these terms:

> Family stability is best viewed as a process of caregiving practices that, when present, can greatly facilitate healthy child development... [and the provision of]...stable and nurturing families can bolster the resilience of children in care and ameliorate negative impacts on their developmental outcomes. (Harden 2004, p.31)

> Permanence is a framework of emotional, physical and legal conditions that gives a child a sense of security, continuity,

commitment and identity. (Department for Education and Schools 2011, p.21)

As we look at the two cases, the deciding factor between their success or failure was one of support, both by the family and the local authority.

What was also shown is that, whether support is present or not, families and children are going to be exposed to a great deal of stress and worry when kinship care is provided.

While support is the decisive factor distinguishing these two cases, this does not mean that this is the formula to success for all placements. In these cases the behaviours of the parents, and the severity of those behaviours, directly or indirectly also played a significant role in the success, or failure, of the placement. However, it would appear that support within the family and from the local authority does play a significant role.

Let us think about the two cases and consider whether stability and permanence were established. In the case of Chelsea, following the breakdown of the mother and baby placement Chelsea moved into a child only placement where she remained until the final court hearing, meaning that she was able to establish a positive attachment (Howe 1995) with her foster carers. This attachment was severed when Chelsea was placed with her paternal aunt, causing Chelsea to make a new bond, then when this placement ended Chelsea had to repeat the exercise twice more, once with her new foster carer and once with her adoptive parents.

If we consider Katy and Paige, while they had managed to remain within the placement for a number of years, it could be argued that while being in a kinship care placement has offered both girls a sense of permanence, the undermining of the placement by their mother provides for an equally valid argument that the placement failed to offer both permanence and stability.

Chelsea's placement failed to provide both stability and permanence as a direct result of Chelsea's fathers' behaviours. For Katy and Paige, while it could be argued that the placement did provide permanence, the same could not be said about stability, due to the actions of the mother following the placement being set up and the granting of the orders.

Conclusion

In concluding this exploration into kinship care in practice, I will refer to the *Family and Friends Care: Statutory Guidance for Local Authorities* (Department for Education and Schools 2011), which has been designed to provide local authority social workers with a framework for working with children who are unable to live with their parents. There is no definition of stability or permanence provided, and while it contains the theoretical and policy context that underpins kinship care today it also states that:

> The Local Authority does not have a duty to assess informal family and friends care arrangements, unless it appears to the authority that services may be necessary to safeguard or promote the welfare of a Child in Need in their area. In such circumstances the Framework for the Assessment of Children in Need and their Families (Department of Health, 2001) provides a suitable model by which local authorities can satisfy themselves that informal family and friends arrangements are appropriate to meet the needs of individual children. (Department for Education and Schools 2011, Chapter 2, paragraph 2.16)

In Chapter 4, which addresses values, principles and objectives, at paragraph 4.5 it states that:

> Policies should promote permanence for children by seeking to enable those who cannot live with their parents to remain with members of their extended family or friends, providing where appropriate a better alternative to growing up in the care of the local authority. Permanence is the framework of emotional, physical and legal conditions that gives a child a sense of security, continuity, commitment and identity. For most looked after children, permanence is achieved through a successful return to their birth family...where this is not possible, family and friends care will often provide an important alternative route to Permanence for the child, particularly where this can be supported by a Residence Order or a Special Guardianship Order or through adoption. (Department for Education and Schools 2011)

In summarising and reviewing the Statutory Guidance, it must be stated that the focus is on the provision of processes, through the provision of advice rather than engaging and supporting placements.

Therefore, along with a number of the studies referenced within this chapter, I conclude that, within statutory social work, the presumption that 'the child is of paramount importance' (HM General Acts 1989, section 1) has been lost in the Processes and Performance Standards, which thereby supports the notion of 'social policing' rather than the processes being child and family focused.

Having reached this conclusion it is important to offer an alternative approach. In doing so, I would like to support *Children First, Kinship Care: A Family Centred Approach* (Children First 2012). This proposes a number of changes in order to improve the outcomes for the children and their families:

> Public Policy that enshrines the right of children to live…[within] …their family network whenever this is in their best interests;

1. Financial allowances, including a national non-means tested benefit for kinship carers…[due to the financial impact experienced following the provision of a kinship care placement];

2. Greater use of Family Group Conferences to inform decisions about support and care for a child…[with a requirement that all chairpersons and social workers are trained to support the family];

3. Support for kinship carers, such as provision of emotional and practical support, an assigned social worker, the strengthening of local support groups, voluntary training, advice and information, and respite opportunities; and

4. [The undertaking of]…research into how best to support children in kinship care placements, including research into the benefits of peer support groups…[and]…training for teachers and social workers, and befriending.

(Children First 2012)

References

BAAF (British Association for Adoption and Fostering) (2012) *Kinship Care, Special Guardianship and Private Fostering*. Available at www.baaf.org.uk/info/kinship-care-and-special-guardianship, accessed on 4 June 2013.

Barnardo's (2011) *On Our Own Two Feet: The Case for a Savings Account Scheme for Looked after Children*. London: Action for Children.

Barratt, S. and Granville, J. (2006) 'Kinship Care: Family Stories, Loyalties and Binds.' In *Creating New Families: Therapeutic Approaches to Fostering, Adoption and Kinship Care.* London: Karnac Publishing.

Brayne, H. and Carr, H. (2010) *Law for Social Workers,* 11th edn. Oxford: Oxford University Press.

Children First (2012) *Kinship Care: A Family Centred Approach.* Available at www.children1st.org.uk/common/uploads/what_we_do/kinship_care.pdf, accessed on 4 June 2013.

Department for Education and Schools (2006) *Care Matters: Transforming the Lives of Children and Young People in Care.* Norwich: Her Majesty's Stationery Office.

Department for Education and Schools (2011) *Family and Friends Care: Statutory Guidance for Local Authorities.* London: Her Majesty's Stationery Office.

Department of Health (2001) *Framework for the Assessment of Children, Young People and their Families.* London: Her Majesty's Stationery Office.

Farmer, E. (2009) 'Placement stability in kinship care.' *Vulnerable Children and Youth Studies 4,* 2, 154–160.

Farmer, E. and Moyers, S. (2008) *Kinship Care: Fostering Effective Family and Friends Placements.* London: Jessica Kingsley Publishers.

Harden, B.J. (2004) 'Safety and stability for foster children: a developmental perspective.' *Children, Families, and Foster Care 14,* 1, 31–44.

Health and Care Professionals Council (2012) *Confidentiality: Guidance for Registrants.* London: Health and Care Professionals Council.

Hill-Tout, J., Pithouse, A. and Lowe, K. (2003) 'Training foster carers in a preventive approach to children who challenge.' *Adoption & Fostering 27,* 1, 47–56.

Howe, D. (1995) *Attachment Theory for Social Work Practice.* Basingstoke: Palgrave Macmillan.

HM General Acts (1989) *The Children Act 1989.* Available at www.legislation.gov.uk/ukpga/1989/41/contents, accessed on 4 June 2013.

HM General Acts (2002) *The Adoption and Children's Act 2002.* Available at www.legislation.gov.uk/ukpga/2002/38/contents, accessed on 4 June 2013.

Jackson, S. (1999) 'Paradigm Shift: Training Staff to Provide Services to the Kinship Triad.' In R. Hegar and M. Scannapieco (eds) *Kinship Foster Care: Policy, Practice and Research.* Oxford: Oxford University Press.

Kinship Care UK (2012) *What Is Kinship Care?* Available at www.kinshipcareuk.org.uk/, accessed on 29 October 2012.

Lutman, E., Hunt, J., and Waterhouse, S. (2009) 'Placement stability for children in kinship care: a long-term follow-up of children placed in kinship care through care proceedings.' *Adoption and Fostering 33,* 3, 28–39.

Ofsted (2012) *Performance Indicator (PAF) Banding and Key Thresholds.* Available at www.ofsted.gov.uk/resources/performance-indicator-paf-banding-and-key-thresholds, accessed on 26 October 2012.

Sinclair, I. and Wilson, K. (2003) 'Matches and mismatches: the contribution of carers and children to the success of foster placements.' *British Journal of Social Work 33,* 871–884.

Social Services Improvement Agency (2007) *What Works in Promoting Good Outcomes for Looked After Children and Young People?* Cardiff: Social Services Improvement Agency.

Stein, M. (2009) *Quality Matters in Children's Services: Messages from Research.* London: Jessica Kingsley Publishers.

Winnicott, D.W. (1984) *Deprivation and Delinquency.* London and New York: Routledge.

CHAPTER 10

A Psychoanalytic Child Psychotherapy Approach to Working with Kinship Care

Graham Music and Geraldine Crehan

Introduction

In this chapter we illustrate how psychoanalytic and developmental thinking can be applied in kinship care cases. We do this primarily via one clinical example, a case in which these ideas allowed us to help the family and the network onto a new and more hopeful trajectory.

Psychoanalytic thinking about work with children and families retains many of its original strengths and features but it also has developed over recent decades. Many of the early psychoanalytic ideas remain extremely pertinent to our practice. These include: the profound impact of early experiences; the way in which we can all be driven by forces outside our consciousness; how we can misinterpret reality; how we can resort to all kinds of defensive mechanisms and strategies to ward off unbearable feelings and thoughts; how we carry beliefs in our inner world which are residues from the past; and how these can distort our understandings of the present in a harmful way. However, psychoanalytic thinking has also developed. We no longer believe it is always necessary to uncover, interpret and work through early experiences in order to effect a healing intervention. We work much more with how relationships unfold here-and-now in the therapy space. We still work using the experience of 'transference', whereby feelings about a person or situation from the past are unconsciously transferred onto a person in the present. Understanding and interpreting these processes can make sense of confusing behaviours. We have also become more attuned to the developmental stage of the child, to what they can tolerate and at what level we should work (Alvarez 2012). We have integrated into our core thinking many of the new findings from affective neuroscience, developmental psychology and attachment theory. We believe that a psychoanalytic psychotherapy which retains the best of its traditional understandings but which can incorporate modern, cutting-edge ideas, offers an ideal lens through which to make sense of our work with families.

Case study: Toby[1]

Toby, a nine-year-old, white British boy, was referred to our service by his social worker. His history was a shocking one. His mother, a crack-cocaine user, had been the victim of domestic violence, and was possibly involved in prostitution. It is unclear exactly what Toby witnessed, especially as many of his terrible experiences would have been preverbal, but violence was a pervasive theme. He might also have seen some sexual acting out. His mother was subject to striking mood changes. At the time of the referral he was living with his maternal grandmother, Julie, and had done so from three years old. This was a voluntary arrangement, with no court order. He had been having contact with his mother but this was extremely erratic. Little was known about his father who disappeared from his life before his first birthday.

Toby's behaviour at school was particularly difficult. He would get into almost daily fights, could barely concentrate in the classroom and needed fairly constant one-to-one attention. He had few friends and was recently excluded from school after an ugly incident which included fighting, and swearing at his teacher. At a recent meeting his head teacher said that she did not think the school would be able to manage him for much longer.

Initial contacts

As always, on receipt of the referral we already had some thinking to do. What really is the main worry, and who is holding it? Who do we invite to the initial meeting? The referral letter triggered a heart-sink reaction in our team of busy, overloaded clinicians who seemed to avert

---

1   For reasons of confidentiality, this example is not based on a particular case but is constructed for illustrative purposes. The case incorporates many elements that are common to referrals received by specialist CAMHS services.

their gaze even more than usual as the team leader attempted to allocate the case. Psychoanalytic practitioners assume that our reactions to cases, even before meeting a family, might well be meaningful. This is linked to the idea of projection, as Klein (1959) and Bion (1962) taught – that the feelings and thoughts we have in a client's presence normally have a meaning, a kind of 'role-responsiveness' (Sandler 1993). While sometimes our reactions are personal responses triggered by our own histories, or by our own current context – such as having too many cases and too little time to see them in – the dynamics in a child or family can also often be re-enacted in the systems and networks around them (Emanuel 2002).

What seemed to be particularly evoked in the team was the sense of being overwhelmed and the wish to shut down. There was an edge to the referral letter which hinted that Toby's behaviours were too much to bear. The school's letter seemed to have a hint of both anger and despair, as well as blame, and there was a clear sense from it that 'someone else' should be taking responsibility and doing something about Toby, that the school had done their bit. Feeling helpless and persecuted can lead any of us to become angry and blaming. There was also a veiled threat. If his behaviour did not improve soon then permanent exclusion loomed large. There already was a sense of a hot potato being passed around.

Given this, it seemed important to help the school to understand and support our approach. We also wanted Julie to understand it. Our experience is that, in many kinship care cases, there is a long-standing history of suspicion of professionals, sometimes going back several generations. We decided to call Julie, Toby's grandmother, first of all, and then arrange a meeting from there. The phone call gave immediate clues. Julie 'did not mind' that a referral was made. She did not see 'why any social worker' should be invited to any meetings, especially as the children's' mother was again pregnant and she was especially concerned that social services would 'interfere' again. She insisted that Toby was a good boy at home mostly. She could bring Toby for sessions but was not keen on meetings herself. From her point of view, she was doing her best by Toby. She wanted her grandson to be helped with his angry behaviour, but thought the school should not let him get away with so much. Again the blame was being passed around. We were also being given a clear message – not an especially welcoming one but one we often encounter in kinship cases – that we professionals are not to be trusted. We decided that one of us would meet Julie initially: without making a therapeutic alliance with her, we would be unlikely to succeed in helping Toby.

At the same time, we did not want to collude with Julie by not linking with other professionals. We told her that we would contact them, and that we hoped that we could all meet to think about Toby together the week after we met with her. In such cases 'splitting' is common. By this we mean that in complex cases any of us may become drawn into identifying with different emotions, feelings or positions represented within the case. For example, we may feel angry with the birth mother, or upset with a judgemental attitude from the school, or frustrated with the wariness of kinship carers. We may feel indignant that a social worker should do more, or maybe we would identify excessively with the child's plight and his or her bad experiences. Such different perspectives somehow need to be contained and held together. When they are not, we often see different bits of the network at loggerheads. Indeed, when anxiety is running particularly high we find that splitting is especially rife, and is the result of what psychoanalytic practitioners would term 'acting out', whereby feelings that have been hard to think about are expressed unconsciously through certain kinds of behaviour.

It was apparent to us from the start that splitting was taking place here. When we contacted the social worker, he was decidedly uninterested, a bit brittle, as if bruised by contact with Julie, and had more or less given up on the family. The school, on the other hand were full of anger and frustration. They had been on the receiving end of Toby's more dramatic behaviours and were struggling.

Initial meetings

We met with Julie a few weeks later. A central tenet of most psychoanalytically informed assessments is to be both open and curious about what we might find, and not to prejudge; as Bion stated, to 'eschew memory and desire' (Bion 1967). In Julie's case this was just as well as we did not meet the person we expected to meet. It was true she was fearful of the judgemental professionals, which she assumed we would be. This transference, the lens through which the therapist is perceived and experienced, was apparent from the moment she walked into the waiting room. Yet she also showed a huge wish to learn and change. It transpired that Julie had difficult memories of professionals from when she had attended such services as a very young mother, and the therapist she saw back then had alerted social services to her husband's violence and drinking. It felt important to name some of this fear and suspicion early on. Being able to bear being what we sometimes call a 'bad object', not needing to be seen as too nice, can offer huge relief. In Julie's case naming her suspicion of us took the sting out of her feelings and allowed her to see us as human and interested in her.

The school

With permission from Julie we did an observation of Toby in school, something we often try to do. This is an opportunity to begin to make sense of a child, speak to key staff members, and unobtrusively observe a child both in a structured classroom context and also in unstructured situations such as the playground or lunch-break. We find that many children can manage clear structures but can fall apart in the ordinary mêlée of school life. There was a striking contrast between Toby the tough-looking 'bruiser', and the evidently vulnerable child lurking just below the surface. In class he tried hard to concentrate but was easily distracted, and as is common in such children, his ability to self-regulate or stay on task was minimal. In psychoanalytic language we might think that he did not have a 'good object' inside him to rely on. Other models of thinking might describe this as a high degree of hypervigilance, or a very sympathetically aroused autonomic nervous system (Porges 2011). Toby seemed to have the expectation that the world was dangerous and scary, which given his early experiences was not surprising. A slightly loud noise led him to judder, other children's shouts left him anxious and when a teacher did not respond quickly to him he slipped quickly into a hurt, angry place.

Even when seemingly being still, Toby was clearly holding himself together with what we would call, after Esther Bick (1968), 'second-skin' defences. Bick described ways in which the personality under stress can attempt to maintain a sense of coherence through using the musculature of the body. For example, Toby's leg would be bouncing away or he would suck his thumb or clothes, just as we see anxious babies do (Beebe and Lachmann 2002). Such subtle signals are inevitably hard for a busy class-teacher to pick up. Things were worse in the playground where he struggled to find a way into groups, being too pushy and not understanding what others expected. Thus, he found himself rejected, and sadly, only through being goaded into fighting did he seem to find any role. The psychology assistant doing the observation felt particularly distressed by this. We know from attachment theory that children with traumatic early lives often struggle with peer relationships (Sroufe 2005) and can have a diminished capacity for empathy. Toby also often resorted to that classic defence first outlined by Anna Freud of 'identification with the aggressor' (Freud 1972), feeling safer and better being angry and attacking than as a victim.

Meeting the professionals and Julie

The next meeting with the social worker and Julie was complex. He arrived with some issues for the agenda. He wanted to know our view on contact with the mother and he also wanted us to discuss the possibility of Julie applying for a Special Guardianship Order, despite Julie's reluctance to take this step. Julie's silence indicated how unhappy she was. We struggled to preserve a fragile alliance with Julie while hoping to establish a helpful relationship with Toby's social worker, and both wanted us to side with them. Such experiences of divided loyalty are common in the relational dynamics of kinship care cases, and were probably partly a re-enactment of the divided loyalty Julie herself felt between Toby and her daughter. As psychoanalytic practitioners we use our own emotional experience – our 'countertransference' – to make sense of the internal dynamics of the young person or family we are seeing. We were to learn later that while Julie was mindful of the benefits of becoming Toby's legal guardian, she also felt that this step would be a betrayal of her daughter. Julie remained hopeful that in time her daughter would 'sort herself out' and be able to resume care of Toby. In psychoanalytic terms, we might see this as a classic case of denying a reality that she did not want to face, a 'turning a blind eye' (Canham 2003). Although Julie was angry with her daughter she also felt protective of her, especially in discussions with professionals.

Toby was like many children who have been let down by their parents: he needed to deny reality and to maintain a positive narrative about an unreliable parent. Simultaneously, feelings of profound hurt and rage may be harboured, and an internal conflict between these two states of mind can exist. Feelings that are repressed or remain outside of conscious awareness, such as anger with birth mother or resentment of Julie, are more likely to be projected onto teachers and social workers who become 'bad objects' in the child's mind, standing in for the parent who has let them down.

Toby struggled to bear this hotchpotch of tumultuous feelings and often 'acted out' dramatically. Psychoanalysis values the capacity to manage difficult feelings and uncertainty and avoid resorting to premature action, something that was easier said than done in this case. Taking swift action can reduce an immediate experience of anxiety, whether this be a school excluding a pupil, or clinicians giving prescriptive advice, but such action may not always be the best solution. Often there can be significant pressure from professionals, from family or from within the clinician to take a very clear view or to jump quickly to offer an intervention. We felt that it was important to bear this pressure and take the time necessary to complete a thorough assessment. This involved monitoring and trying to make sense of the powerful pressures that were projected around the group and which sometimes rendered it difficult to think about Toby's needs.

We also offered Toby some individual assessment sessions and were heartened by how well he responded, in particular how he calmed down and became reflective in the presence of a therapist who was interested in his feelings and bearing them with him. We decided to offer some individual psychotherapy. However, we were also aware that a lot of work was needed with the family and network, and so went for a two-pronged approach, working regularly with Julie and the professional network alongside sessions for Toby. Invariably, child psychotherapists will offer family work in addition to individual psychotherapy and this is especially pertinent in kinship care cases.

Therapy with Toby

In therapy Toby presented as vigilant, wary and controlling of adults. He frequently challenged the capacity of his therapist to tolerate his behaviour as he relentlessly criticised her ability to be helpful. He would often throw toys at her 'by accident'. Psychoanalytic practitioners have found the concept of 'Double Deprivation' (Henry 2004) helpful in working with children like Toby. The initial deprivation is the early experience of neglectful parenting and the secondary deprivation is found in the internal world of the child. Their internalised representations of unreliable or frightening parental figures often mean that they cannot accept the real, actual help being offered in the present.

Many children like Toby are trying to ward off feelings of self-hate and self-blame. We often see a split in the personality, as described by Fairbairn (1962) who suggested that children feel safer blaming themselves than the parent who should be caring for them but is not. At least if they blame themselves they can retain some illusion of control, an omnipotent belief that they can do something about it, which is much less frightening than relying on abusive and neglectful parents. With children like Toby, the self-blame is hard to bear and it is again often projected angrily onto others, such as peers or teachers.

Initially it was hard for Toby to allow vulnerable aspects of his personality to be visible or thought about; vulnerability creates high anxiety which Toby defended against by identifying with an aggressive state of mind. Experiences of feeling frightened and denigrated were frequently projected onto the therapist as he threw objects and continually criticised them. The theory of 'projective identification', originally formulated by Klein (1946) and later developed by Bion (1962) helped make sense of what was happening. When the infant is subject to frightening and chaotic experiences their immature ego quickly becomes overwhelmed especially as they do not have language through which they may understand and convey their experience to another. Such early intolerable emotions are often communicated through behaviour. The therapist must receive the projections and make sense of their emotional content, finding ways to communicate gently an understanding of what is happening, both verbally and non-verbally.

Psychoanalytic technique is not only concerned with helping children manage difficult experiences but also with helping them move towards a more positive emotional state. Many children like Toby are in fact fearful of feeling hope and of feeling good. At least they have a familiarity with hopelessness, rage and distrust. Helping Toby to trust in his own capacities, and to believe that he can be thought about and cared for, makes space in the mind for the more difficult feelings to also be processed.

This all takes time, requiring courage on both sides and a subtle sense of a child's developmental needs. We may be drawn into colluding with falsely positive states, and we may also prematurely force a child to face what he or she cannot bear. As the therapy developed, Toby was able to acknowledge a belief that his mother did not love him because she 'took drugs and told his dad to go away'. He was also able to say that he loved 'nan' and wanted to stay with her. Fleetingly, he expressed rage at the absence of his father in his life. Supporting Toby in staying with some of these emotions helped him to identify the different feelings he had towards his grandmother and towards his mother, which helped in sustaining his relationship with his grandmother. Giving form to these very painful thoughts and wishes enabled Toby gradually to have more control over his rage and his impulsive aggression, alongside gaining a growing sense of hope and optimism about himself.

For Toby, an enduring fear was that he was unlovable. After all, his mother had chosen drugs over him. His feeling of being unloved was manifested in many other ways such as accusing his social worker and therapist of only caring because they 'get paid'. An important difference between kinship care and foster care is that the child often expresses a feeling that they 'belong' to the family and are being 'claimed', rather than being in receipt of professional foster care. In time, Toby moved towards healing this split and he was able to be appreciative of many of the professionals who were clearly on his side as well as really feeling 'claimed' by Julie.

Working with the family and network

Toby made great strides in his therapy but this could not have happened without much work with both Julie and the professional network. The adults in a child's life need to provide what Winnicott called a 'holding environment' (Winnicott 1958), and for this they too often need emotional 'holding' and 'containment' (Bion 1962). Although initially ambivalent about attending sessions for herself, as Julie became increasingly committed to Toby's therapy we met regularly and thought about Toby as well as her daughter. In one meeting Toby's mother joined us but sadly her continued drug abuse made this impossible to persevere with.

Often in kinship care cases, experiences of trauma, abuse and neglect span several generations and carers may have limited internal resources to parent a child. This has been described as there being 'ghosts in the nursery' (Fraiberg, Adelson and Shapiro 1975). Any internal representations of good parental figures may be fragile and not adequate to the task. Julie bravely managed to acknowledge that her daughter had a difficult start to life and that she had struggled to raise her. She could also let us know that her own mother had serious mental health difficulties and she was 'passed from pillar to post' when growing up. In some ways, Julie's willingness to care for Toby and her wish to be a loving grandmother was a reparative act that at an unconscious level may have been redressing the inadequacies of the parenting she received and the parenting she had been able to give. As she mellowed she became more trusting and less suspicious, and this had a knock-on effect on her relationship with her social worker who she allowed to help her more openly.

Alongside this work we kept in contact with school who were helped to make sense of Toby's behaviour and what precipitated it, and they became increasingly sympathetic to him. The initial observation findings were fed back both to the pastoral support teacher and the class teacher, and this and ongoing meetings led to a change in both how Toby was perceived and in how they managed him. There was a softening towards him, and the school began to be more sensitive to his states of mind. They also ensured that time was set aside to 'check in' with him, and maybe most importantly, they began to be able to spot danger signals *before* he began to 'kick-off'.

As Toby felt less attacked, and developed more trust, he calmed down and a vicious circle seemed to turn into a virtuous one. This new sympathy was at times of course sorely tested, especially when Toby's behaviour deteriorated when there were breaks, holidays and changes in routine. This was often when the network erupted into blame and recriminations and then our role was to try to gather this together, to ensure that the adults were working reflectively together and not enacting the powerful emotions that abounded.

Conclusions

In this chapter we have tried to portray how psychoanalytic understanding can contribute to therapeutic work in kinship care cases. We have described how bearing difficult to manage feelings, and facing warded off thoughts can lead to psychic integration, greater sense of ease and less likelihood of acting out. Much of this work goes right back to Freud. We continue to pay great attention to defensive processes and aim, in a compassionate way, to help clients find ways of facing those issues which they defend against. Freud (1917) also wrote much on processes of mourning and much of the important internal work clients do is to mourn for what they have lost or never had. In Toby's case this included facing and mourning the reality of what his mother was not capable of giving him, and in Julia's case it included facing up to what she had not given her own daughter and also what she had not received from her own parents.

We have highlighted processes such as projective identification and how sometimes we project unwanted parts of ourselves onto others and how hard to bear emotions, and the powerful dynamics of families and cases, can be powerfully re-enacted within networks. We have focused on how infantile defences and ways of holding oneself together, such as self-soothing or dramatic enactments, can be resorted to when feelings become unmanageable, and also how these defensive patterns can persist into late childhood and indeed into adulthood, when no alternative means of managing them are on hand. We have also suggested that we need to find ways to build hope, optimism and strength in a child's inner world, as well as helping to bear difficulties.

This way of working requires that a thoughtful, reflective and emotionally attuned mind is put into action, a mind that can bear a range of feelings and can think thoughts that have been unmanageable. Such a function is these days often conceptualised in terms of a more sophisticated and emotionally attuned part of the brain helping to manage and regulate more primitive brain areas. It requires bearing what seems unbearable but also holding onto hope when others have lost it. Such hope must never be falsely optimistic but be based on a real understanding of how facing and staying with difficult experiences can pay dividends, as we have seen in Toby's case.

References

Alvarez, A. (2012) *The Thinking Heart: Three Levels of Psychoanalytic Therapy with Disturbed Children*, 1st edn. Oxford: Routledge.

Bion, W.R. (1962) *Learning from Experience*. London: Heinemann.

Bion, W.R. (1967) 'Notes on memory and desire.' *Psychoanalytic Forum 2*, 3, 271–280.

Beeb, B. and Lachmann, F.M. (2002) *Infant Research and Adult Treatment: Co-constructing Interactions*. New York: Analytic Press.

Bick, E. (1968) 'The experience of the skin in early object relations.' *International Journal of Psycho-Analysis 49*, 484–486.

Canham, H. (2003) 'The relevance of the Oedipus myth to fostered and adopted children.' *Journal of Child Psychotherapy 29*, 1, 5–19.

Emanuel, L. (2002) 'Deprivation × 3.' *Journal of Child Psychotherapy 28*, 2, 163–179.

Fairbairn, W.R.D. (1962) *An Object-relations Theory of the Personality*. New York: Basic Books.

Fraiberg, S., Adelson, E. and Shapiro, V. (1975) 'Ghosts in the nursery: a psychoanalytic approach to the problems of impaired infant-mother relationships.' *Journal of the American Academy of Child and Adolescent Psychiatry 14*, 3, 387–421.

Freud, A. (1972) 'Comments on aggression.' *International Journal of Psycho-Analysis 53*, 163–171.

Freud, S. (1917) 'Mourning and Melancholia Vol. 14.' In J. Strachey (ed.) *The Complete Psychological Works of Sigmund Freud*. London: Hogarth.

Henry, G. (2004) 'Doubly Deprived.' In P. Barrows (ed.) *Key Papers from the Journal of Child Psychotherapy.* London: Routledge.

Klein, M. (1946) 'Notes on some schizoid mechanisms.' *International Journal of Psycho-Analysis 27,* 99–110.

Klein, M. (1959) 'Our adult world and its roots in infancy.' *Human Relations 12,* 4, 291.

Porges, S.W. (2011) *The Polyvagal Theory: Neurophysiological Foundations of Emotions, Attachment, Communication, and Self-regulation.* New York: WW Norton.

Sandler, J. (1993) 'On communication from patient to analyst: not everything is projective identification.' *International Journal of Psycho-Analysis 74,* 1097–1107.

Sroufe, L.A. (2005) *The Development of the Person: The Minnesota Study of Risk and Adaptation from Birth to Adulthood.* New York: Guilford Press.

Winnicott, D.W. (1958) *Through Pediatrics to Psychoanalysis: Collected Papers.* New York: Basic Books.

CHAPTER 11

Support Groups

What they Do and How they Help

Jackie Wyke

The aim of this chapter is to address how support groups form part of an overall strategy for supporting grandparents who care for their grandchildren. It will look at how they work and why they can be helpful. I will tap into primarily the experience of the Grandparents' Association. In order to inform this chapter, the experiences of three support group leaders have been specifically drawn on.

The Grandparents' Association celebrated its twenty-fifth anniversary in 2012 and was originally founded by a group of grandparents whose grandchildren had been put into care, adopted from care or were not allowed any contact with them. The organisation's mission is to improve the lives of children by working with and for all grandparents, especially those who:

- have lost or are losing contact with their grandchildren because of divorce, family feud or other problems

- are caring for their grandchildren on a full time basis

- have childcare responsibilities for their grandchildren, or

- are interested in the educational and welfare needs of their grandchildren.

Our youngest grandparent is 28, our oldest grandparent to access our services is an 89-year-old great-grandmother raising her 15-year-old great-granddaughter. The average age of our grandparents is 50.

Our research informs us that one in every three people over the age of 50 is a grandparent and that by the age of 54 one in every two people is a grandparent. More than a third of grandparents spend the equivalent of three days per week caring for their grandchildren and over the past two generations the number of children cared for by grandparents has jumped from 33 per cent to 82 per cent. The value of this care is estimated to save around one billion pounds per year. Over half of our members (56 per cent) are bringing up their grandchildren full time.

The latest annual report from the Grandparents' Association identified that there are in excess of 80 groups nationally supporting over 800 grandparents. This supports, indirectly, approximately 2000 children. Thus, the running of groups is a central part of the overall support the Association provides. To quote the report:

> Such groups are essential for those grandparents who have childcare responsibilities and are essential for the well-being of both children and the grandparents as they reduce the social isolation that many feel in these situations and enable children to learn more social skills. (Grandparents' Association 2012, p.14)

Kinship care and the need for support

Before we can launch into support groups, we need to address some fundamentals in relation to kinship care and its very reason for being.

The overarching vision for the Department for Education, the main body in the UK that looks after the needs of children, is for 'a highly educated society in which opportunity is more equal for children and young people no matter what their background or family circumstances'. Those children who are in danger of not achieving the best outcomes are defined by the Children Act 1989 as 'children in need', and such children have an entitlement to higher levels of service:

> A child whose vulnerability is such that they are unlikely to reach or maintain a reasonable level of health, or development, or their health or development would be significantly impaired, without the provision of services by the local authority, or they are disabled. (Section 17 (10))

Kinship care is seen as a preferential option for children. Many 'children in need' are in kinship care arrangements. The Casey Foundation, in their Stepping Up for Kids Report (Casey Foundation 2011) describes kinship carers as:

> Across every generation and culture, grandparents, other relatives, and close family friends have stepped forward to raise children whose

parents can no longer care for them. This time-honoured tradition, known as kinship care, helps protect children and maintains strong family, community, and cultural connections. When children cannot remain safely with their parents, other family and friends can provide a sense of security, positive identity, and belonging. (p.3)

Research from Bristol University around the 2001 Census in their *Spotlight on Kinship Care* research (Nandy and Selwyn 2011) identified that in the United Kingdom approximately 173,200 children were living with relatives without their parents present in the household. This represents just over one per cent of children, which is broadly in line with international figures (EveryChild 2010). This includes the two main types of kinship care:

- private, or informal, kinship care: an arrangement in which extended family members raise children without child protective services involvement

- public kinship: situations in which families care for children involved with the child welfare system. Kinship foster care describes the subset of child welfare-involved children who are placed with relatives, but remain in the legal custody of the state.

One major piece of guidance that is applicable to Kinship Care Support Groups is the *Family and Friends Care: Statutory Guidance for Local Authorities* (Department for Education 2011). This guidance sets out the Department for Education's aims for Children and Young People: 'To improve outcomes for children and young people who, because they are unable to live with their parents, are being brought up by members of their extended families, friends or other people who are connected with them' (paragraph 1.1) and 'Children and young people who are unable to live with their parents should receive the support that they and their carers need to safeguard and promote their welfare, whether or not they are looked after' (paragraph 1.2).

Despite this, however, these levels of support are not always provided. Forty-five per cent of authorities do not have a family and friends care policy,[1] despite this being a legal requirement. Roth, Aziz and Lindley (2012) identified that 56 per cent of policies failed to signpost families

1   The FRG update of 24/10/12 identified 57 per cent now have a policy, 88 per cent have a named contact and all policies should be having their first year review in September 2012.

and friends carers to local universal support services. This means that practitioners do not have a clear direction and family and friends carers are left without information about what help is available for them and the children they are raising. Little work appears to have been done to ensure that partner agencies understand the difficulties and needs of family and friends carers.

This is not just a British problem. The Save the Children Report into Kinship Care (Save the Children 2007) identifies: 'While kinship care is the most common form of out-of-home care, it is also the care option least systematically recorded, monitored or supported' (p.4).

Those people providing high levels of care are twice as likely to be permanently sick or disabled as a direct consequence of the stress of caring. This includes kinship carers. A recent study (Templeton 2010), which looked at the experiences and needs of grandparents who were caring for their grandchildren because of parental substance abuse, clearly showed that grandparents felt isolated, with feelings of embarrassment and being 'cast aside' (p.38), and also that they believed their grandchildren needed others to talk to. In both cases, they expressed the need to have others, whether other grandparents or grandchildren or not, who were 'there', so that they were not, in the words of one grandmother, 'trapped alone' (p.40).

From an international perspective, the Save the Children Report into Kinship Care (Save the Children 2007) identifies that the following support may be beneficial in kinship care (p.12):

(a) information and advice on rights, entitlements, eligibility and how to access services

(b) healthcare, including prevention, treatment and rehabilitative services, e.g., for HIV and AIDS infection, drug and alcohol abuse, and disabilities

(c) education, including catch-up classes and life skills training, and HIV and AIDS awareness raising

(d) day care and respite care

(e) parenting courses, the promotion of positive parent–child relationships and conflict resolution skills

(f) financial support, including benefits, vouchers, and in-kind payments

(g) income generation and vocational training

(h) mediation and conciliation services

(i) psychosocial services, including direct work with children.

Providing support through groups

Caring for grandchildren can be lonely and isolating and it is all too easy to lose touch with friends, most of whose own children will have grown up and so have less in common, as well as it being difficult to get out to see friends. Thus, support groups can fulfil a vital role.

A good definition for a support group or self-help group is provided by the British Stammering Association's guidance for support groups (see British Stammering Association n.d.). It identifies a self-help group as:

- a group of people meeting with common problems or experiences of stammering

- a group that people join to meet their own needs, and provide support for other members

- a group of people wanting to take on some responsibility for themselves

- a group of people working together cooperatively

- a group of people helping themselves by helping others.

Looking more specifically at kinship care, the EU Kinship Carers Report (2010) identifies the following areas which cover the majority of kinship care families' needs:

1. Emotional needs of grandchildren:

    (a) via support groups (Mayer 2002)

    (b) training around drug, alcohol and dependency training and assistance with loss and grief (Mayer 2002)

    (c) encouraging intergenerational activities to strength family structures (Mayer 2002)

    (d) mentoring for communication problems between grandparents and grandchildren (Mayer 2002)

(e) children's social workers receive training in working with
vulnerable adults (Forrester and Harwin 2008).

2. Emotional needs of grandparents:

(a) school psychologists to have information about resources in
the community (Mayer 2002)

(b) before and after school activities, classes on grand parenting,
discipline, behavioural problems, etc. (Mayer 2002)

(c) extra time at teacher conferences to inform grandparents how
to reach teachers (Mayer 2002)

(d) support for grandparents in parental efficacy to strengthen
families (Landry-Meyer 1999).

3. Financial support issues:

(a) Sheran and Swann (2007) identify many private kinship
carers do not take up cash assistance mainly due to the fact
they are unaware of what is available

(b) grandparents often need information and assistance in
identifying additional sources of income (Flint, Perez-
Porter 1997).

4. Legal issues (Mayer 2002).

5. Transitions and reorganisation (Mayer 2002) perhaps
achieved via:

(a) parenting classes

(b) grandparent led families encouraged to seek help and
resources beyond the family unit (for instance baby sitters
groups, senior centres, etc.). However, in the UK while these
groups may be called kinship carers, they are not entitled to
respite care as other caring groups are

(c) counselling to stabilise the family unit while it regroups.

Burnette (1999) cited in the EU Kinship Care Literature Review
describes support groups as the most popular source of education
and support for the growing number of grandparents rearing their
grandchildren. Studies showed a reduction in depressive symptoms

among those attending a group, and that the group was used as a coping strategy.

The Department for Education guidance (DfE 2011) goes further in relation to its description of support groups:

> Groups can help to combat the isolation which many carers feel when they take on the role, particularly when they are dealing with the complex needs of vulnerable children, for which they had not planned. Support groups can be particularly important for carers and others who are not in receipt of services from the local authorities. (para 4.38)

> Successful groups usually offer time for discussion between their members as well as offering opportunities for visitors with expertise to address some meetings. They may also service a social function, and arrange activities for children. (para 4.39)

> Support groups for special guardians and prospective special guardians, children subject to special guardianship orders and their parents are included in the services prescribed by the Special Guardianship Regulations 2005 for which a local authority MUST make arrangements. (para 4.41)

> Local authorities should also work with partner agencies and the voluntary sector to find ways to encourage peer support and access to support groups. (para 4.38–40)

We can therefore posit that support groups for kinship carers are often promoted as a way of reducing isolation for carers and children. Such groups can be of great value, but unless they are planned and run with the appropriate knowledge of group processes they will not work as intended.

To meet these needs, there can be many different types of support group. Groups may be ongoing, or time limited. They may be specific to kinship carers, or attended by kinship carers because of a particular issue, such as a group for parents and carers of a child with autism. They may be set up to campaign for a particular issue. Groups may be set up and run by professionals, either as part of a local authority's service to children and families (Pitcher 2002), or as a therapeutic group (Kennedy and Keeney 1987; Vardi and Buchholz 1994). Alternatively, a group may be peer led. Self-help groups have been developing for people with long-term conditions over many years; it is more recently that they are being referred to as peer support groups. These groups will be facilitated by a peer volunteer and may be fully independent. Some, while maintaining their independence, are affiliated to large voluntary sector organisations. In such cases coordinators usually support peers to set up and lead self-help initiatives.

The grandparent and toddler group

The distinctive group run by the Grandparents' Association (2013) is the grandparent and toddler group:

> Grandparent and toddler groups offer the opportunity for grandparents and their grandchildren to interact and form relationships with other children and adults. They give children the chance to experience a range of materials and play activities to support their learning and development. The groups provide grandparents with the opportunity to socialise with other grandparents and support one another to inspire play activity ideas to use with their grandchild(ren) at home and if they are involved in the running of the group, gain useful skills. (p.6)

Networks and support groups are a vital theme of the Association and the first group was set up in 2001 in Harlow in Essex. The remit of our groups is to combat the loneliness among carers who are often cut off from their own peer groups when looking after young children and who cannot fit into the usual age of parents' groups because of their age.

There are currently 34 groups linked directly with the Grandparents' Association, and a further 15 which are affiliated. Grandparents' Association groups insist on stringent quality checks and the group leaders are all checked against the Criminal Records Bureau (CRB). There is clear guidance about safety.

In our Leeds office we recently conducted research between professionals who refer clients to use our services, and service users themselves. Our research was called 'Needs and Impacts Survey Leeds 2012' (informal publication). Seventy-four per cent of professionals identified that social support groups/contact with other grandparents would make the *most* difference to grandparents. Sixty per cent of grandparents (n = 73) identified that social support groups would help them, and 38 per cent identified social support groups as making the *most* difference to them.

A recent initiative has been to accredit a children's centre as a 'good practice hub' when it meets the approval criteria as follows:

- It explicitly includes grandparents and recognises that grandparents are an important group with specific needs who frequently play an instrumental role in the care of their grandchildren.

- It recognises the emotional attachment and sensitivities that grandparents have to their grandchildren, and uses this knowledge to inform methods of engagement and support.

- It has tacitly supported, or is willing to support, the setting up of a grandparent and toddler group for the grandparents and toddlers of the children's centre reach area. Due to its set up and delivery, this will be regarded as a model of good practice for others to learn from and to draw upon for guidance and support.

- It acts as a point of contact to signpost those interested in developing their own group to the grandparent and toddler group for guidance, thereby providing a model of good practice to other children's centres (as well as to volunteer group leaders and group leader trainers, or professionals working with families in a locality), and other relevant agencies wishing to provide such services to grandparents.

- It has identified ways of engaging with grandparents and has developed materials and approaches that meet these needs and signposts grandparents to other services or sources of information.

Currently, there are four such good practice hubs: in Coram's Fields, London; in Aylesbury, Buckinghamshire; in Paulsgrove, Portsmouth; and in Leeds.

Feedback from the recent survey to group leaders tends to indicate that support groups were started initially from a personal need and that existing groups such as mother and toddler groups were unsuitable with grandparents feeling they did not fit in and would be unable to make friends with people who were not in the same position as themselves: 'Joining a group helped me to socialise with people my own age and my grandchild is able to play with new children. The volunteers running the club are very friendly too' (feedback quoted in our 2011–2012 Annual Report).

The new start groups seemed to stem initially from personal needs from the feedback from the survey responses received. Most have formed through word of mouth with grandparents in crisis, as has been the case in other countries (Doucette-Dudman 1996).

Survey responses indicate that the average size of a group is 15 and that membership tends to be fluid with the age of the child being looked after. Most members leave the group when their child enters the education system full time. All group members agreed that there is a need for empathy and knowledge of the complex care issues to effectively lead a group and that movement of members is around 25 per cent.

It is important to set ground rules for the group, as this prevents people becoming dominant, or pursuing a narrow personal agenda. All group leaders identified that confidentiality must be covered when new members join the group and members are given notes about confidentiality and other policies applicable to the group. Boundaries are established when individuals join the group, and the Grandparents' Association provides a toolkit to group leaders in relation to welcome letters, registration forms and similar. Group members identified that there is a process for allowing people to speak and tell their stories but the focus of the group is on the children receiving the care and not on individual members.

Our survey asked group leaders to identify tips for running a successful group. Responses included:

- Set ground rules and be organised.

- Make meetings at mutually convenient times (to suit the members).

- Involve volunteers in the running and management of the group including befriending new, shy members.

- Be organised and have effective communication channels.

- Have a common understanding of the types of problems that may occur.

They were also invited to suggest pitfalls, from their experience. Responses included:

- Find ways of limiting how much some people talk about their issues.

- Help group members to understand that help and advice cannot extend to time outside the group. One commented: 'Leading a group could easily become a full-time job'.

People are encouraged to become members of the Grandparents' Association, but many do not do so.

There are usually at least two social events per year one in the summer and one linked to Christmas. Refreshments are provided as standard with dues being paid by members to cover the costs (most group leaders use the subs to support the social activities too). All refreshments provided are usually soft drinks for the children, biscuits for carers and children and in some venues tea and coffee. Subs are usually collected at each session (approximate cost £1.50 per session) again to cover room hire and refreshment costs with any surplus going to supporting social activities. Where there is contact from the press and media, these are referred upwards to the Grandparents' Association, and general visitors, who are not grandparents, are not encouraged due to safeguarding issues. Tasks usually tend to be shared around the group members to ensure the balance is not being borne too heavily by one member alone. Advertising is usually done via the Grandparents' Association and sometimes via children's centres but very often by word of mouth.

The group may split when size makes it too large to adhere to health and safety issues and children become overwhelmed by the size of the group. A group may need to close if membership is limited and does not cover the costs of renting the meeting room.

As regards the value of a group, the thoughts of the group leaders were:

Regular contact is caring.

You know there will be someone to ask about an issue in attendance or if not someone will be able to find out.

A group is an efficient way of sharing information. There is local knowledge of who to go to or ask for more information. Other group members may be able to answer from first-hand knowledge and experience. Also, from the point of view of the Grandparents' Association, discussion generates ideas and information for wider circulation and is useful for research.

Our findings are echoed by those of other research, such as the Mental Health Foundation (2012). This includes the pitfalls which were identified. People can become too dependent and need more support than is available, leeching into the private time of group leaders which could make the role a full-time position if conditions are not clearly established on joining the group in relation to contact/availability outside of group. The group leader needs to ensure they do not take on the responsibility of solving members' issues, but merely act as a signpost to other members who may have first-hand experience or point members in the direction of known local contacts who can help. Poorly trained peer supporters can take on a 'saviour role' (p.18).

Further areas for research in relation to support groups

As more and more experience is gained by the Grandparents' Association and other organisations such as Grandparents Plus and the Family Rights Group, as well as in other parts of the world, it would be fruitful to gain a fuller understanding of the following areas:

1. How does attending a group help at different stages in the kinship care process, for example when considering whether to take a child on; soon after placement; when there are difficulties during adolescence; or where there are court applications by birth parents? Perhaps one could posit that age can be a barrier for carers attending well established groups such as mother and toddler groups and that members attending groups feel the need to belong to a certain familiar structure. This could this be linked to Maslow's Hierarchy of Needs (Maslow 1943) in the sense of individuals needing to feel a sense of love and belonging. This might be seen in relation to an individual's movement through the recognised phases of the grieving process (Kübler-Ross 1969, pp.51–146) or 'transition curve' (Fisher 2012). If we used Kübler-Ross's model, it would perhaps show individuals moving towards 'acceptance'.

2. It would be helpful to investigate individual members' motivation for attending the groups, and why some choose not to attend, or why they leave. What do they want to get out of it? Some may use the group to make a transition into other kinds of

organisation, while others may not. This too could be firmly linked to Maslow's 'hierarchy of needs'.

3. It would be useful to investigate how different kinds of groups may suit different needs, situations and personalities. We have already referred to peer-led groups as opposed to those led by a professional, for example. What are the relative benefits and disadvantages of alternatives such as peer befriending (Grandparents First 2012, p.8), or occasional conferences and gatherings for kinship carers, or support via social networking sites and email – all of which can be provided in areas of sparse population, or where a carer has limited ability to leave the house? How can all these types of peer support be linked up, on both an organisational level and on a theoretical level?

References

British Stammering Association (n.d.) *A Guide for Starting and Managing a Self-help Support Group*. London: BSA. Available at www.stammering.org/shgs_manual_.pdf, accessed 31 May 2013.

Burnette, D. (1999) 'Custodial grandparents in Latino families: patterns of service use and predictors of unmet needs.' *Social Work 44*, 1, 22–34.

Casey Foundation (2011) *Stepping Up for Kids Report*. Available at www.aecf.org/~/media/Pubs/Initiatives/KIDS%20COUNT/S/SteppingUpforKids2012PolicyReport/SteppingUpForKidsPolicyReport2012.pdf, accessed on 30 August 2013.

Department for Education (2011) *Family and Friends Care: Statutory Guidance for Local Authorities*. London: Her Majesty's Stationary Office..

Doucette-Dudman, D. with La Cure, J. (1996) *Raising our Children's Children*. Minneapolis, MT: Fairview Press.

EveryChild (2010) *Every Child Deserves a Family*. Available at www.everychild.org.uk/docs/Every%20Child%20Deserves%20a%20Family_CFV.pdf, accessed on 31 October 2012.

Fisher, J. (2012) Available at www.businessballs.com/personalchangeprocess.htm, accessed on 4 June 2013.

Flint, M.M. and Perez-Porter, M. (1997) 'Grandparent caregivers: legal and economic issues.' *Journal of Gerontological Social Work 28*, 63–76.

Forrester, D. and Harwin, J. (2008) 'Parental substance misuse and child welfare: outcomes for children two years after referral.' *British Journal of Social Work 38*, 1518–1535.

Grandparents' Association (2012) *Annual Report, 2011–2012*. Harlow: Grandparents' Association, Moot House, The Stow, Harlow, CM20 3AG, UK.

Grandparents' Association (2013) *A Guide to Setting Up and Running a Grandparent and Toddler Group*. Harlow: Grandparents' Association.

Grandparents First (2012) *Newsletter of Grandparents Plus*, Autumn 2012, Issue 23.

Kennedy, J.F. and Keeney, V.T. (1987) 'Group psychotherapy with grandparents rearing their emotionally disturbed grandchildren.' *Group 11*, 1, 15–25.

Kübler-Ross, E. (1969) *On Death and Dying*. New York: Macmillan.

Landry-Meyer, L. (1999) 'Research into action: recommended intervention strategies for grandparent caregivers.' *Family Relations 48*, 4, 381–389.

Maslow, A.H. (1943) 'A theory of human motivation.' *Psychological Review 50*, 4, 370–396.

Mayer, M. (2002) 'Grandparents rearing grandchildren: circumstances and interventions.' *School Psychology International 23*, 4, 371–385.

Mental Health Foundation (2012) *Exploring Peer Support as an Approach to Supporting Self-Management*. Available at www.mentalhealth.org.uk/publications/, accessed 12 August 2013 (free to download).

Nandy, S. and Selwyn, J. (2011) *Spotlight on Kinship Care: Using Census Microdata to Examine the Extent and Nature of Kinship Care in the UK*. Bristol: Bristol University. Available at www.bristol.ac.uk/sps/research/projects/completed/2011/rj5314/execsum.pdf, accessed on 21 May 2013.

Pitcher, D. (2002) 'Going to live with Grandma.' *Professional Social Work*, June, 14–15.

Richards, A. and Tapsfield, R. (2003) *Funding Family and Friends Care: The Way Forward*. London: Family Rights Group.

Roth, D., Aziz, R. and Lindley, B. (2012) *Understanding Family and Friends Care: Local Authority Policies – the Good, the Bad and the Non Existent*. London: Family Rights Group. Available at www.frg.org.uk/images/e-publications/ffc-report-4.pdf, accessed on 31 October 2012.

Save the Children (2007) *Kinship Care: Providing Positive and Safe Care for Children Living Away from Home*. London: Save the Children. Available at www.crin.org/docs/kinship%20care,pdf, accessed on 1 November 2012.

Sheran, M. and Swann, C.A. (2007) 'The take-up of cash assistance among private kinship care families.' *Children and Youth Services Review 29*, 8, 973–987.

Templeton, L. (2010) *The Experiences and Needs of Grandparents who Care for their Grandchildren because of Parental Substance Misuse*. Birmingham: Aquarius Action Projects.

Vardi, D. and Buchholz, E. (1994) 'Group psychotherapy with inner city grandmothers raising their grandchildren.' *International Journal of Group Psychotherapy 44*, 1, 101–122.

Further guidance in relation to support groups

www.prisonersfamilies.org.uk/uploadedFiles/2010_Family_Member_In_Prison/Setting_up_a_Support_Group.pdf

www.stammering.org/shgs_manual_.pdf

www.nacsdc.org/aware/groundrules-mahre.pdf

www.crsprogramquality.org/storage/pubs/hivaids/support_grps.pdf

www.diabetesinmichigan.org/PDF/General/SGLeader08.pdf

Websites for further investigation

http://www.mentoruk.org.uk/2010/07/311/

www.mentorfoundation.org

www.grandparents-association.org.uk

www.education.gov.uk

CHAPTER 12

What do White Kinship Carers Need to Consider when Caring for Children of Black 'Mixed Race'?

Nicholas J. Banks

This chapter recognises the tension between the preferred terminology of professionals and the preferred self-definition of individuals of 'mixed race' background. While professionals tend to prefer terms such as 'mixed parentage' and/or 'dual parentage', recent research suggests that the individuals themselves prefer the clear, non-ambiguous term of 'mixed-race' (Caballero 2010; Song and Aspinall 2012). With this in mind, the term 'black mixed race' is used in this chapter to refer to children where at least one parent is of African or African-Caribbean or Asian decent with the other parent being of white European decent.

There is no systematic recording of national child substitute placement figures based on racial classification in the UK and therefore it is not possible to begin to estimate kinship placement patterns and outcome for any group of children. Within the general population, the 2001 census identified that mixed-race people, particularly those of mixed black/white and mixed/Asian white, are an increasing proportion of British society, with some 677,118 people identifying themselves in the 2001 census as 'mixed'. This figure is said to be almost three times more than the figure recorded in 1991 (Owen 2005). With what is known about the over representation of black 'mixed-race' children in the UK care system (Thoburn 2005; Wood 2009), such a growth in the general mixed-race population may have implications for a growth of black 'mixed-race' children in kinship care placement.

'Children are children, aren't they?'

Many white kinship carers of black mixed-race children may ask themselves, given that they are caring for children from their own family, why their care should be seen as giving any particular cause for concern or special attention. After all, 'children are children, regardless of colour, aren't they?' While this view may be generally correct, there will remain particular issues which are only likely to show themselves in caring for mixed-race children which white kinship carers will not experience when only caring for white children. For example, depending on where white kinship carers live, and depending on the cultural and ethnic mix of the population where they live, children of black mixed race (from here on referred to as BMR), may be seen as a 'rarity' or attracting specific attention due to their perceived 'difference' from the local population. It will not be that uncommon to expect individuals who perceive BMR children as 'unusual' to ask invasive questions that would not ordinarily be tolerated when making enquiries of strangers (Dalmage 2000; Song and Aspinall 2012). Invasive questioning may be as basic as 'Is he/she yours?' or 'Is he/she adopted?' The usual British 'social reserve' may be much less in evidence than normally shown where the general white population perceive themselves as entitled and within their rights to exercise their curiosity with invasive questioning. Some white kinship carers may be asking the question at this point 'Why is natural curiosity an issue?' Well, for the BMR child it may confirm, depending on their age, experience, self-esteem and confidence, issues of difference or separateness from the wider community and, more importantly perhaps, difference and separateness from their kinship social network, where they are perceived by others as 'not belonging'. This sense of 'not belonging' may develop into additional areas of concern, particularly if the BMR child has experienced issues of loss of, or rejection by, his birth parents. Questions of 'Where do I belong?' and 'Who am I?' may begin to develop into increasing, 'racially triggered' anxiety.

Samuels (2009) takes the view that the task of raising a BMR child within a white family requires additional attention to the process of a shared parent-child racial status. Shared experience, rather than a shared racial heritage, needs to inform the process of promoting racial identity. She also makes the point that BMR children, within white families, do not have a clear visual marker of belonging, as would occur in 'mixed-race' families where there is at least one parent of mixed background. As such, a child of BMR background may not see or experience the family as a place of safe retreat, but more that of additional threat due to the legitimacy of their perceived belonging if questioned. Thoburn's (2005) research finding was that for most BMR children, 'Skin colour and other physical characteristics, as well as aspects of heritage and culture of the birth family and the substitute family, are central to identity and worth' (pp.112–113). Samuels (2009) makes the important point that the process of socialisation and establishing identity in white families will bring definite challenges if these are undertaken by carers whose understanding and functioning have not previously required of them the skills of how to cope with racial stigma and racism, as the children that they intend to parent will require such skills for healthy psychological development.

The concept of 'micro-aggression'

In addition to the more obvious overt and sometimes insensitive questioning that BMR children and white kinship carers may experience in the wider community, there may also be more subtle issues of concern of which neither the BMR child, nor his white kinship carers, have experience. They are likely to be poorly equipped to identify and assess the potential impact on a child, and how this is best managed. The term 'micro-aggressions' (Sue 2010) is useful to consider here. Sue (2010) sees the experience of micro-aggressions as:

> The constant and continuing everyday reality of slights, insults, invalidations and indignities visited upon marginalised groups by well-intentioned, moral and decent family members, friends, neighbours, co-workers, students, teachers, clerks, waiters and waitresses, employers, health care professionals and educators. The power of micro-aggressions lies in their invisibility to the perpetrator who is unaware that he or she has engaged in a behaviour that threatens and demeans the recipient of such a communication. (p.xv)

Here, one gains some insight into the higher levels of social analysis in the dynamics of communication required by white kinship carers looking after BMR children. How might such an experience or process manifest itself in everyday life?

I will give an example from my own early background when first coming to the UK from the USA as a young BMR adolescent. Having come from the USA, one can assume that my level of English language would be at least comparable to my white UK peer group. My accent, although different, should, in the context of Hollywood and its influence in the UK, have been readily understood. A teacher, well-meaning, and presumably attempting to be sensitive to my learning needs, approached me on the morning of my first day, speaking in a laboured, slow, precise and deliberate manner, asking 'What...is...your...name?' Initially, not having experienced this before or seen myself as lacking basic English language skills, I assumed that the teacher had some neurological difficulty affecting her rate of speech production. When I told her my name again, the rather ordinary Western European name of 'Nicholas Banks', in what I assumed to be plain English, the teacher appeared to not understand what I was saying and became demonstrably anxious saying that she would have to get a pen and paper for me to write my name down, as she was unsure what I was saying. Assuming that the teacher had some hearing or speech and language difficulties which I needed to compensate for in my communication to her, I told her my name in the same laborious, slow set of consonant spacing that she had initially used when communicating with me. However, once having written down the name, she became somewhat confused as to why she had not immediately understood what I had said, and then proceeded to suggest (in a covert manner this time) that I had not spoken clearly. I was therefore blamed for her unconscious presumption that I would have a more 'exotic', incomprehensible name that would generate some difficulties for her recognising the utterance as a name. This was in an a outer London school in an area that was mainly white, with there being only one other child of non-white origin, a Trinidadian Asian, who spoke with a particularly pronounced London accent, which I later believed may have come about as a result of her compensation for what may have been similar experiences to me, in an English school environment, in her social development. The experience for me was a clear demonstration of a teacher's perspective that I was different, unlikely to be understood and then, when found to be not as different as she had first expected, became somewhat agitated at her own error, and attempted to project the cause of the error in her perception onto me. Some people reading this may think that I was over-sensitive and should have taken the teacher's attempts to communicate as a sensitive approach to difference. This memory has stayed with me for over 40 years as a clear example of an unintended micro-aggression and still forms part of my matrix of experience of how white people may respond in a well-meaning way to difference that causes some tension in the recipient of the 'well-meaning' action. Research suggests that the classroom dynamics may not have changed much over time (Archer

2008; Black 2004; Crozier 2006; Crozier 2009; Haynes, Tikly and Caballero 2006).

BMR young people may also experience the growing assumption that they are more likely to commit crimes and be muggers and rapists or drug pushers, due to unchallenged social stereotypes. The early stop and search (SAS) laws and the statistics around who was stopped by the police support this, as many ethnic minorities will also point out about powers of SAS associated with the Terrorism Act. Micro-aggressions all have the affect of giving a clear indication to children of BMR that they are not worthy, are not trustworthy and lack recognisable social integrity. BMR individuals, who are on the receiving end of micro-aggressions may come, over time, to doubt their ability to interpret social messages. As Sue (2010) identifies, such communications effect highly stressful situations due to confusion between an intended meaning and one's direct experience. Relationships that one had previously assumed to be positive become altered as the BMR individual begins to reassess their experience. Such unintended messages undermine a child's self-esteem and racial identity. They are stressful experiences in which children, in particular, may experience an event as hostile, but lack the capacity to intellectually identify their experience and explain or express this to others to seek support. If a child is punched in the playground, it is relatively easy for them to describe what has happened, with the teacher or parent understanding what the child is complaining about and offering the necessary support. A BMR child experiencing not being picked for important social events within a school (e.g. a black Jesus or Mary in the Christmas play) or experiencing themselves as being on the outside of the white peer group, is much less able to explain their experience and, when attempting to explain this to a white kinship carer, may be much less understood because of a white kinship carer's inability to understand and empathise with what the issue is about. With increasing micro-aggressions, children's presentation may change over time with them becoming more hyper-vigilant, sullen and resentful with increasing experience of being seen as different, less worthy, and with their growing awareness of marginalised status. Such an impact may have considerable influence on a child's social and emotional development and also their educational development. This all makes the life and social experience of a BMR individual seem overtly hostile and negative. Isn't this much too depressing? Some may also ask, isn't this 'much too dark' a picture? Again, looking at the last sentence, one sees the very subtle impact of a potential micro-aggression in alerting a BMR child as to how colour, 'darkness', is construed within the English language. Reflect on the implications of that phrase for a minute in the context of micro-aggressions.

Moving on, a further question may be asked: 'Do young children really notice colour?' Surely this is an adult preoccupation. Root (1998) suggests that many carers of BMR children will attempt to instil them with a resilient sense of self by making comments that 'Colour doesn't matter, we are all the same, you're no different'. While this may have attractions to a white kinship carer's view of how the world should be, it is not likely to be reflected in the BMR child's daily lived experience. It is not that unusual for BMR children to grow up within colour-blind families with white relatives. Samuels (2009) noted, in her study of transracially placed mixed children, that they described their parents as frequently having high levels of colour blindness. Samuels also found that few of the white carers were described as taking a proactive stance in talking about colour, difference and racism, and left this to when a crisis occurred that was brought to their attention by the children. Indeed, it would be an unusually insightful white family that openly and accurately discussed 'race' and colour differences in a productive manner which helped a child have a rooted sense of who they are and their belonging. What does colour blindness mean and how is such a perspective unhelpful in supporting a BMR child's social development needs? Helms (2008) suggests that colour blindness is a means by which we pretend that we do not notice one another's skin colour. At a general level, this tends to be seen as a means for achieving social justice. However, such a notion tends to deny the reality of the significance of 'race' in society as regards employment opportunity, educational opportunity and outcome and black and ethnic minority experiences in the criminal justice system.

Some may question 'Isn't colour blindness a means of ensuring that individuals are seen on their merits, rather than their skin colour?' This view assumes that the objective merits of an individual will triumph and be more visible and actively acted upon, than more deeply held, often unconscious, prejudice. Holding the notion of colour blindness also starts from the presumption that ethnic minorities' experiences are the same as white people's and that the experiences and 'world views' of white people are the yardstick by which all other experiences should be assessed. An example of how world views may differ depending on one's own cultural and ethnic background, is that of the black poet Benjamin Zephaniah (Mills 2003), who refused his OBE (Order of the British Empire), an award bestowed by the Queen in recognition of significant contribution to Britain. For many white individuals, such an award is likely to be associated with feelings of increased self-esteem and a high level of achievement for what is essentially recognition of one's contribution to (white) British society. However, Benjamin Zephaniah's perspective was:

> I get angry when I see that word 'Empire'. It reminds me of slavery, it reminds me of thousands of years of brutality, it reminds me of how my foremothers were raped and my forefathers brutalised. It is because of this concept of empire that my British education led me to believe that the history of black people started with slavery and that we were born slaves and should therefore be grateful that we were given freedom by our caring white masters. It is because of this idea of empire that black people like myself, don't even know our true names or our true historical culture. (Mills 2003)

Such a perspective clearly identifies that Great Britain and its empire is not seen as a great achievement by all.

Supporting the development of identity

When considering the notion of 'colour blindness' Helms suggests a view that everyone has the same opportunities regardless of 'race', should be seen as a form of 'power evasion'. This is to say that a lack of acknowledgement of colour and its significant social influence on one's opportunities in society would reflect a huge level of denial of psychiatric proportions. White kinship carers, in reflecting on their view of the need to deny colour and difference, may benefit from considering their own white identity development as a white person. In considering your own white identity and its development, think of how you have come to develop your own world view. First, in considering what a world view may be, think of this as a pair of spectacles through which a person comes to see or perceived their world and, most importantly, interpret meanings and social nuances. For example, if you are asked the question 'What is it like to be white?', how would you respond? Most people, in my many years of training experience, have voiced the initial view 'I have never thought about it, I just accept it'.

Some theorists (Neville, Worthington and Spanierman 2001) see this as form of what is referred to as 'white privilege', or never having to reflect on or experience one's white self from the perspective of less powerful, black groups, and never having to think about one's racial identity. Helms (2008) provides a useful model of white identity development. She describes her model of white identity as beginning with a situation (the stage of 'Contact') in which every white individual develops, through social experience (see Neville *et al.* 2001), a perspective in which it is seen as better to be perceived as white than non-white. Helms (2008) sees this as a particularly subtle and pervasive position, so taken for granted and seen as the norm, that it is always possible for white individuals to ignore this, and to deny that it would have any influence on their way of being. Helms considers that such a position, if it remains unexplored, and an essentially colour-blind perspective is adopted, does not allow a white individual to develop what she sees as a healthy white, non-racist identity. Helms (2008) also suggests that through a lack of exploration of their own white identity, the white individual accepts and internalised racism and colludes with what they obtain through the benefits of white privilege. This may not necessarily be an overt, active racist stance, but is seen by Helms as one of innocence, ignorance or having no view about 'race' and 'racism'. Such an individual is seen by Helms as '"race"-less', and as not giving much thought to the influence of 'race' in society. As a white kinship carer, being in such a position is not likely to enable you to meet and support the needs of a BMR child. This is because you will not be able to understand, identify or emphasise with the child's experiences of micro-aggressions and will not be able to provide them with the level of support and understanding they require. You are likely to further contribute to their experience of micro-aggression by denying that their experiences have validity and/or misunderstanding these and not helping the child to make sense of them and develop the necessary social defences. However, it is hoped that over time, a kinship carer in this stage will begin to develop some insight through the cumulative experience of how people respond to them with a BMR child and is likely to be placed in a position where they can no longer ignore the social implications of 'race'. Such a situation may come about through a crisis type experience. For example, a white kinship carer may be with their BMR child when he or she encounters a racial slur such as 'blackie' or 'nigger'. Here, Helms (2008) takes the view that during such a crisis, the white individual will need to confront their world view of colour blindness and its implications for any BMR child in their care. It is at the point of some social crisis that the white kinship carer is likely to lose their historical protective strategy of colour blindness. Here, they can no longer deny that 'race' is of social significance.

Helms (2008) describes the second stage of her white identity development model as that of 'disintegration-reintegration' – entering into a confused state where the white individual is forced to confront the fact that they are white, that white privilege exists and that they have partaken of white privilege through economic and political membership of a powerful white group. Helms (2008) sees the white individual in this stage as developing a complex pattern of cognitive distortion where they then come to believe that white people are in superior positions because of social merit, not white privilege. Helms (2008) notes that this next stage, the 'reintegration' phase, may show itself as a particularly persistent position over time. As part of this complex pattern of distortion in the reintegration phase, a kinship carer may also take the position that their BMR child is different to others and attempt to deny that the BMR child is anything other than white. Such a denial of reality will be particularly disturbing for the BMR child's healthy social and emotional development and may contribute significant disturbance to the BMR child's sense of identity and ability to connect both to white individuals and ethnic minority groups. Here, the kinship carer may take the view that if their BMR child can be helped to integrate into white culture, deny difference, and be seen as a white person, this is the best that can be achieved. Evidence does not support this view. Research in the USA with transracially placed children who live in mainly white areas with white families found black children showed some level of emotional disconnection with their racial difference and found it difficult to mix with other black people in later adolescence (DeBerry, Scarr and Weinberg 1966; Patton 2000). Samuels (2009) went so far as to suggest in her study, that being raised in a multiracial family does not reduce the role of 'race' in a child's life, but may exacerbate and complicate an (adopted) person's sense of difference and emphasise the need for parents to teach children how to cope and manage in a racialised society. For white kinship carers this is an important message and I would suggest that they never forget or deny the reality that one of the first things we notice about an individual, as well as their gender, is their 'race'. 'Race' provides important conscious and unconscious social clues about an individual and their place in society.

Helms (2008) then goes on to discuss the next stage, one of 'pseudo-independence', where a white person maintains a positive view of whiteness but does not see this as one of superiority and may have a liberal view that ethnic minority groups can be supported through special programmes. However, intellectualisation and denial still occur even when inequality is recognised: high levels of denial allow the white individual to disassociate themselves from the white privilege system. Helms (2008) believes that if there is continuing social challenge to the white person in the pseudo-independence stage, with a recognition that ethnic minority individuals do not wish to be white or assimilate into the predominant white British culture, then they may move onto the next stage of immersion versus emersion, where here, the white individual is able openly to understand the impact of racism and how white privilege contributes to this. Here, a white individual is able to remove themselves from the emotional guilt which may cause them to stick in the reintegration phase and cope with the cognitive or intellectual issues of white history and racist connections. In this stage the white individual takes an active stand in attempting to challenge racism and its impact. For a white kinship carer, this will mean being proactive in helping their BMR child to understand that racist experience is not a comment on the child's status and worth, but more a comment on living in an unequal society with high levels of denial and lack of awareness of white privilege and its contribution to a racist system. A white kinship carer should adopt the position of actively developing and support their BMR child's social awareness of the impact of racism (McHale *et al.* 2006; Rockquemore and Laszloffy 2005). A white kinship carer should also challenge individuals and systems such as the school and other social systems or groupings, for example the Scouts and Guides and similar, when the BMR child experiences micro-aggressions.

The final stage of Helms' (2008) white identity model is one of autonomy, where a white individual is said to actively search out experiences and opportunities to challenge racism and similar forms of oppression in their wider community and actively seek out cross-racial experiences that permit the individual to develop open and supportive experiences of individuals regardless of 'race' and culture. In the stage autonomy a person develops into feeling safe and secure within their experience of their whiteness. The previous emotions of guilt and suspicion which led the white individual to seek self-protection by denial and minimisation in the stages of 'disintegration-reintegration' are more adaptively managed with a greater degree of openness and self-exploration in evidence. Here, one is at the optimum level, as a white kinship carer, to be able to better meet the needs of a BMR child.

Conclusion

Research suggests that white carers can have a positive influence on raising BMR children if they are aware of the additional tasks in parenting required to achieve successful outcomes (Ryde 2009). This chapter identifies that an important additional task is one of acknowledging the different world experience of BMR people and how white kinship carers will need to be proactive and committed to providing their BMR children with the necessary approach and strategies to overcome any racialised adversity that they may experience in their early and later adult development. An important parenting task is one of preparing children to cope with adversity in life, with an extra dimension to this task required for white kinship carers of BMR children.

References

Archer, L. (2008) 'The impossibility of minority ethnic educational "Success"? An examination of the discourses of teachers and pupils in British secondary schools.' *European Educational Research Journal 7*, 1, 89–107.

Black, L. (2004) 'Differential participation in whole class discussions and the construction of marginalised identities.' *The Journal of Educational Enquiry 5*, 1, 34–54.

Caballero, C. (2010) *Lone Mothers of Children from Mixed Racial and Ethnic Backgrounds: A Case Study.* Bristol: Single Parent Action Network (SPAN).

Crozier, G. (2006) '"There's a war against our children": black educational underachievement revisited.' *British Journal of Sociology of Education 26*, 5, 585–598.

Crozier, G. (2009) 'South Asian parents' aspirations versus teachers' expectations in the United Kingdom.' *Theory Into Practice 4*, 290–296.

Dalmage, H.M. (2000) *Tripping on the Color Line: Black-white Multiracial Families in a Racially Divided World.* Piskataway, NJ: Rutgers University Press.

DeBerry, K.M., Scarr, S. and Weinberg, R. (1966) 'Family racial socialisation and ecological competence: longitudinal assessments of African American transracial adoptees.' *Child Development 67*, 2375–2399.

Haynes, J., Tikly, L. and Caballero, C. (2006) 'The barriers to achievement for White/ Black Caribbean pupils in English schools.' *British Journal of Sociology of Education* 27, 5, 569–583.

Helms, J.E. (2008) *A 'Race' is a Nice Thing to Have: A Guide to Being a White Person or Understanding the White Persons in your Life*, 2nd edn. Hanover, MA: Micro-training Associates Inc.

McHale, S.M., Crouter, A.C., Kim, J.Y., Burton, L.M., Davis, K.D. and Dotterer, A.M. (2006) 'Mothers' and fathers' racial socialisation in African American families: implications for youth.' *Child Development* 77, 1387–1402.

Mills, M. (2003) 'Rasta poet publicly rejects his OBE'. *The Guardian*, 27 November.

Neville, H., Worthington, R. and Spanierman, L. (2001) 'Race, Power, and Multicultural Counseling Psychology: Understanding White Privilege and Color Blind Racial Attitudes.' In J. Ponterotto, M. Casas, L. Suzuki and C. Alexander (eds) *Handbook of Multicultural Counseling*. Thousand Oaks, CA: Sage.

Owen, C. (2005) 'Looking at Numbers and Projections: Making Sense of the Census and Emerging Trends.' In T. Okitikpi (ed.) *Working with Children of 'Mixed-race'*. Russell House Publishing.

Patton, S. (2000) *Birth Marks: Transracial Adoption in Contemporary America*. New York: New York University Press.

Rockquemore, K.A. and Laszloffy, T. (2005) *Raising bi-racial Children*. Lanham, MD: Altamira Press.

Root, P.P.M. (1998) 'Experiences and processes affecting racial identity development: Preliminary results from the Bi-Racial Sibling Project.' *Cultural Diversity in Mental Health 4*, 3.

Ryde, J. (2009) *Being White in the Helping Professions: Developing Effective Intercultural Awareness*. London: Jessica Kingsley Publishers.

Samuels, G.M. (2009) '"Being raised by white people": navigating racial difference among adopted multiracial adults.' *Journal of Marriage and Family 71*, February, 80–94.

Song, M. and Aspinall, P. (2012) '"Mixed-race" Young People's Differential Responses to Misrecognition in Britain.' In R. Edwards, S. Ali, C. Caballero and M. Song (eds) *International Perspectives on Racial and Ethnic Mixedness and Mixing*. London: Routledge.

Sue, D.W. (2010) *Micro-aggressions in Everyday Life: 'Race', Gender and Sexual Orientation*. Hoboken, NJ: John Wiley and Sons Inc.

Thoburn, J. (2005) 'Permanent Family Placement for Children of Dual Heritage: Issues Arising from a Longitudinal Study.' In T. Okitikpi (ed.) *Working with Children of Mixed Parentage*. Russell House Publishing.

Wood, M. (2009) 'Mixed ethnicity, identity and adoption: research, policy and practice.' *Child and Family Social Work 14*, 431–439.

PART 3

International Contexts

CHAPTER 13

Australia and New Zealand

Assessing Parenting Capacity in Kinship Care

Marilyn McHugh and Paula Hayden

Introduction

Families are experts in their own experience and know more about their own strengths and vulnerabilities. Our job is to engage with them in ways that encourage collaboration and build solid foundations from which to develop a positive intervention plan. (Salomen and Sturmfels 2011, pp.4–5)

Australia has one of the highest rates of statutory kinship care. In 2010–2011, almost half (48 per cent) of all out-of-home care (OOHC) placements were with relative/kinship carers (AIHW 2012). The increasing use of kinship care as the preferred placement option raises issues of how the state assesses the suitability of these placements for children, and in turn how this assessment is experienced by the families themselves. This has been the subject of research, and has also given rise to some innovative practice. This and other aspects of assessing parenting capacity are described in this chapter.

In Australia the high kinship care use is attributed to:

- legislative preference in OOHC for the least 'intrusive' option – placing children requiring care with extended family, particularly for Indigenous children

- difficulties in recruiting/retaining foster carers nation-wide, and

- lesser cost of kinship compared to foster care placements (Boetto 2010; McHugh and valentine 2011; Paxman 2006; Spence 2004).

Indigenous children in Australia comprise 4.9 per cent of all children aged 0–17 years. Indigenous children ($n = 12,358$) compared to non-Indigenous ($n = 24,929$) are highly over-represented in the OOHC system, with a rate ten times that of non-Indigenous children (AIHW 2012). The Aboriginal Child Placement Principle (ACPP) ensures, that where possible and appropriate, all Indigenous children are placed either with the child's extended family; or within the child's Indigenous community; or with other Indigenous people. In 2011 nearly two-thirds (64.2 per cent) of Indigenous children were placed with relatives, kin or other Indigenous caregivers. Just over half (51.8 per cent) of non-Indigenous children were similarly placed (AGPC 2012, Table 15A.45).

New Zealand has a significant proportion of Indigenous people (15 per cent Māori) and similar to Australia, Māori children are more likely to be in OOHC than other children. New Zealand legislation enshrines the rights of Māori children to be cared for by family and Family Group Conferencing (FGC) is widely used in child protection matters in deciding who is best placed to care for Māori children. In 2011 44 per cent of OOHC placements were with family/whanau (i.e. relative/kin) caregiver, compared to 36 per cent with foster carers (NZ/MSD 2012). Despite the increasing use of kinship care there is limited research, especially with Māori carers (Worrall 2009).

In Australia and New Zealand statutory kinship care is part of general foster care programmes. Reforms in the implementation of specific kinship care policy and programmes are progressing in both countries (for the State of Victoria see Thompson Goodall Associates 2011). For many agencies however, there is a lack of structured frameworks and specific worker training in the assessment and support of kinship care placements. Training is required to address worker attitudes, values and beliefs around kinship care (Boetto 2010; McHugh 2009; Worrall 2009).

In Australia kinship carer assessment tools, in (and within) the eight jurisdictions by different agencies, are highly variable and there is no generally accepted model of kinship carer assessment. In Australia and New Zealand most kinship care assessment tools are variations or adaption of tools use for assessing foster carers (Yardley, Mason and Watson 2009; NZ/CYF 2007). Prior to the introduction of the Winangay tool (see below) research indicated that most standard assessment processes were culturally inappropriate for Indigenous kinship carers (Bromfield *et al.* 2007).

In Australia and New Zealand many kinship placements are 'unplanned'. At times grandparents take grandchildren into their care to secure their safety (Brennan and Cass forthcoming; McHugh 2009; Worrall 2008). The need for assistance at some stage of the placement can lead grandparent families, often reluctantly, to contact agencies. Formal assessments can occur at any stage, for example prior to placement, at a specific point ('crisis' period), or some months later in the placement. The alternating time frame for kinship assessment, often with children already placed, appears to have engendered less detailed/structured assessments, sometimes seen as 'enabling' rather than 'approving' carers to continue caring. A degree of 'flexibility', rarely defined, appears to be a key feature in conducting kinship carer assessments (McHugh 2009; Yardley *et al.* 2009).

National and international literature indicate that kinship carers, compared to unrelated foster carers, are usually grandparents, older, often single (grandmothers), in poorer health, with low incomes and lower levels of education (overview in McHugh and valentine 2011). These characteristics are intensified with Indigenous and Māori kinship carers, who experience higher levels of socio-economic disadvantage, relative to most other family groups in their respective societies (Brandon 2004; NZ/MSD 2007).

Studies by Australia and New Zealand researchers, comparing foster care with kinship care, note that kinship carer assessment is more perfunctory, and appropriate information, training and support (financial and non-financial) for kinship carers is often lacking. Studies give recognition to the similarities of the *needs* of kinship and unrelated foster carers and the children in their care, while highlighting the 'lesser' and variable treatment accorded to kinship carers (Boetto 2010; Families Australia 2008; Horner *et al.* 2007; Jenkins *et al.* 2010; McHugh 2009; McHugh and valentine 2011; Smyth and Eardley 2008; Spence 2004; Thompson Goodall Associates 2011; Worrall 2005, 2007, 2008, 2009; Yardley *et al.* 2009).

Some researchers suggest the general lack of appropriate information, training and support for kinship care placements is based on the erroneous assumption that extended families have the capacities to provide the necessary care, with little or no intervention by government agencies (Mason *et al.* 2002; Spence 2004).

Assessing parenting capacity

Foster care by unrelated carers is different to care by kin/relatives. In assessing the suitability of family members (predominantly grandparents in the Australian and New Zealand context) workers have to take into account:

- the balance between familiarity and identity between members of the kinship triad (e.g. child, mother, grandparent)

- the ability of kinship/relative carers to meet sometimes complex needs and the particular challenges of maintaining boundaries, and

- based on a previous different relationship, how the links as an insider to the family are maintained.

The aim here is to discuss the parenting capacities required of statutory kinship carers in Australia and New Zealand and to present issues that may impact on these capacities. In the development of a conceptual model for kinship care, O'Brien (2012) suggests six key parental capacities are required of kinship carers. Summarising O'Brien (2012, p.6), these capacities include:

1. keeping children safe and supported

2. understanding and meeting children's educational, social, physical (including health), identity, cultural and emotional needs[1]

3. self insight

4. understanding/dealing with family dynamics and carer understanding of own position in the dynamics

5. acceptance of placement support and understanding agency relevance in family lives, and

6. understanding the job of kinship (foster)[2] care.

---

1   In Australia the mental and other health needs of children in foster and kinship care have been found to be substantial (Chambers *et al.* 2010). For all children, particularly children from other cultures (especially Indigenous) understanding the importance of maintaining cultural connections is paramount (Bromfield *et al.* 2007). While 'health' and 'cultural' needs are not specifically mentioned by O'Brien (2012) they have been included in the list.

2   Terminology describing kinship care differs in countries. In NZ 'family/whanau caregiver' is used and in Australia 'kinship/relative care' is used, not 'kinship foster care'.

The first two listed capacities are directly related to parenting, by all parents, while the following four capacities (3–6) are more tangential to parenting. From the perspective of child welfare/protection agencies, capacities 3–6 are critical in statutory kinship care, though may not be viewed the same way by kinship carers. In the assessment process a degree of tension between carers and workers may materialise as discussion around the agency and kinship carers' role/responsibilities is explored. In ensuring the safety and protection of children, workers, as 'outsiders' in the family, walk a fine line in ensuring that 'intervention' into family life is kept to a minimum while ensuring adherence to standards. Ensuring capacities 3–6 are seen by carers as 'required capacities' requires well-trained, skilled and experienced caseworkers. O'Brien's interlinked parental capacities are explored in the following sections.

Keeping children safe and supported

As noted by O'Brien (2012, p.11) central to the kinship care model is the belief that extended family can keep children safe. This is borne out in numerous studies finding kinship carers are overwhelmingly committed to keep children safe. All placements have potential risk/safety concerns around them but some have a stronger relevance or resonance for kinship carers compared to foster carer. For example, contact with birth parents is seen as critical for placement stability. Unlike foster care, kinship carers are often responsible for arranging and maintaining contact/access with birth parents (many with substance abuse problems). Ensuring children are kept safe on access visits (often unsupervised), and that boundaries are observed by parents, is a source of carer anxiety and stress. Adversely impacting on children are court orders for contact not adhered to by carers and/or parents (Brennan and Cass forthcoming; Dunne and Kettler 2008; Worrall 2009; Yardley *et al.* 2009).

In Indigenous kinship care, family group conferencing or family meetings with Aboriginal/Māori are necessary, to ensure appropriate and safe child placements are made. At family meetings an Aboriginal/Māori worker should be available to provide advice on cultural issues, family and community politics. An 'agreed' decision is crucial, as placement decisions, not in accordance with family views, may break down due to a lack of support from the wider family and community In Aboriginal/Māori kinship families safety issues can arise due to overcrowding, or when a large sibling group (common in Aboriginal/ Māori families) are kept together, over-stretching carer capacity to meet children's needs. Longstanding generational conflict or feuding within wider Aboriginal/Māori families and irregular or informal contact arrangements can at times exacerbate safety issues (McHugh 2009; Williams and Satour 2005; Worrall 2009).

It is essential for workers undertaking kinship care assessments to understand the complications that can arise in relationships between the children, their carers and their parents. Agency involvement, such as supervising contact, may be essential in ensuring safety (McHugh 2009; Worrall 2009). How children are supported in the placement is closely linked to the second capacity discussed below.

Understanding and meeting children's educational, social, physical (including health), identity, cultural and emotional needs

The ethos of kinship care encompasses family continuity, sustaining family links and assisting children's identity formation (NSW Ombudsman 2008; Worrall 2008). In some areas of children's needs, their grandparents' awareness may be limited. This may be due to a lack of understanding of:

- current parenting practices and values (i.e. the generation gap)

- challenging behaviours, special needs or health problems

- developmental milestones

- impact of abuse and trauma, and

- meeting cultural and emotional needs (McHugh 2009; McHugh and valentine 2011; Worrall 2005, 2009).

Given the irregular nature of some kinship placements, it is not unusual for carers not to have access to relevant information about the potential needs of children (NSW Ombudsman 2008).

Grandparents can struggle with contemporary education systems and often cannot assist grandchildren with homework/schoolwork. In social situations (e.g. sports, school events, playgroups, etc.) grandparents can feel socially isolated with little connection with the (younger) parents of their grandchildren's peers. More problematic for grandparents carers is the fact that, even knowing children's needs, it can be difficult to access and finance the required services and support (Brennan and Cass forthcoming; McHugh 2009; Yardley *et al.* 2009).

Carers cannot commit to meeting children's needs unless they understand what those needs are; and their needs are often psychological as well as practical (Dunne and Kettler 2008). Grandparents can struggle with grief/anger/disappointment around birth children's issues, shame around having grandchildren in care, resentment at loss of friends, lifestyle and/or paid work, and the financial expenses associated with caring. They require substantial support and services, including respite, to ensure they can acknowledge and meet their needs and children's needs (McHugh 2009; Worrall 2009).

Health and education assessments for children entering OOHC are essential. Ensuring case plans list identified needs and how they are to be addressed in a timely manner is even more critical. For Māori/ Aboriginal children cultural plans – supporting Indigenous children's identity and connection to family, land and culture – form an important part of their case plans (NSW Ombudsman 2008; Rankin and Mills 2008).

Self insight

The parental capacity of 'self insight' is not clarified by O'Brien (2012). In the context of kinship care, at issue, is the carer's ability to see clearly and intuitively into the nature of the complex situation (i.e. placement) that has arisen, which is often one not of their choosing. It is difficult to gauge at what point carers can self-reflect on the situation that many are 'thrown' into, often with little warning, and how they plan to cope. Over the life of the placement carers are required to deal with fluid and changing relationships with family and friends, some positive and some negative, while negotiating the complex and challenging nature of statutory care with agency workers and other professionals. Their need to understand the myriad tasks they face in 'parenting again' for one or more children who have been traumatised, occurs amid high and mixed emotions.

The gaining of insight for kinship carers is a developing process. Building trust and a positive relationship between agencies and carers in the assessment process requires a degree of worker expertise, particularly if carer confidence in their abilities is not to be undermined. In a study from the State of Victoria (Victorian Government/DHS

2007), kinship carers suggested that the following would assist them in the assessment process:

- information about: realistic appraisals of the demands and impact of the placement; scoping of the child's future needs; knowledge about handling family reactions and future family relationships; and understanding of the birth parents' involvement and contact

- qualities necessary in their caseworkers were: maturity, experience, understanding and respect; appreciation of a carer's situation/ story; understanding the carer's mixed emotions/divided loyalties with parents and grandchildren; ability to involve extended family in decisions/planning; and an understanding of drug/alcohol addiction.

In the initial stages of the placement and involvement with the agency, it is unlikely that carers will have full insight into the complexities of a placement. With knowledge comes insight. In New Zealand and in most Australian jurisdictions, the lack of initial training, which is required of foster, but not of kinship carers, results in kinship carers struggling to understand the 'system' and their role and responsibilities. Without appropriate training and education, carers are unaware of how to access relevant information and gain knowledge of entitlements (financial and non-financial) and how best to meet children's needs. Research in Victoria involving four non-government kinship care agency workers found that a high majority (70 per cent) of carers would benefit from formal training to a 'great' or 'very great' extent. 'Insufficient training potentially puts their wellbeing at risk as well as that of the child or young person' (Thomson Goodall Associates 2011, pp.51–52). Similarly, interviews with Aboriginal carers in NSW ($n = 68$) revealed a desire for training on issues important to them (NSW Ombudsman 2008).

Understanding and dealing with family dynamics

Despite difficulties in managing the family dynamics arising from kinship placements numerous studies indicate that carers offer stability and security while maintaining family contact. A grandparent's decision to provide care can cause tension, conflict or resentment with other family members, including carers' spouses or partners, often upsetting previous good relationships. Other grandchildren are known to 'miss out' on contact with grandparents. Adult children in families may disapprove of their parents' decision to care, or raise concerns at the stress and strain on their parents. For some kinship carers, relationships with other family members (including spouse/partners) can be strengthened and emotional and material support offered when kinship placements occur. Rarely do unsettled family dynamics appear to be the cause of placement breakdown (Brennan and Cass forthcoming; McHugh 2009; QLD Government/DoC 2012; Worrall 2008).

Divided family loyalties can elevate the stress levels of kinship carers. For example, grandparents may feel they 'do not want to alienate the parents, often their own adult children, but they see the effects of the parents' behaviour on the grandchildren' (COTA 2003, p.24). Some birth parents, hostile towards the placement, can attempt to undermine it (QLD Government/DoC 2012). Researchers have defined this conflict in core family values in caring for all family members and treating all family members equally as the 'double bind' of family relationships (Campbell and Handy 2011). Caught in the midst of these dynamics grandparents struggle satisfactorily to resolve their internal and external conflicts with other family members.

Accepting placement support and understanding agency relevance in family lives

Studies indicate that many kinship carers are highly conflicted in their relationships with state agencies with some carers finding assessment processes intrusive and demeaning. A lack of ongoing caseworker support accentuates any negative feelings. In contrast other kinship carers express delight and appreciation in receiving financial assistance and placement support. Through kinship carer groups (a growing advice and support mechanism throughout Australia and New Zealand) carers gain insight and information about their rights, entitlements and how the 'system' works, and they become more attuned to agency relevance in their lives (Brennan and Cass forthcoming; Doolan and Nixon 2003; NSW/Ombudsman 2008; McHugh 2009; Worrall 2008).

The research from Victoria referred to above (Thomson Goodall Associates 2011) found almost all (88 per cent) kinship carers accepted the support offered by the agencies. The researchers concluded that: 'hopefully this willingness to accept support has an impact…by establishing good patterns and relationships from the commencement of the placement' (p.55). Kinship carers who were interviewed for the study commented that since being transferred to the non-government agency they feel 'more supported, recognised and understood' and 'their efforts are acknowledged and appreciated'. For some carers 'this was the first time that they had an opportunity to openly discuss their current struggles and fears for the future' (Thomson Goodall Associates 2011, pp.65–66).

Understanding the job of kinship (foster) care

> Society has no idea how hard this type of care giving is. As we age our finances become fixed but as the children grow their financial needs increase. More recognition for the job we do!

> Knowing they are loved and this is not a job. We are blessed to have them in our lives. Makes for a happy family.

These two kinship carers' quotes in Worrall's study (2009) highlight the vast continuum of carer understanding of the *job* of kinship care. In one study, an Aboriginal carer further separated her role from the notion of care work: 'I'm raising him…I'm not caring for him…he's part of my family' (McHugh 2009, p.99). This strong disassociation for many kinship carers, not perceiving their role as 'work/job', is why workers need to understand and engage with kinship carer from a different perspective. How workers approach this issue appears to influence how support that is 'offered' (or not) by workers is 'accepted' (or not) by families. As kinship carers can be highly conflicted in their relationship with agencies it is the responsibility of workers to develop trusting relationships with carers, assisting them to gain a more nuanced understanding of the roles and responsibilities of being a kinship carer.

Promising practice in Australian kinship care

Recognising the inappropriateness of standard assessment tools, especially for Aboriginal people, led to the development of a unique assessment tool (Winangay Aboriginal Kinship Care Assessment) by a team of Australian Aboriginal and non-Aboriginal workers in 2010 (see Winangay.com.au). The tool is embedded in a culturally appropriate model acknowledging the unique role of kinship carers 'raising', not caring for, children. The strength-based tool, based on an ecological framework, uses an 'exchange of information' approach in assessing the parental capacities, strengths and needs of kinship carers.

Designed to be completed by workers and kinship carers, the outcomes of the discussions inform a joint 'Action Plan' outlining unmet needs, concerns, services and support. The tool incorporating children and young people's views addresses their issues/concerns as part of the Action Plan (McHugh and valentine 2011).

In the Winangay model, questions are embedded into the assessment process which promotes reflection on the part of the kinship carer, for example, in regard to:

- circumstances prior to the child coming to live with them

- impact on family members and relationships, and

- balancing the needs of all family members.

In discussing their 'family', kinship carers are encouraged to use family photos to tell their story. The tool comes with a series of visual pictorial cards (Strength and Concerns Cards) for the workers to use, allowing carers to scale themselves, in relation to their strengths and concerns. The use of the cards facilitates discussion on:

- environment and basic needs

- the kinship carer

- children and their wellbeing, and

- carers' actions and how they will work with others.

The format of the resource is deliberately informal and uses earthy colours and Aboriginal graphics and images. The questions are in plain English and flow in a manner that encourages conversations. Each card focuses on a key factor, identified in research and practice wisdom, as key to successful outcomes for Aboriginal children and kinship carers. The cards allow carers to identify their strengths and areas of concern, placing them on a continuum from 'real' concern to 'deadly' strength.[3] Visually displaying key areas of unmet needs enables the Action Plan to reflect required supports and services.

Topics covered include:

- meeting basic needs

- existing supports available to kinship carers

---

3   Deadly is an Aboriginal slang word for 'really good'.

- support they provide to other family members, and

- supports/services required to meet the children's needs.

The process provides an opportunity for carers to take ownership of the process, to identify what keeps them strong as a carer and what facilitates their learning. It allows carers to reflect on their own past experiences, in particular the impact of child welfare polices and intergenerational trauma, which may impact on their capacity to care, their ability to advocate for children and themselves, and how they will balance competing demands.

The strong emphasis in the assessment is keeping children safe in the home and beyond. Kinship carers have responsibilities for orchestrating a myriad of differing relationships – including family members, teachers, workers and other professionals. The tool explores how carers can do this and the support they might require in managing contact with birth and wider family members, or negotiating with others to best meet children's needs. The tool can be used to monitor and review changes in the family over time, with workers and carers using the Strengths/Concerns continuum to ensure that identified supports and strategies are being provided, supporting carers to continue meeting children's needs.

Feedback from workers in several Australian jurisdictions on the Winangay Aboriginal Kinship Care Assessment Tool is very encouraging and has led to adaption of the tool for non-Aboriginal kinship carers. Workers indicate that the tool enables them to build a strong, respectful and transparent relationship with carers to identify strengths, needs and concerns and collaboratively develop the Action Plan. Workers note that kinship carers value the opportunity to determine where they are on the Strengths and Concerns scale. In the words of one carer: 'What's important to us is included in the Action Plan. We work with the worker to decide what we all have to work on'.

Australia and New Zealand, as in other countries, have begun to develop a better understanding of statutory kinship care and the parental capacities required by carers. In further developments the focus should be on 'shifting the way assessments are done by redistributing power from workers to carers, contributing to new stronger ways of kinship carers, workers and kids working together' (Hayden, Ryan and McHugh, 2011: Canadian First Nations worker's response at the Winangay presentation).

References

AGPC (Australian Government Productivity Commission) (2012) *Report on Government Services 2012*. Canberra: AGPS. Available at www.pc.gov.au/gsp/rogs/2012, accessed on 4 June 2013.

AIHW (Australian Institute of Health and Welfare) (2012) *Child Protection Australia*, Child Welfare Series, No 53. Canberra: AIHW. Available at www.aihw.gov.au/WorkArea/DownloadAsset.aspx?id=10737421014, accessed on 4 June 2013.

Boetto, H. (2010) 'Kinship care: a review of the Issues.' *Family Matters 85*, 61–67. Available at www.aifs.gov.au/institute/pubs/fm2010/fm85/fm85g.pdf, accessed on 4 June 2013.

Brandon, P.D. (2004) 'Identifying the diversity in Australian children's living arrangements.' *Journal of Sociology 40*, 2, 179–192.

Brennan, D. and Cass B. (eds) (forthcoming) *'Run Faster, Nana': Grandparents as Primary Carers of their Grandchildren: A National, State and Territory Analysis*. Social Policy Research Centre, The University of New South Wales.

Bromfield, L.M., Higgins, J.R., Richardson, N. and Higgins, D.J. (2007) 'Why standard assessment processes are culturally inappropriate, Paper 3: *Promising Practices in Out-of-Home Care for Aboriginal and Torres Strait Islander Carers and Young People: Strengths and Barriers*, Australian Institute of Family Studies. Available at http://192.135.208.240/nch/pubs/reports/promisingpractices/summarypapers/paper3.pdf, accessed on 4 June 2013.

Campbell, J. and Handy, J. (2011) 'Bound to care: custodial grandmothers' experience of double bind family relationships.' *Feminism & Psychology 21*, 431–439.

Chambers, M., Saunders, A.M., New, B.D., Williams, C.L. and Stachurska, A. (2010) 'Assessment of children coming into care: Processes, pitfalls and partnerships.' *Clinical Child Psychology & Psychiatry 15*, 4, 511–527.

COTA (Council on the Ageing) (2003) *Grandparents Raising Grandchildren*. Melbourne: Australian Institute of Family Studies.

Doolan, M. and Nixon, P. (2003) 'The importance of kinship care.' September, *Social Work Now. 25*, 12–20.

Dunne, E.G. and Kettler, L.J. (2008) 'Grandparents raising grandchildren in Australia: exploring psychological health and grandparents' experience of providing kinship care.' *International Journal of Social Welfare 17*, 333–345.

Families Australia (2008) *Better Support for Grandparents: Issues and Recommendations*. Canberra: Families Australia.

Hayden, P., Ryan, F. and McHugh, M. (2011) 'Winangay Aboriginal Kinship Care Assessment Tool.' Presentation at the IFCO Conference *Fostering Hope...Together, we can make a difference*, Victoria, BC, Canada, 10–15 July.

Horner, B., Downie, J., Hay, D. and Wichman, H. (2007) 'Grandparent-headed families in Australia.' *Family Matters 76*, 76–84.

Jenkins, B., Brennan, D., Cass, B. and valentine, k. (2010) 'Information Provision and Kinship Care.' Paper presented at the AIFS Conference, *Sustaining Families in Challenging Times*, July, Melbourne.

Mason, J., Falloon, J., Gibbons, L., Spence, N. and Scott, E. (2002) *Understanding Kinship Care*. Report on a research project undertaken by the University of Western Sydney and the Association of Children's Welfare Agencies, NSW.

McHugh, M. (2009) *A Framework of Practice for Implementing a Kinship Care Program*. Report prepared for the Benevolent Society, Social Policy Research Centre, The University of New South Wales, Sydney.

McHugh, M. and valentine, k. (2011) *Financial and Non-Financial Support to Formal and Informal Out-of-Home Carers*, SPRC, UNSW, Occasional Paper No. 38. Canberra: Australian Government, Department of Families, Housing, Community Services and Indigenous Affairs.

NSW Ombudsman (2008) *Supporting the Carers of Aboriginal Children*, March. Available at www.ombo.nsw.gov.au/__data/assets/pdf_file/0012/4080/Supporting-the-carers-of-Aboriginal-children-June-2008-FINAL-REPORT.pdf, accessed on 4 June 2013.

NZ (New Zealand), MSD (Government, Ministry of Social Development) (2012) *The Statistical Report for the Year Ending June 2011*. Wellington: Ministry of Social Development. Available at www.msd.govt.nz/documents/about-msd-and-our-work/publications-resources/statistics/statistical-report-2011.pdf, accessed on 4 June 2013.

NZ (New Zealand), CYF (Government, Child, Youth and Family (2007) *Understanding the Experience and Needs of Caregivers*. Available at www.cyf.govt.nz/documents/about-us/publications/reports/caregivers-speak.pdf, accessed 4 June 2013.

NZ (New Zealand), MSD (Ministry of Social Development) (2007) *The Social Report*. Wellington: Ministry of Social Development.

O'Brien, V. (2012) *A New Conceptual Model for Kinship Care Assessment*, WP 26. Dublin: UCD School of Applied Social Science.

Paxman, M. (2006) *An Issues Paper: Outcomes for Children and Young People in Kinship Care*. Ashfield, NSW: Centre for Parenting and Research, NSW Department of Community Services.

QLD (Queensland) Government, DoC (Department of Communities) (2012) *Kinship Care: A Literature Review*. Brisbane. Available at www.communities.qld.gov.au/resources/childsafety/foster-care/kinship-care-literature-review.pdf, accessed on 4 June 2013.

Rankin, D. and Mills, A. (2008) 'Establishing health and education assessments for children entering care.' *Social Work Now* December *41*, 35–39.

Salomen, N. and Sturmfels, D. (2011) 'Making the most of child and family assessments in child protection.' *Social Work Now 47*, 3–9.

Smyth, C. and Eardley T. (2008) *Out of Home Care for Children in Australia: A Review of Literature and Policy*, SPRC Report No. 3/08, prepared for the Department of Families, Housing, Community Services and Indigenous Affairs, Social Policy Research Centre, The University of New South Wales, Sydney.

Spence, N. (2004) 'Kinship care in Australia.' *Child Abuse Review 13*, 263–276.

Thomson Goodall Associates (2011) *Review of the Anglicare Victoria and Berry Street Kinship Care Program* (unpublished) (Summary available from Berry Street: www.berrystreet.org.au, accessed on 4 June 2013).

Victorian Government, Department of Human Services (DHS) (2007) *Kinship Care: Relatives and Family Friends Caring for Children: Report on Consultations*. Melbourne: Placement and Support Unit, Child Protection and Family Services, Office for Children, DHS.

Williams, A. and Satour, J. (2005) 'Kinship Care: Mapping Progress in Central Australia', paper presented at the National Foster Care Conference, *Living and Learning Together: A Celebration and Appreciation of Diversity*, 29–31 July, Alice Springs.

Worrall, J. (2005) *Grandparents and Other Relatives Raising Kin Children in Aotearoa/ New Zealand.* Report commissioned by the Grandparents Raising Grandchildren Charitable Trust, Auckland: Grandparents Raising Grandchildren Trust.

Worrall, J. (2007) *Grandparents Raising Grandchildren: A Handbook for Grandparents and Other Kin Carers*, 3rd edn, Auckland: Grandparents Raising Grandchildren Trust.

Worrall, J. (2008) 'Kin care: understanding the dynamics.' *Social Work Now* December, 4–11.

Worrall, J. (2009) *Grandparents and Whanau/Extended Families Raising Kin Children in Aotearoa/New Zealand.* Report commissioned by the Grandparents Raising Grandchildren Charitable Trust, Auckland.

Yardley, A., Mason, J. and Watson, E. (2009) *Kinship Care in NSW: Finding a Way Forward.* Sydney: Social Justice Social Change Research Centre, University of Western Sydney and Association of Childrens Welfare Agencies.

CHAPTER 14

Kinship Care among Families Affected by HIV in South Africa

Caroline Kuo, Lucie Cluver and Don Operario

South Africa faces one of the worst HIV epidemics globally, with 5.6 million people living with HIV and 314,000 people dying from AIDS each year (UNAIDS 2012). Because the South African epidemic is largely driven by heterosexual infection, and concentrated among adults of child-bearing age, it has had particularly devastating consequences upon families (Karim and Karim 2002). Not surprisingly, patterns of kinship care have shifted in response to family members living with HIV and dying from AIDS. The epidemic has also altered the psychological landscape for HIV affected families, particularly for kin caregivers who confront the challenges of caring for children orphaned by AIDS, tending to ill family members, coping with the death of someone close to them, and perhaps even coping with their own illness. This chapter provides an overview of the impact of the HIV epidemic on patterns of kinship care, the psychological consequences of kinship care, and existing systems of support for kin caregivers. We hope that by focusing on South Africa, which faces one of the worst epidemics in the world, this chapter will offer insights into the formulation of appropriate responses to support kin caregivers in other severely affected settings.

Shifting patterns of kinship care

In South Africa, the placement of children into kinship care was well established prior to the HIV epidemic (Madhavan 2004). Indeed AIDS orphanhood is not the sole driver of kinship care placements in South Africa today. For example, nearly a quarter of children (24 percent) live with neither biological parent, even though both parents are alive (Hall 2012). South Africa's longstanding practices of kinship care emerged from a number of historical factors including apartheid policies which frequently separated families, and migratory work which resulted in biological parents leaving children under the care of extended family for short and long periods of time (Cock, Emdon and Klugman 1986; Lemon 1991; Niehaus 1994). However, the HIV epidemic has undoubtedly impacted kinship care in South Africa (Ford and Hosegood 2005; Hill, Hosegood and Newell 2008). This is largely due to the 1.9 million children orphaned by AIDS (Monasch and Boerma 2004; UNAIDS 2012), and the millions more who may be placed into kinship care when their parents become ill.

The majority of children orphaned by AIDS are cared for by extended family members, with far fewer children being placed into residential care (UNICEF 2006). This suggests that the placement of children within the kinship care system is not a new consequence of the HIV epidemic in South Africa. Rather, important changes in household composition may be taking place in response to the HIV epidemic. While systematic and detailed national data on the composition of households engaged in kinship care are unavailable in South Africa (UNICEF 2008), regional longitudinal data indicate increasing numbers of fostered children and higher dependency ratios (Madhavan and Schatz 2007). These data may be indicative of an increase in the numbers of children being placed in kinship care as well as a rise in permanent, rather than temporary, kinship care arrangements. The placement of children with kin caregivers is conducted largely without the involvement of administrative or judicial authorities (UNICEF 2008). However, because many HIV-affected households also experience poverty, the need to access government social grants may be resulting in an increasing number of kinship care arrangements that involve administrative and judicial authorities.

Child-headed households or households where all members are under 18 years of age may also be a newly emerging pattern in kinship care. Unfortunately, there is limited available longitudinal data, making it difficult to ascertain whether there has been a statistically significant rise in child-headed households during the course of the HIV epidemic (Mturi 2012). Existing data from national household surveys and demographic and surveillance data suggest that the prevalence of child-headed households remains low in South Africa (Hall and Meintjes 2012; Hill et al. 2008; Hosegood et al. 2007). Even though there are few child-headed households, children who serve in the role of kin caregivers face challenges. Few studies have been conducted on this vulnerable sub-population of kin caregivers, and all the studies were qualitative in nature. Together, these studies suggest that children serving as kin caregivers have difficulty accessing social services and generating income; experience food insecurity; and face challenges to their psychosocial wellbeing including coping with grief (Donald and Clacherty 2009; Pillay 2012; vann Dijk and van Driel 2009). Many of these challenges start prior to orphanhood, in the period when children's parents or kin caregivers become ill. During this period, children may act as "young carers" within their families, a term we use to describe children who partake in caregiving duties to adults living with a disability or another illness in their home.

The psychological consequences of the HIV epidemic

The HIV epidemic has profound consequences for family outcomes in South Africa. A growing body of literature documents a diverse range of outcomes related to the experience of individual or household HIV. For example, studies or reviews have examined the sexual risk behaviors and educational outcomes of children orphaned by AIDS in South Africa (Arndt and Lewis 2005; Case and Ardington 2006; Operario et al. 2011; Parikh et al. 2007). Studies have also documented adverse nutritional and economic conditions faced by households affected by HIV including those caring for orphaned children (Bachman DeSilva et al. 2008; Bachmann and Booysen 2003, 2004; Kaschula 2008). Importantly, we are beginning to understand the psychological consequences of the HIV epidemic on families.

Growing evidence shows that South African children orphaned by AIDS are more likely to face higher rates of depression, post-traumatic stress, and internalizing and externalizing disorders compared to non-orphaned children (Cluver, Gardner and Operario 2007; Cluver, Gardner and Operario 2009; Cluver, Operario and Gardner 2009). Evidence on the negative psychological consequences of AIDS orphanhood has also been replicated in studies across sub-Saharan Africa and elsewhere in the world; an analysis of 24 quantitative studies from a recent systematic review of the global literature on the psychosocial outcomes of HIV-affected children showed that in 77 percent of these studies, children affected by AIDS were more likely to report depression, trauma, somatization, anxiety, loneliness, suicidal ideation, and hopelessness compared to children from non-HIV affected families (Chi and Li 2012). Ongoing work in South Africa is also investigating the psychological consequences of being a young carer (Cluver *et al.* 2010). Studies of this important population elsewhere in the world show that while some aspects of being a young carer can be positive, including for example, growth in emotional maturity (Robson *et al.* 2006), young carers also face a number of psychological challenges (Bauman *et al.* 2006; Martin 2006; Skovdal and Ogutu 2009). Similar to children orphaned by AIDS, children affected by parental HIV illness are likely to report poor emotional, behavioral, and social adjustment during parental illness and this persists during orphanhood (Chi and Li 2012). Some of the possible reasons driving elevated psychological risk among HIV-affected children is the unique "clustering" of traumatic and/or stressful life events, HIV-related stigma, and the impoverishing effect of HIV (Chi and Li 2012).

Importantly, we are also now beginning to understand the psychological impacts of being a kinship caregiver in the era of HIV but the literature on adults providing kinship care to HIV-affected children is much more limited than the literature on children orphaned and otherwise affected by AIDS. The psychological impacts faced by kin caregivers may be related to the provision of care for orphaned children, caring for a sick family member, and/or coping with the bereavement of a loved one. Similar to the literature on psychological distress among orphaned children, South African studies indicate that kin caregivers in HIV-affected households were more likely to report poor health, including poor psychosocial outcomes compared to non-affected households (Bachman DeSilva *et al.* 2008; Kuo and Operario 2010; Kuo, Operario and Cluver 2012). Studies elsewhere document similar findings (Lv *et al.* 2010). In the context of these shifting patterns of kinship care, and an emerging understanding of the psychosocial consequences faced by kin caregivers, it is vital to consider strategies for supporting and protecting the resilience of families.

Systems to protect the resilience of kin caregivers

South Africa has one of the most extensive social protection systems for kin caregivers within the sub-Saharan African region (Patel and Triegaardt 2008). These social protections are particularly important for those caring for orphaned children, who are far more likely to come from poor households (Hall and Meintjes 2012). South Africa's social protection system is rooted in the extensive welfare reforms of the democratic government that followed apartheid in 1994 (Republic of South Africa 1997). While the system was initially designed to address socio-economic inequalities rooted in generations of differential racial access to resources, the system has grown into a crucial safety net for families affected by HIV. These social protections are enshrined in a number of government policies and strategy documents. Of particular importance for kin caregivers of children who are orphaned and vulnerable is the National Action Plan for Orphans and Other Children Made Vulnerable by HIV and AIDS (South African Department of Social Development 2009). These social protections also include a number of services, provided by the government as well as non-governmental and community-based organizations. Finally, social protections are transferred to families through various social grants. Five types of grants are of paramount importance to kin caregivers.

The first grant is the foster care grant. This is awarded to families that care for a child that has completed a social work assessment determining that they are in need of care (due to being orphaned, abandoned, at risk, etc.). The child is then formally placed with the family by the courts, and followed through time by a social worker. Families are given a grant of 770 Rand (89 US dollars/£57) per month to help support the child, and re-assessed every two years until the child reaches 18 years of age (Department of Social Development 2008). Although families may access the foster grant for a child that is unrelated to them, most caregivers who access the foster care grant are kin caregivers, most often extended relatives of the child. For example, a report that analyzed the profile of those utilizing the foster care grant showed the large majority of recipients were extended relatives of the child (41% were grandparents, 30% were aunts, 12% were other relatives) (De Koker, de Waal and Vorster 2006).

The second grant is the child support grant. The child support grant is a means-tested non-contributory cash transfer targeted at children living in poverty. The grant is awarded to a child's primary caregiver who meets financial needs-based criteria, and consists of 280 Rand (32 US dollars/£20) per month. Recently, eligibility rules changed so that caregivers who are children over the age of 16 years can also receive the grant. This is an important change that helps meet the needs of children who may be serving in the role of kin caregivers in child-headed households (Department of Social Development 2008).

The third and fourth grants are designed to support those caring for adults or children with disabilities. These are the disability grant which meets the needs of adults with a disability, and the care dependency grant which meets the needs of adults caring for a child with a disability. Both grants provide a maximum of 1800 Rand (209 US dollars/£133) per month for individuals who pass a medical examination and who are not receiving institutional care (Department of Social Development 2008). Increasingly, these grants are being used to assist individuals living with HIV (with disability assessed based on a CD4 count assessment) and individuals providing support to them during their illness (Phaswana-Mafuya, Peltzer and Petros 2009).

The final grant utilized by kin caregivers is the old age pension. Similar to the child support grant, this grant is a means-tested non-contributory cash transfer. It is targeted at older adults who may need financial supplementation in their aging years and amounts to a maximum of 1200 Rand (139 US dollars/£89) per month for adults age 60–75 years, and a maximum of 1220 Rand (142 US dollars/£91) per month for adults age 75 years or older (Department of Social Development 2008). Given that so many older adults, particularly grandmothers, play a role in caring for both orphaned and vulnerable children in South Africa, this grant is a key source of social protection.

Clearly, these grant programs function as an important safety net for those in poverty. Notably, these grants also have been found to lower the risk of common mental disorders (Plagerson *et al.* 2010). While grants serve as important sources of socio-economic and psychological protection, they are not without their challenges. One major challenge includes the creation of perverse incentives. For example, in the case of the disability grant, individuals living with HIV and poverty may face a tension between the desire to receive the disability grant and the desire to maintain their health. Since the disability grant requires that individuals meet a certain threshold of disability – as determined by a low CD4 count – individuals taking anti-retroviral medication would improve their health at the risk of becoming ineligible for the disability grant (de Paoli, Mills and Gronningsaeter 2012; Hardy and Richter 2006). Other challenges arise from the gendered nature of social protection utilization and the consequences for the grant recipient when grants are redistributed to household members to alleviate poverty (Samson *et al.* 2004) and to meet basic needs such as food and education (Delany *et al.* 2008; Schatz 2007a). For example, women who receive the old age pension redistribute their pension within households to pay for subsistence needs including food, shelter, and clothing (Schatz 2007a). While these redistributions have positive effects on household members including improvements in child health (Duflo 2003), they may have potentially negative consequences on the wellbeing of kin caregivers, particularly women who play a predominant role as kin caregivers for orphaned and vulnerable children during the epidemic (Foster et al. 1995; Freeman and Nkomo 2006; Howard et al. 2006).

Efficacious family-centered interventions and rigorously evaluated community programs also serve as key strategies to support kin caregivers. Notably lacking are efficacious mental health interventions that take a family approach in South Africa. One example of an efficacious family intervention to address psychological health and HIV behavioral outcomes is the Collaborative HIV Prevention and Adolescent Mental Health Project-Plus Program, originally tested in the United States (McKay et al. 2008). This program is driven by social action theory, and is designed to improve family psychosocial outcomes as well as HIV behavioral outcomes. It consists of 10- to 90-minute sessions delivered over ten weekends. It incorporates a cartoon-based manual to engage with participants and overcome the barrier of low literacy and such innovative low-cost approaches may be particularly relevant in other highly affected settings throughout sub-Saharan Africa. The sessions focus on HIV knowledge and decreasing HIV stigma; authoritative parenting, caregiver decision-making and caregiver monitoring of children; family comfort discussing sexual risky behaviors; promoting social networks, social control, and social cohesion (Bell et al. 2008). The program also addresses complex family forms in South Africa including adaptation and testing for use with biological parents as well as kin caregivers (Bhana et al. 2010; Petersen et al. 2006). There are several other psychological interventions for HIV-affected families currently being tested in South Africa. These include for example, a randomized control trial of an intervention to support the family functioning and emotional wellbeing of mothers disclosing their HIV positive status to school-age children (Principal Investigator, Dr Ruth Bland) and adapting an existing evidence-based family intervention called Project Style to the South African context with the aim of preventing HIV and alcohol/drug use (Principal Investigator, Dr Geri Donenberg). In South Africa and in other highly HIV-affected settings, there is a need to develop more family-based approaches to address the psychological needs of kin caregivers and the children under their care.

There are also a number of community based programs which support kin caregivers in South Africa. These programs address a range of child and kin caregiver needs. While these programs have not been rigorously tested for efficacy in randomized controlled trials, external evaluations indicate that these types of community-based programs provide essential sources of support to kin caregivers. One exemplary example in South Africa is the Children in Distress Network, which links hundreds of non-governmental, faith-based, and community-based organizations together to better leverage services to orphaned and vulnerable children and their caregivers. Through this network, kin caregivers can access skills training, education, and assistance in accessing the social safety net (Stewart *et al.* 2012). However, community-based programs are faced by the challenge of scalability. Moreover, those that address psychosocial outcomes also face the issue of rigor in regards to effectiveness (Richter *et al.* 2009). It is crucial that community-based programs utilize evidence-based approaches to improving the psychosocial outcomes of families and also evaluate the effectiveness of their approaches to enhance the possibility of disseminating innovative community-based responses elsewhere.

Conclusions

Undoubtedly, South African patterns of kinship care will continue to respond in a fluid manner to the HIV epidemic and other challenges to family structures (Mathambo and Gibbs 2009). However, there are significant research gaps that would greatly expand our understanding of kinship care in South Africa and in other highly affected regions. First, systematic sources of national data on kinship care arrangements are lacking in highly affected regions like sub-Saharan Africa. This poses difficulties for systematically ascertaining how kinship patterns have changed due to AIDS mortality. Second, large-scale quantitative studies are needed to assess the challenges faced by children who serve as kin caregivers and young carers. Third, we need a better understanding of the psychological consequences of the HIV epidemic on kin caregivers, including longitudinal studies that document how the process of HIV illness, AIDS orphanhood, and bereavement might affect psychosocial outcomes. This evidence can inform the formulation of evidence-based interventions to address the psychosocial and other needs of kin caregivers. Such interventions can help bolster the strong safety net provided by government programs and policies and other types of non-governmental organization.

South Africa has developed an outstanding social safety net for kin caregivers and the children under their care. Lessons can be drawn on the importance of South Africa's structural system of support for kin caregivers and the children under their care for other highly affected settings. However, the global economic crisis poses a dual challenge to HIV-affected communities, particularly in sub-Saharan Africa, which is also highly dependent on international aid for social programs more generally. It is vital to ensure continued investment in existing safety nets for kin caregivers, and to efficiently administer these systems to promote long-term sustainability. In South Africa, and elsewhere, more research needs to done to increase our understanding of the patterns and consequences of redistribution of social grants and other sources of support for kin caregivers. Specifically, an improved understanding of how redistribution impacts women who serve as kin caregivers is particularly crucial, given the gendered dimensions of kinship care as well as the gendered utilization social grant programs in South Africa (Hosegood and Timaeus 2006; Schatz 2007b). Finally, given that the kinship care system may be responding in a dynamic manner to crises such as the HIV epidemic, these support systems need to be carefully regulated and efficiently administered to increase the effectiveness with which kin caregivers can support their families and to ensure that vulnerable children are able to access and utilize available safety nets.

References

Arndt, C. and Lewis, J. (2005) 'The macro implications of HIV/AIDS in South Africa: a preliminary assessment.' *South African Journal of Economics 68*, 5, 380–392. doi: 10.1111/j.1813-6982.2000.tb01283.x

Bachman DeSilva, M., Beard, J., Cakwe, M., McCoy, K. *et al.* (2008) 'Vulnerability of orphan caregivers vs. non-orphan caregivers in KwaZulu-Natal.' *Vulnerable Children and Youth Studies 3*, 1, 102–111.

Bachmann, M. and Booysen, F. (2003) 'Health and economic impacts of HIV/AIDS on South African households: a cohort study.' *BMC Public Health 1*, 3, 14.

Bachmann, M. and Booysen, F. (2004) 'Relationships between HIV/AIDS, income and expenditure over time in deprived South African households.' *AIDS Care 16*, 7, 817–826.

Bauman, L., Foster, G., Silver, E., Berman, R. *et al.* (2006) 'Children caring for their ill parents with HIV/AIDS.' *Vulnerable Children and Youth Studies 1*, 1, 56–70.

Bell, C., Bhana, A., Petersen, I., McKay, M. *et al.* (2008) 'Building protective factors to offset sexually risky behaviors among black youths.' *Journal of the National Medical Association 100*, 8, 936–944.

Bhana, A., McKay, M., Mellins, C., Petersen, I. and Bell, C. (2010) 'Family-based HIV prevention and intervention services for youth living in poverty-affected contexts: the CHAMP model of collaborative, evidence-informed programme development.' *Journal of the International AIDS Society 13* (Supplement 2), S8.

Case, A. and Ardington, C. (2006) 'The impact of parental death on school outcomes: longitudinal evidence from South Africa.' *Demography 43*, 4, 401–420.

Chi, P. and Li, X. (2012) 'Impact of parental HIV/AIDS on children's psychological well-being: a systematic review of global literature.' *AIDS and Behavior*, 1–21.

Cluver, L., Gardner, F. and Operario, D. (2007) 'Psychological distress amongst AIDS-orphaned children in urban South Africa.' *Journal of Child Psychiatry and Psychology and Allied Disciplines 48*, 8, 755–763.

Cluver, L., Gardner, F. and Operario, D. (2009) Caregiving and psychological distress of AIDS-orphaned children. *Vulnerable Children and Youth Studies 4*, 3, 185–199.

Cluver, L., Kganakga, C., Kuo, C. and Casale, M. (2010) '*Parenting, disability and HIV/AIDS: Understanding impacts on children in AIDS-affected families.*' Paper presented to the Symposium on Children and HIV: Family Support First – Working Together to Achieve Universal Support and Access to Treatment, Vienna, Austria, 16–17 July.

Cluver, L., Operario, D. and Gardner, F. (2009) 'Parental illness, caregiving factors and psychological distress among children orphaned by acquired immune deficiency syndrome (AIDS) in South Africa.' *Vulnerable Child and Youth Studies 4*, 3, 185–198.

Cock, J., Emdon, E. and Klugman, B. (eds) (1986) *The Care of the Apartheid Child: An Urban African Study.* Johannesburg: Ravan Press.

De Koker, C., de Waal, L. and Vorster, J. (2006) *A Profile of Social Security Beneficiaries in South Africa.* Stellenbosch: Datadesk, Department of Sociology and Social Anthropology at University of Stellenbosch, and South African Department of Social Development.

de Paoli, M., Mills, E. and Gronningsaeter, A. (2012) 'The ARV roll out and the disability grant: a South African dilemma?' *Journal of the International AIDS Society 15*, 6.

Delany, A., Ismail, Z., Graham, L. and Ramkissoon, Y. (2008) *Review of the Child Support Grant: Uses, Implementation and Obstacles.* Johannesburg: Community Agency for Social Enquiry.

Department of Social Development (2008) For current rates see: www.services.gov.za/services/content/Home/ServicesForPeople/socialbenefits, accessed 30 August 2013.

Donald, D. and Clacherty, G. (2009) 'Developmental vulnerabilities and strengths of children living in child-headed households: a comparison with children in adult-headed households in equivalent impoverished communities.' *African Journal of AIDS Research 4*, 1, 21–28.

Duflo, E. (2003) 'Grandmothers and granddaughters: old age pension and intra-household allocation in SouthAfrica.' *World Bank Economic Review 17*, 1, 1–25.

Ford, K. and Hosegood, V. (2005) 'AIDS mortality and the mobility of children in KwaZulu Natal, South Africa.' *Demography 42*, 757–768.

Foster, G., Shakespeare, R., Chinemana, F., Jackson, H. *et al.* (1995) 'Orphan prevalence and extended family care in a peri-urban community in Zimbabwe.' *AIDS Care 7*, 1, 3–17.

Freeman, M. and Nkomo, N. (2006) 'Guardianship of orphans and vulnerable children: a survey of current and prospective South African caregivers.' *AIDS Care 18*, 4, 302–310.

Hall, K. (2012) 'Children in South Africa.' In Children's Institute (ed.) *Children Count: Statistics on Children in South Africa*. Cape Town: University of Cape Town.

Hall, K. and Meintjes, H. (2012) 'Children in South Africa.' In Childern's Institute (ed.) *Children Count: Statistics on Children in South Africa*. Cape Town: University of Cape Town.

Hardy, C. and Richter, M. (2006) 'Disability grants or antiretrovirals? A quandary for people with HIV/AIDS in South Africa.' *African Journal of AIDS Research 5*, 1, 85–96.

Hill, C., Hosegood, V. and Newell, M. (2008) 'Children's care and living arrangements in a high HIV prevalence area in rural South Africa.' *Vulnerable Child and Youth Studies 3*, 1, 65–77.

Hosegood, V., Floyd, S., Marston, M., Hill, C. *et al.* (2007) 'The effects of high HIV prevalence on orphanhood and living arrangements of children in Malawi, Tanzania and South Africa.' *Population Studies 61*, 327–336.

Hosegood, V. and Timaeus, I. (eds) (2006) *HIV/AIDS and Older People in South Africa*. Washington, DC: National Academies Press.

Howard, B., Phillips, C., Matinhure, N., Goodman, K., McCurdy, S. and Johnson, C. (2006) 'Barriers and incentives to orphan care in a time of AIDS and economic crisis: a cross-sectional survey of caregivers in rural Zimbabwe.' *BMC Public Health 6*, 27, 1–11.

Karim, A. and Karim, S. (2002) 'The evolving HIV epidemic in South Africa.' *The International Journal of Epidemiology 31*, 37–40.

Kaschula, S. (2008) 'Wild foods and household food security responses to AIDS: evidence from South Africa.' *Population and Environment 29*, 162–185.

Kuo, C. and Operario, D. (2010) 'Health of adults caring for orphaned children in an HIV endemic community in South Africa.' *AIDS Care 5*, 4, 344–352.

Kuo, C., Operario, D. and Cluver, L. (2012) 'Depression amongst carers of AIDS-orphaned and other-orphaned children in Umlazi Township, South Africa.' *Global Public Health 7*, 3, 253–269.

Lemon, A. (ed.) (1991) *The Apartheid City*. Cape Town: David Philip Publishers.

Lv, Y., Zhao, Q., Li, X., Stanton, B. *et al.* (2010) 'Depression symptoms among caregivers of children in HIV-affected families in rural China.' *AIDS Care 22*, 6, 669–676.

Madhavan, S. (2004) 'Fosterage patterns in the age of AIDS: continuity and change.' *Social Science and Medicine 58*, 7, 1443–1454.

Madhavan, S. and Schatz, E. (2007) 'Coping with change: household structure and composition in rural South Africa, 1992–2003.' *Scandanavian Journal of Public Health 35*, 3, 85–93.

Martin, R. (2006) 'Children's perspectives: roles, responsibilities and burdens in homebased care in Zimbabwe.' *Journal of Social Development in Africa 21*, 1, 106–129.

Mathambo, V. and Gibbs, A. (2009) 'Extended family childcare arrangements in a context of AIDS: collapse or adaptation?' *AIDS Care 21* (Supplement 2), 22–27.

McKay, M., Block, M., Mellins, C., Traube, D. *et al.* (2008) 'Adapting a family-based HIV prevention program for HIV-infected preadolescents and their families.' *Social Work and Mental Health 5*, 3–4, 355–378.

Monasch, R. and Boerma, J. (2004) 'Orphanhood and childcare patterns in sub-Saharan Africa: an analysis of national surveys from 40 countries.' *AIDS 18*, suppl 2, 55–65.

Mturi, A. (2012) 'Child-headed households in South Africa: What we know and what we don't.' *Development Southern Africa 29*, 3, 506–516.

Niehaus, I. (1994) 'Disharmonious spouses and harmonious siblings: conceptualising household formation among urban residents in Qwaqwa.' *African Studies 53*, 115–135.

Operario, D., Underhill, K., Chuong, C. and Cluver, L. (2011) 'HIV infection and sexual risk behaviour among youth who have experienced orphanhood: systematic review and meta-analysis.' *Journal of the International AIDS Society 14*, 25.

Parikh, A., DeSilva, M., Cakwe, M., Quinlan, T. *et al.* (2007) 'Exploring the Cinderella myth: intrahousehold differences in child wellbeing between orphans and non-orphans in Amajuba District, South Africa.' *AIDS 21*, Supplement 7, S95–S103.

Patel, L. and Triegaardt, J. (eds) (2008) *South Africa: Social Security, Poverty Alleviation and Development.* New York: Palgrave Macmillan.

Petersen, I., Mason, A., Bhana, A., Bell, C. and McKay, M. (2006) 'Mediating social representations using a cartoon narrative in the context of HIV/AIDS: the Ama Qhawe Family Project in South Africa.' *Journal of Health Psychology 11*, 2, 197–208.

Phaswana-Mafuya, N., Peltzer, K. and Petros, G. (2009) 'Disability grant for people living with HIV/AIDS in the Eastern Cape of South Africa.' *Social Work in Health Care 48*, 5, 533–550.

Pillay, J. (2012) 'Experiences of learners from child-headed households in a vulnerable school that makes a difference: lessons for school psychologists.' *School Psychology International 33*, 1, 3–21.

Plagerson, S., Patel, V., Harpham, T., Kielmann, K. and Mathee, A. (2010) 'Does money matter for mental health? Evidence from the child support grants in Johannesburg, South Africa.' *Global Public Health 11*, 1–17.

Republic of South Africa (1997) *White Paper for Social Welfare* (No. 18166). Pretoria: Republic of South Africa.

Republic of South Africa (2009) *National Action Plan for Orphans and Other Children Made Vulnerable by HIV and AIDS for 2009–2012.* Pretoria: Republic of South Africa.

Richter, L., Sherr, L., Adato, M., Belsey, M. *et al.* (2009) 'Strengthening families to support children affected by HIV and AIDS.' *AIDS Care 21*, Supplement 1, 3–12.

Robson, E., Ansell, N., Huber, U., Gould, S. and Van Blerk, L. (2006) 'Young caregivers in the context of the HIV/AIDS pandemic in sub-Saharan Africa.' *Population, Space and Place 12*, 2, 93–111.

Samson, M., Lee, U., Ndlebe, A., Mac Quene, K. *et al.* (2004) *The Social and Economic Impact of South Africa's Social Security System.* Pretoria: Republic of South Africa.

Schatz, E. (2007a) 'Caring and contributing: the role of older women in rural South African multi-generational households in the HIV/AIDS era.' *World Development 35*, 8, 1390–1403.

Schatz, E. (2007b) '"Taking care of my own blood": Older women's relationships to their households in rural South Africa.' *Scandanavian Journal of Public Health 69*, 147–154.

Skovdal, M. and Ogutu, V. (2009) '"I washed and fed my mother before going to school": Understanding the psychosocial well-being of children providing chronic care for adults affected by HIV/AIDS in Western Kenya.' *Globalisation and Health 5*, 8.

South African Department of Social Development (2009) *National Action Plan for Orphans and Other Children Made Vulnerable by HIV and AIDS for 2009–2012.* Pretoria: Republic of South Africa.

Stewart, M., Konstant, T., Coetzer, A., Dlamini, L., Mahlase, G., Williams, J. and Rangasami, J. (2012) Evaluation Report: Children in Distress Network. Pietermaritzburg: Children in Distress Network.

UNAIDS (2012) 'Country Factsheet: South Africa.' Geneva: UNAIDS.

UNICEF (2006) 'Africa's Orphaned and Vulnerable Generations: Children Affected by AIDS.' Geneva: UNICEF.

UNICEF (2008) 'Working Paper: Alternative Care for Children in Southern Africa: Progress, Challenges and Future Directions.' Nairobi: UNICEF.

vann Dijk, D. and van Driel, F. (2009) 'Supporting child-headed households in South Africa: whose best interests?' *Journal of Southern African Studies 35*, 4, 915–927.

CHAPTER 15

The Views of Children in Kinship Care, their Caregivers and their Birth Parents

Key Themes from the United States

James P. Gleeson

More than 2.7 million children in the United States are raised by relatives, and in the past decade this number has grown six times faster than the number of children in the general population (Annie E. Casey Foundation 2012). Most kinship care arrangements are informal with no involvement of the child protection system. About 104,000 children living with relatives are in the custody of the child protection system (formal kinship care), representing 26 percent of children in foster care. While kinship care is common among all racial and ethnic groups, African American children are two to three times more likely to be raised by grandparents or other relatives compared to other US children (Kreider and Ellis 2011).

Three decades of increasingly rigorous research provides convincing evidence that, on average, formal kinship care arrangements in the USA are more stable than placement with non-related foster parents and children in kinship care tend to fare better on most behavioral and mental health indicators compared to children in foster care with non-relatives, even after controlling for the differences in the level of functioning at the time of initial placement (Gleeson 2012). However, there are differences among kinship caregiving families. For example, while kinship care tends to be stable, disruptions do occur. Some of the factors that threaten stability of these living arrangements include conflicts with biological parents, behavioral and mental health problems and special needs of children and adolescents, and health limitations of kinship caregivers.

Perhaps more important than average differences between different types of living arrangements is the range of unique experiences among kinship caregiving families. A few studies dig a bit deeper and describe the views, feelings, and experiences of children in kinship care, kinship caregivers, and parents of children living with kin. While the majority of these studies are not based upon representative samples and therefore do not generate findings that can be generalized to all families involved in kinship care, they do reveal a variety of views and experiences that helping professionals may encounter when they come into contact with these families. In this chapter I summarize themes from several of these studies, limiting my focus to research conducted in the USA. I conclude the chapter with implications these themes have for practice with families involved in kinship care in the US context.

Children's views and experiences
What children like and dislike about kinship care
A number of studies indicate that children living in formal kinship care are more likely to be satisfied with their living arrangement (Wilson and Conroy 1999), to like the people they live with, to have contact with their biological parents and siblings, to talk with adults in their life about dating and school (Chapman, Wall and Barth 2004) and to feel like part of the family (Hegar and Rosenthal 2009) compared to children in foster care or group care. However, children reared by kin often indicate a desire for even more contact with their parents and siblings, and describe a number of likes and dislikes specific to their situation. Children participating in Gleeson *et al.*'s (2008) informal kinship care study indicated that they liked interaction with the caregiver and other extended family members, the way the caregiver provided for them, and the atmosphere of the home. Several children stated that they liked living with someone who loved them and who was "somebody that I love". However, 21 of the 56 children interviewed were able to identify at least one thing they did not like about living with the current caregiver, including absence of their parents, conflicts with household members, safety and cleanliness of the community or household environment, discipline issues, and activities in the caregiver's home, such as watching the news on television, reading a book daily, staying in the house (often because of the caregiver's fear of violence in the community), cleaning the house, and going certain places with the caregiver.

Life is better but I still miss my parents

It is clear that many children recognize that their life is better with the relative caregiver than it had been or would otherwise be, and appreciate the "many acts of kindness" (Altshuler 1999), love, thoughtfulness, investment, and commitment to their welfare displayed by caregivers (Messing 2006). Some children also demonstrate compassion for the caregiver and an understanding of the stress and physical health challenges that some caregivers experience just to ensure that the children have a safe and stable home and loving family. Despite this recognition and appreciation, children in formal and informal kinship care arrangements are not immune to feelings of loss, anger, resentment or longing for acceptance by their biological parents (Messing 2006; Sands, Goldberg-Glen and Shin 2009).

It's different but it's kind of like a normal house

While children tend to view living with kin as normal and not stigmatizing (Brown, Cohon and Wheeler 2002), some acknowledge that living with a relative other than their parents is different from the experience of many other children (Messing 2006). One child in an informal kinship care arrangement described the experience this way:

> It's kind of like a normal house…maybe most kids think…that like they're sad because like their grandma has custody of 'em. I mean like I'm not really sad because then I get to spend more time with her. (Gleeson *et al.* 2008, p.218)

Helping children adjust

Although some youth do not experience living with relatives as novel or disruptive (Brown *et al.* 2002), others understand the living arrangements to be a result of a breakdown in family functioning (Altshuler 1999). Not all children have a clear understanding or memory of why they are not able to live with at least one of their parents. Children who are able to remember the move from their parent's home to the relative's home also remember the way adults helped them manage the transition. Children in formal kinship care interviewed by Altshuler (1999) emphasized the need for children to be involved in decisions about their living arrangements and the need to ensure that caseworkers and caregivers are concerned about the wellbeing of children and communicate this to the children. Helping children through this transition is just as important when the child protection system is not involved. In Gleeson *et al.*'s (2008) study of informal kinship care, children described ways caregivers helped them feel welcome in their homes by meeting their physical and material needs, meeting their emotional needs for affection and recognition, teaching and supporting them, respecting the children and "being proud to care for them."

Stability, permanence, and a sense of belonging

A number of qualitative studies with children in kinship care report close relationships with caregivers and a sense of belonging to a family (Altshuler 1999; Brown *et al.* 2002; Gleeson *et al.* 2008; Messing 2006). Some describe long histories of shared residence in households where youth, parents, and other kin reside together from time to time (Brown *et al.* 2002; Messing 2006). Yet some children living with their grandparents express concerns about the permanence of their living arrangements, worrying about what would happen to them if their grandparents die or became too ill to care for them.

Most children interviewed by Gleeson *et al.* (2008) seemed to have a feeling of security and a belief that they would have a place to live in the future that included family, but this was not true for all. Five children expressed a degree of uncertainty; one of these children appeared sad and anxious, stating "My grandma said she is going to kick me out at 18…" (Gleeson *et al.* 2008, p. 223).

Where children want to live and feel most at home

While many children in kinship care report that they feel most at home with their current caregiver, others report that they feel most at home with their mother, father, or another relative with whom they are not currently living. When asked what helps them feel at home, children in Gleeson *et al.*'s (2008) study described activities, the safe and comfortable atmosphere of the home, contact with many family members, gifts they receive on birthdays, the food provided, or their personal possessions. One child said, "…I feel comfortable here. I know that nobody won't hurt me. I can usually go to sleep…" (p.216).

It is common for children in kinship care to state that they would like to live with at least one of their parents and their siblings in the future.

Yet many state a preference for living with their current caregivers, in part because they fear that their parents will be unable to care for them and keep them safe. It is also common for children to express the desire to take care of family members (Gleeson *et al.* 2008; Messing 2006). For example, one child participating in Gleeson *et al.*'s informal kinship care study said she would like to live with her current caregiver *and* her mother, so her mother would have a better life. Another child said he wanted to grow up to become famous so he could take care of his entire family.

Caregivers' views and experiences
Costs and benefits of caregiving

Much of the research focusing on the impact of kinship care on caregivers has been conducted with grandparents raising grandchildren. These custodial grandparents report more health problems and higher levels of psychological distress, parenting stress, depression, and burden compared to grandparents who do not have primary responsibility for raising their grandchildren (Harrison, Richman and Vittimberga 2000; Kelley *et al.* 2000; Lee, Ensminger and LaVeist 2005; Linsk *et al.* 2009; Musil 2000; Musil and Standing 2005; Sands and Goldberg-Glen 2000). These increased levels of stress, burden, distress, and health problems are associated with children's behavior problems, school adjustment and performance, caring for larger numbers of children, conflict with birth parents and other family members, multiple losses, lack of social support, complex legal situations, and financial strain. Other costs and challenges include restricted freedom, differences raising a relative's child compared to their own, and fear of what would happen to the children if something happened to them (Gleeson *et al.* 2008; Kolomer and McCallion 2005). In addition, a sense of isolation, lack of support, loss of adult intimate relationships, and loss of contact with friends and associates affect both formal and informal kinship caregivers, often after they have assumed responsibility for the child due to family obligation and a belief that nobody else in the family could or would step up to care for the children (Gleeson *et al.* 2009; Osby 1999).

Despite the stress and burden, grandparents and other kinship caregivers often report considerable satisfaction and meaning that comes from raising grandchildren (Waldrop and Weber 2001). Some go so far as to describe the children as blessings or gifts (Gleeson *et al.* 2008), yet others describe the responsibility of raising a relative's child as a burden and a blessing (O'Brien, Massat and Gleeson 2001; Smith-Ruiz 2008). While many caregivers in Gleeson *et al.*'s (2008) study described strong, positive relationships with the children, others described the relationship as frustrating and overwhelming at times. A few caregivers indicated that it was difficult developing close bonds with the relatives' children. When reflecting on their own experience, kinship caregivers fall into a number of categories: those who would do it again despite the challenges, those who are unsure, those who indicate they definitely would not care for a relative's child again, and those who would give it careful consideration before caring for a relative's child because they do not believe that it should be necessary, believing that parents should be able to raise their own children.

Child protective service system involvement tends to be associated with greater access to financial support and services and consequently somewhat lower levels of caregivers stress (Bunch, Eastman and Griffin 2007). However, some caregivers report stress that is induced by the child protective service system through lack of responsiveness (Cimmarusti 1999), failure to value the caregivers' many years of child-rearing experience (Osby 1999; Petras 1999), pressure to take children into their homes without time to think this over (Kolomer and McCallion 2005), or pressure to adopt related children (O'Brien *et al.* 2001). Some caregivers express the belief that child protection agencies take advantage of the caregivers' love and commitment to the children (Cimmarusti 1999; Kolomer and McCallion 2005; O'Brien *et al.* 2001).

The need for support and services

Many informal and formal kinship caregivers and their families need ongoing support and access to services to help them deal with the burden and stress associated with raising a relative's child. Kinship caregivers with the highest levels of stress, greatest levels of expressed need, and greatest burden are most likely to benefit from informal social support as well as formal services (Goodman, Potts and Pasztor 2007) and are most likely to ensure that they and the children complete treatment that addresses the need (Timmer, Sedlar and Urquiza 2004). However, some caregivers, either because of a lack of other supports or as a first option, report that spirituality, or their reliance on God or a higher power, is their primary source of support and coping mechanism (Anderson 2006; Cimmarusti 1999; Petras 1999; Smith-Ruiz 2008).

The importance of parents

Caregivers in Gleeson et al.'s (2008) study reported at least annual contact with 80 percent of mothers and 50 percent of fathers of the related children in their care; and at least weekly contact with 20 percent of mothers and a small percentage of fathers. They also reported considerable variability in the quality of these relationships. Over one-third of caregivers rated their own relationship with the focus child's mother as very friendly with no conflict or only minor conflict. Nearly as many caregivers rated their relationship with the child's father in the same way. Some caregivers expressed frustration with the parents' drug use or other problems that prevented them from assuming the role of the child's primary caregiver. Others expressed understanding of the challenges faced by the parents related to substance abuse, mental health, or becoming a parent at a young age. Yet other caregivers praised the parents for their efforts to deal with challenges they faced (e.g. progress made in drug treatment), for involvement in their children's lives, for love for their children. Many caregivers expressed their own disappointment, frustration and anger with parents for letting their children down or failing to assume responsibility for their children. Others feared that the parents might resume custody of their children but then not care for them adequately. Some warned of the rollercoaster ride that is the relationship with some parents of children in kinship care.

Many caregivers emphasize how important the parents are to their children, and seemed to honor and encourage this relationship (Gibson 2005; Gleeson et al. 2008). A number of caregivers stress the need to support children's relationships with their parents and not to say anything bad about the parents to their children. Many caregivers participating in Gleeson et al.'s study identified positive aspects of the parent–child relationship even when there appears to be little hope that the parent would assume primary caregiving responsibility for the child. Some caregivers describe parents as maturing and demonstrating increasing responsibility for their children, while others described parents as having child-like relationship with their children, similar to peers or siblings. Caregivers described a role reversal in some relationships, with children worrying about their parents and in some ways acting as the parents' caregivers. A number of caregivers mentioned that the children missed their parents greatly and that the parents of some of these children took little interest in them. Some caregivers described the children as openly angry with their parents, with some children confronting the parents about their failure to do the things necessary to assume care of them. Other caregivers described the children's feelings toward their parents as neutral or ambivalent.

Parents' involvement and views

Parent–child contact tends to be more frequent when children are living with kin than with non-related foster parents, and the nature of parental involvement tends to vary with the type of kinship care arrangement. Parents' relationships with children and caregivers are important and are associated with outcomes, whether positive or negative, for both. Life satisfaction is highest, and depression lowest, for custodial grandmothers when parent–child, parent–caregiver, and caregiver–child relationships are all close; the reverse is true when the caregiver reports no close relationships among any members of the triad (Bunch, Eastman and Griffin 2007; Goodman 2003, 2007). Similarly, children function better if they have a close relationship with the relative caregiver, the parent, or both. Grandchildren who are emotionally isolated from both parent and grandparent, and grandchildren in families with no close bonds between any members of the triad, showed the highest levels of behavioral dysfunction.

What parents like and dislike about kinship care

Interviews with 20 mothers and five fathers participating in substance abuse treatment while incarcerated and while their children were cared for by kin revealed positive feelings regarding kinship care and thankfulness that their children were living with kin, mixed with feelings of jealousy, anger, and criticism of the caregiver (Smith *et al.* 2004). Twenty-seven mothers and three fathers of children in informal kinship care arrangements interviewed by Gleeson *et al.* (2008) described similar positive and negative views. Many parents indicated that they were happy that their children were living with people who loved them, were safe and well cared for, were doing better in school and were having the opportunity to get to know their relatives. Negative views included loss of the parent role and the fear of being forgotten by their children. One parent indicated that she was fearful of "oversteppin' my bounds" by asserting the parent role, possibly causing conflict with the kinship caregiver.

Parents participating in Smith et al.'s (2004) study expressed awareness of the harm that their substance abuse and incarceration had done to their children. Parents also acknowledged the burden that the relative caregiver had assumed and expressed concern for their children and their caregivers, a desire for personal contact with their children, and apprehension about what would happen when they were released.

Separation and loss

Parents of children in kinship care describe a range of feelings they experience when they are with their children and when they are away from them (Gleeson et al. 2008; Gleeson and Seryak 2010; Smith et al. 2004). Interviews with parents of children in informal kinship care reveal feelings of love, warmth, happiness, joy, pride, enlightenment, or inspiration when they are with their children and feelings of loss when they are not (Gleeson and Seryak 2010). Parents' feelings of loss parallel those experienced by children who miss their parents.

Hopes and dreams

Incarcerated parents with children in kinship care also describe parallel hopes and dreams for their children and for their own brighter futures (Smith et al. 2004). These parents and other parents of children in informal kinship care describe future goals and dreams for their children and themselves that include academic and career success, responsible behavior, avoiding gang involvement, and having a happy life (Gleeson et al. 2008; Gleeson and Seryak 2010). Many parents described their plans to support their children's success by encouraging them, advocating for them, getting their own lives in order, and providing a positive example for their children.

Relationships with children and caregivers

Parents of children in informal kinship care arrangements describe a range of relationships with their children (Gleeson et al. 2008; Gleeson and Seryak 2010). Some describe very close, loving relationships, characterized by frequent and open communication. Others describe the erosion of trust that their behavior had caused and efforts to rebuild that trust with their children. Yet, others describe their relationships with their children as strained and uncertain. One parent described it this way, "I kinda wanna hurry up and get back together because I wanna find out where I stand with them…" (Gleeson and Seryak 2010, p.91). Some parents describe very active roles in their children's lives and their own efforts to assume or resume the primary parent role. Others describe their relationships with their children as "…friends, instead of mama and daughter" (Gleeson and Seryak 2010, p.91). Some parents acknowledge their own frustration and inability to tolerate their children's behavior, resulting in avoidance of their children.

The range of relationships between parents and caregivers is equally wide. While some parents describe very close and loving relationships with their children's caregiver, others describe conflict and strain in this relationship (Gleeson *et al.* 2008). Some describe their relationship with the caregiver as being "like best friends" or "like sisters" (Gleeson and Seryak 2010, p.92).

Extended family support

The quality and nature of the relationship between parents of children in kinship care, kinship caregiver, and extended family also have an impact on outcomes for parents. In several small sample studies, mothers reported substantial support from the caregiver and the extended family, and they reported appreciation for that support (Blakey 2012; Harris 1999; Strozier *et al.* 2011). Substance abuse was a factor that contributed to the kinship care arrangements for nearly all of the mothers in these studies and the type of support was associated with the degree to which the mothers successfully assumed or resumed a primary parenting role. For formal kinship care, the type of support also appeared to be related to the likelihood that parents would regain custody of their children. Blakey's (2012) interviews with 26 women whose children were taken into the custody of the child protective service system and placed with relatives revealed that "family support with parameters" and "limited family support" were associated with a high likelihood of reunification, whereas "enabling family support" was associated with mothers' failure to take responsibility for her children and permanent loss of custody. Family support with parameters and limited family support communicated expectations to the mother that she had only a limited amount of time to do what was necessary to assume responsibility for care of the children. If caregivers simply supported mothers uncritically, this allowed mothers to come and go as they pleased, to continue to use drugs, yet have contact with their children when they desired, with no expectations of assuming responsibility for their care. Strozier *et al.* (2011) found similar enabling patterns in interviews with incarcerated mothers who regularly left their children with the grandmother while engaging in substance abuse and other activities, later regretting the way that they abdicated their parenting role.

Coparenting relationships

Parents are more likely to share parenting responsibilities when kinship care is informal rather than formal, and when the relationship between the parent and caregiver is good (Green and Goodman 2010). Strozier *et al.* (2011) interviewed incarcerated mothers and their children's grandparent caregivers to assess their ability to share parenting. Coparenting relationships that displayed high solidarity included compromise and joint problem solving, shared child-rearing philosophies, cooperation, teamwork, good communication, affirmation, empathy, and emotional support for each other. Low solidarity relationships included power struggles, conflict over the quality of parenting, unresolved disputes about discipline, and undermining or overturning discipline. Mothers in some low solidarity families were characterized as disenfranchised, detached, and disconnected from parenting. Mothers and grandmothers in low solidarity families tended to be despondent, guilty, and fearful about the future. Mothers in particular expressed their disappointment in themselves and guilt and remorse for their drug use and the impact it has had on their children. Grandmothers tended to blame themselves in some ways for the failures of the mothers.

Conclusions and implications for practice

Research on kinship care conducted in the USA highlights the benefits of both formal and informal kinship care arrangements in comparison to placement in foster care with non-relatives or group care. This research has driven a number of policy initiatives that place a high priority on placement with kin and support for stable and permanent kinship care living arrangements. While this research and its impact are important, equally important is the research that looks more deeply into the unique and varied experiences of children, caregivers, and parents in families engaged in kinship care. For example, research that examines these unique experiences shows us that while it may be true that most children living with kin experience a sense of belonging, stability, and permanence, this is not true for all children. And, while many children want to live with their parents, some are afraid that they will not be safe or have their needs met by the parents, unless their current caregiver or another relative is also living in the home. Similarly, caregivers and parents of children in kinship care have a range of unique and varied experiences. In addition, this research reveals that seemingly contradictory views and feelings can be experienced simultaneously by the same person. Caregivers who experience high levels of burden and stress may also experience high levels of satisfaction and derive a great deal of meaning from their caregiving role. The most important implication for practice is the need to individualize, ask questions, and listen to children, parents and caregivers.

Some of the themes that deserve exploration with children, parents, and caregivers are experiences of loss and disappointment as well as belonging, satisfaction, and appreciation; costs as well as benefits; the roles of parents, caregivers and other extended family members; and the hopes and dreams that children, parents, and caregivers have for themselves and each other.

References

Altshuler, S.J. (1999) 'The Well-being of Children in Kinship Foster Care.' In J.P. Gleeson and C.F. Hairston (eds) *Kinship Care: Improving Practice Through Research*. Washington, DC: Child Welfare League of America, Inc.

Anderson, N.E. (2006) It's easier with God: spirituality as a coping mechanism for African-American female kinship caregivers. Unpublished doctoral dissertation, University of Illinois at Chicago.

Annie E. Casey Foundation (2012) *Stepping up for Kids: What Government and Communities Should Do to Support Kinship Families*. Baltimore, MD: Annie E. Casey Foundation.

Blakely, J.M. (2012) 'The best of both worlds: how kinship care impacts reunification.' *Families in Society 93*, 2, 103–110.

Brown, S., Cohon, D. and Wheeler, R. (2002) 'African American extended families and kinship care: how relevant is the foster care model for kinship care?' *Children and Youth Services Review 24*, 1/2, 53–77.

Bunch, S.G., Eastman, B.J. and Griffin, L.W. (2007) 'Examining the perceptions of grandparents who parent in formal and informal kinship care.' *Journal of Human Behavior in the Social Environment 15*, 4, 93–105.

Chapman, M.V., Wall, A. and Barth, R.P. (2004) 'Children's voices: the perceptions of children in foster care.' *American Journal of Orthopsychiatry 74*, 3, 293–304.

Cimmarusti, R.A. (1999) 'Caregiver Burden in Kinship Foster Care.' In J.P. Gleeson and C.F. Hairston (eds) *Kinship Care: Improving Practice Through Research*. Washington, DC: Child Welfare League of America, Inc.

Gibson, P. (2005) 'Intergenerational parenting from the perspective of African American grandmothers.' *Family Relations 54*, 2, 280–297.

Gleeson, J.P. (2012) 'What Works in Kinship Care.' In P.A. Curtis and G. Alexander (eds) *What Works in Child Welfare, Revised Edition*. Washington, DC: CWLA.

Gleeson, J.P., Hsieh, C., Anderson, N., Seryak, C. *et al.* (2008) *Individual and Social Protective Factors for Children in Informal Kinship Care: Final Report*. (Grant #90-CA-1693). Chicago: Jane Addams College of Social Work and Jane Addams Center for Social Policy and Research, University of Illinois at Chicago. Available at www.uic.edu/jaddams/college/kincare/research/research.html, accessed on 4 June 2013.

Gleeson, J.P. and Seryak, C. (2010) '"I made some mistakes ... but I love them dearly." The views of parents of children in informal kinship care.' *Child and Family Social Work 15*, 87–96.

Gleeson, J.P., Wesley, J., Ellis, R., Seryak, C., Talley, G.W. and Robinson, J. (2009) 'Becoming involved in raising a relative's child: reasons, caregiver motivations and pathways to informal kinship care.' *Child and Family Social Work 14*, 300–310.

Goodman, C. (2003) 'Intergenerational triads in grandparent-headed families.' *Journal of Gerontology: Social Sciences 58B*(5), S281–S289.

Goodman, C. (2007) 'Intergenerational triads in skipped-generation grand families.' *The International Journal of Aging Human Development 65*, 3, 231–258.

Goodman, C.C., Potts, M.K. and Pasztor, E.M. (2007) 'Care giving grandmothers with vs. without child welfare system involvement: effects of expressed need, formal services, and informal social support on caregiver burden.' *Children and Youth Services Review 29*, 428–441.

Green, Y.R. and Goodman, C.C. (2010) 'Understanding birthparent involvement in kinship families: influencing factors and the importance of placement arrangement.' *Children and Youth Services Review 32*, 1357–1364.

Harris, M.S. (1999) 'Comparing Mothers of Children in Kinship Foster Care: Reunification vs. Remaining in Care.' In J.P. Gleeson and C.F. Hairston (eds) *Kinship Care: Improving Practice Through Research*. Washington, DC: Child Welfare League of America, Inc.

Harrison, K.A., Richman, G.S. and Vittimberga, G.L. (2000) 'Parental stress in grandparents versus parents raising children with behavior problems.' *Journal of Family Issues 21*, 2, 262–270.

Hegar, R.L. and Rosenthal, J.A. (2009) 'Kinship care and sibling placement: child behavior, family relationships, and school outcomes.' *Children and Youth Services Review 31*, 670–679.

Kelley, S.J., Whitley, D., Sipe, T.A. and Yorker, B.C. (2000) 'Psychological distress in grandmother kinship care providers: the role of resources, social support, and physical health.' *Child Abuse and Neglect 24*, 311–321.

Kolomer, S.R. and McCallion, P. (2005) 'Depression and caregiver mastery in grandfathers caring for their grandchildren.' *International Journal of Aging and Human Development 60*, 4, 283–294.

Kreider, R.M. and Ellis, R. (2011) 'Living Arrangements of Children: 2009.' In *Current Population Reports.* Washington, DC: US Census Bureau.

Lee, R.D., Ensminger, M.E. and LaVeist, T.A. (2005) 'The responsibility continuum: never primary, coresident and caregiver – heterogeneity in the African-American grandmother experience.' *International Journal of Aging and Human Development 60,* 4, 295–304.

Linsk, N., Mason, S., Fendrich, M., Bass, M., Brubhughate, P. and Brown, A. (2009) '"No matter what I do they still want their family": stressors for African American grandparents and other relatives.' *Journal of Family Social Work 43,* 25–43.

Messing, J.T. (2006) 'From the child's perspective: a qualitative analysis of kinship care placements.' *Children and Youth Services Review 28,* 1415–1434.

Musil, C.M. (2000) 'Health of grandmothers as caregivers: a ten month follow-up.' *Journal of Women and Aging 12,* 2, 120–145.

Musil, C.M. and Standing, T. (2005) 'Grandmothers' diaries: a glimpse at daily lives.' *International Journal of Aging and Human Development 60,* 4, 317–329.

O'Brien, P., Massat, C.R. and Gleeson, J.P. (2001) 'Upping the ante: kinship caregivers' perceptions of changes in child welfare policies.' *Child Welfare 80,* 6, 719–748.

Osby, O. (1999) 'Child-rearing Perspectives of Grandparent Caregivers.' In J.P. Gleeson and C.F. Hairston (eds) *Kinship Care: Improving Practice Through Research.* Washington, DC: Child Welfare League of America, Inc.

Petras, D.D. (1999) 'The Effect of Caregiver Preparation and Sense of Control on Adaptation of Kinship Caregivers.' In J.P. Gleeson and C.F. Hairston (eds) *Kinship Care: Improving Practice Through Research.* Washington, DC: Child Welfare League of America, Inc.

Sands, R.B. and Goldberg-Glen, R.S. (2000) 'Factors associated with stress among grandparents raising their grandchildren.' *Family Relations 49,* 1, 97–105.

Sands, R.G., Goldberg-Glen, R.S. and Shin, H. (2009) 'The voices of grandchildren of grandparent caregivers: a strengths-resilience perspective.' *Child Welfare 88,* 2, 25–45.

Smith, A., Krisman, K., Strozier, A.L. and Marley, M.A. (2004) 'Breaking through the bars: exploring the experiences of addicted incarcerated parents whose children are cared for by relatives.' *Families in Society 85,* 2, 187–195.

Smith-Ruiz, D. (2008) 'African American grandmothers providing extensive care to their grandchildren: socio-demographic and health determinants of life satisfaction.' *Journal of Sociology and Social Welfare 35,* 4, 29–52.

Strozier, A., Armstrong, M., Skuza, S., Cecil, D. and McHale, J. (2011) 'Coparenting in kinship families with an incarcerated mother: a qualitative study.' *Families in Society 92,* 1, 55–61.

Timmer, S.G., Sedlar, G. and Urquiza, A.J. (2004) 'Challenging children in kin versus nonkin foster care: perceived costs and benefits to caregivers.' *Child Maltreatment 9,* 3, 251–262.

Waldrop, D.P. and Weber, J.A. (2001) 'From grandparent to caregiver: the stress and satisfaction of raising grandchildren.' *Families in Society 82,* 5, 461–472.

Wilson, L. and Conroy, J. (1999) 'Satisfaction of children in out-of-home care.' *Child Welfare 78,* 1, 53–69.

Epilogue

Looking Forward in Kinship Care

David Pitcher

This book does not present a unified view of kinship care. Rather, a variety of perspectives and emphases are presented by the authors. Yet they have one thing in common: in the words of one researcher from a previous century, 'there are some matters which cannot be studied in the closet' (Borrow 1841, 1905, p.335). From each chapter there emerge real people, in real situations, attempting to make sense of life as it has worked out for them, in their family. Kinship care has real costs, pitfalls and benefits.

The contributors to this book leave us in no doubt that, despite the assumptions of some, kinship care is rarely straightforward, and is often very complex as historical family patterns (Young; Essex and Turnell; Flegg), shifting cultural beliefs (Ziminski; Music and Crehan; Banks), and different interests among family members (Flegg; Pitcher, Farmer and Meakings; Simmonds) come together to throw up ever varying situations, which often have to be understood by professionals and who are outside the family and who yet have significant influence on it (McHugh and Hayden; Hawkins; Gough).

What overall themes emerge from these chapters?

1. Within kinship care, relationships change, but are rarely severed (Jackson 1999, p.109). This is different from other forms of intervention, such as adoption. Roles and responsibilities and living arrangements all shift, but the people around the child remain the same. Even those not directly affected have some change of position in relation to the child. While this brings great benefits to a child in terms of his or her identity, it can make things very complicated, sometimes in ways that may not be immediately obvious.

2. Within kinship care, there is usually some level of ambivalence: 'Did things *have* to be this way?' This may be felt by the carers,

who usually have to change their life plans in order to provide care. It may be felt by the children, or by other family members. It may be felt by professionals, who have constantly to balance their responsibilities to ensure placements are adequate with the call to 'enable' placements, about which they may have mixed feelings, as described by Marilyn McHugh and Paula Hayden. This ambivalence needs to be embraced and seen as normal, rather than denied.

3. There is a need for clarity, and a proper understanding both within the agency and within the family, from the very beginning of a placement. Beyond this, there needs to be a more refined understanding of the part played by professionals, particularly by the local authority or its equivalents. Outside intervention needs to happen at the right time, and in the right way.

Professional assistance is part of overall support by the wider society. It may take the form of financial support, as shown in the South African experience by Caroline Kuo and her colleagues. It may take the form of including kinship carers within family support strategies, as Jackie Wyke describes. It may involve different levels of advice or therapy, as people make sense of changing roles and expectations amid a situation for which, most likely, they were unprepared. Jeanne Ziminski reflects on this, as do John Simmonds and Anna Gough, and also points to how legal and professional authority, and professional expertise, can be used to assist this process. What is clear is that any intervention from outside the family needs to be clearly thought out and carefully planned. Unless they are properly thought through and planned, as both Tom Hawkins and Erica Flegg show, a situation can result that makes life worse for everyone. We still have a great deal more to learn.

This book does not aim to say everything about kinship care, or to be the final word. It is a milepost at a certain point in time. Further research is needed and is suggested throughout by the authors of this book. Areas for further research include the following:

1. There needs to be detailed recording and analysis of the actual experience of children. This can be varied, and will contain surprises. Amy O'Donohoe's narrative is of great value, as it captures kinship care as it was experienced over time. More accounts, in real life detail and made available for reference and analysis, would be of real importance. This needs to include the

experiences of children and young people who are not necessarily happy in their family arrangement, but where – for various reasons – this falls short of actual breakdown (Liddy 1970).

2. A variety of theoretical models should be applied to kinship care. This includes those traditionally used within social care – such as attachment theory and also the ideas of Jung and his successors. In addition, models not traditionally associated with family work, such as Complexity Theory (Miller and Page 2007; Stevens and Hassett 2007; Warren-Adamson 2009 and 2011), which would bring many new insights to our understanding of kinship care. Psychoanalytic theory has as yet shed but little light on kinship care, and the contribution of Geraldine Crehan and Graham Music is important in this regard and needs to be built upon. Such work would bring the double benefit of cross-fertilisation, bringing kinship care into the awareness of theorists, and make the insights of those theories accessible to practitioners and family members within kinship care.

3. As our understanding of kinship care develops and deepens, it would be beneficial to have detailed and accessible examples of how issues are worked out:

    • on a policy level, for example how a cultural shift, such as that envisaged by Andrew Turnell and Susie Essex, can be attempted or achieved. What are the obstacles? Are there any unforeseen consequences?

    • on the level of professional practice. How are various dilemmas with siblings, or mothers, resolved? What interventions have been successful, and which have not worked?

One good example of this, presented in an accessible form, can be seen in the work of Chris Warren-Adamson (2009). More are needed.

In my view, it would be especially useful to understand the interface between help which involves temporary care, and meeting a child's need for permanence. In the light of John Simmonds' analysis, where would care during a parent's two-year prison sentence fit in? When might rehabilitation to a parent be considered? It is clear from a recent British legal case, *Re B* (Re B (A Child) [2009] UKSC 5, 19 November 2009), which came before the newly constituted Supreme Court, that clarity is badly needed here.

4. There needs to be developed an understanding of kinship care as it is practised within other cultures, including how it fits in with belief structures and socio-economic circumstances. Beyond this, there needs to be an analysis of what happens when these practices interface with other host cultures, for example, when a traditional family arrangement within an immigrant family needs to be assessed by a social worker from a dominant Western culture.

5. Kinship care may often be called 'family and friends care', but there is as yet little in the literature about care by friends as opposed to family (whether or not 'blood' related). Does the age of the child matter? Or the degree of permanence? Are family-type roles, such as godparents, different to neighbours or parents of school friends? What kinds of arrangements exist, and how (if at all) are they different?

Kinship care will always be important, as long as there are people who live in families and in a world in which lives take unexpected courses. Although this has always be the case, recent work, including by those who have contributed to this book, means that kinship care will no longer be invisible as it has long been. As Jim Gleeson shows in this volume, it is remarkable how much has been learned in the last 20 years; and psychological research, practice in social care, legal judgments and social policy all appear to be moving in step to consolidate kinship care's position as the option of choice for children who cannot live with one or both parents. This is true internationally. I suspect that kinship care touches a nerve with most of us because it makes us ask, 'How would I respond?' in a situation that could happen to any one of us, at any time.

Because kinship care will always be with us, achieving a proper understanding of all the experiences, thoughts and emotions which make it up will be something of universal and permanent value. My hope for this book is that it will be one step along this path.

References

Borrow, G. (1841/1905) *The Zincali: An Account of the Gipsies of Spain.* London: John Murray.

Jackson, S. (1999) 'The Paradigm Shift: Training Staff to Provide Services to the Kinship Triad.' In R.L. Hegar and M. Scannapieco (eds) *Kinship Foster Care: Policy, Practice and Research.* New York and Oxford: Oxford University Press.

Liddy, L. (1970) 'The Self-Image of the Child Placed with Relatives.' *Smith College Studies in Social Work 40*, 2, 164–176.

Miller, J.H. and Page, S.E. (2007) *Complex Adaptive Systems: An Introduction to Computational Models of Social Life.* Princeton and Oxford: Princeton University Press.

Stevens, I. and Hassett, P. (2007) 'Applying complexity theory to risk in child protection practice.' *Childhood 14*, 1, 128–144.

Warren-Adamson, C. (2009) 'Exploring kinship care through practitioner collaborative enquiry.' *Adoption and Fostering 33*, 3, 76–84.

Warren-Adamson, C. (2011) 'Evaluating Complexity in Community Based Programmes.' In A.N. Maluccio, C. Canali, T. Vecchiatto, A. Lightburn, J. Aldgate and W. Rose (eds) *Improving Outcomes for Children and Families: Finding and Using International Evidence.* London: Jessica Kingsley Publishers.

The Contributors

Dr Nicholas J. Banks is a consultant chartered clinical psychologist in private practice working as an expert court witness. He was a lecturer in social work for ten years and taught on the childcare element of the course and also as a senior lecturer in counselling and psychotherapy. He is a consultant to the Post Adoption Centre (London), the Adoption Support Agency of Registered Therapists and a past consultant to the British Agencies for Adoption and Fostering (BAAF). He is the author of a book on counselling and psychotherapy and numerous academic and professional journal articles on child care and development, sexual abuse, parental contact, fostering and adoption.

Dr Lucie Cluver is a social worker, and a lecturer in evidence-based social intervention at Oxford University, and in psychiatry at the University of Cape Town. She works with the South African government, UNICEF, USAID and Save the Children to provide evidence for policy with AIDS-affected children.

Dr Geraldine Crehan is a child and adolescent psychotherapist now working in the Child and Adolescent Mental Health Team (CAMHS) in Guildford, Surrey. She has a particular interest in the mental health needs of children who have suffered early neglect and abuse. She worked for several years in the Tavistock Centre's Fostering, Adoption and Kinship Care Team.

Susie Essex was, until her recent retirement, a consultant family therapist with North Bristol Health Trust. With Andrew Turnell, she has written *The Resolutions Approach: Working with 'Denied' Child Abuse.*

Professor Elaine Farmer is Professor of Child and Family Studies in the School for Policy Studies at the University of Bristol, prior to which she spent several years as a social worker. She has researched and published widely on child welfare and child protection. Her first study on formal kinship care was published as *Kinship Care: Fostering Effective Family and Friends Placements* (2008). The first part of her current study on informal kinship care (with Julie Selwyn and Sarah Meakings), examining prevalence, was published as *Spotlight on Kinship Care* (2011).

Erica Flegg is an experienced risk assessor and psychotherapist in the field of family violence. She is a recognised expert witness, and is frequently called to give evidence to the courts in family law cases (and formerly in criminal cases). Erica has a particular clinical interest in the psychology of gender, and in assessing mothers' ability to protect their children. She has developed a treatment model to enhance mothers' protectiveness and to work with parents for family safety.

Dr James (Jim) P. Gleeson is an associate professor at the Jane Addams College of Social Work, University of Illinois at Chicago. His research and publications focus on kinship care policy and practice, child welfare training, how child welfare workers learn, and evaluation of child welfare programmes and practice. Jim is a member of the review board for the *Child Welfare* journal and is a member of the editorial board for the *Journal of Public Child Welfare.*

Dr Anna Gough is a registered clinical psychologist in the independent sector. She has undertaken psychological assessments for the Family Courts since 2002, including kinship assessments. Anna has published qualitative research in specialist clinical areas of borderline personality disorders and eating disorders. She has a particular interest in individual narratives and the co-construction of identity, shaped by her personal experience of adoption from overseas.

Tom Hawkins is a lecturer in social work at the University of Plymouth, Cornwall College, Camborne. He has over 16 years' experience of working with children and young people and their families within residential, child protection, fostering and private law settings. Despite his teaching commitments and having become disabled in recent years, Tom also practises as an independent social worker. Over the course of his career Tom has developed research interests in kinship care, assessing and demonstrating protective parenting, and child protection assessment tools, processes and frameworks.

Paula Hayden is a consultant practitioner in foster care and kinship care based in Sydney, Australia. Paula has contributed to the development of culturally appropriate assessment tools for kinship carers from the Aboriginal community.

Dr Caroline Kuo is an assistant professor in the Department of Behavioral and Social Science at Brown University. She has conducted research on the effects of AIDS-related familial deaths on the outcomes of children orphaned by AIDS and their caregivers, and has documented patterns of kinship care in HIV-endemic communities.

Dr Marilyn McHugh is a research fellow at the Social Policy Research Centre at the University of New South Wales. She has conducted several foster and kinship carer studies. One recent study was for the Australian Government, Canberra: Department of Families, Housing, Community Services and Indigenous Affairs (FaHCSIA), *Financial and Non-Financial Support to Formal and Informal Out-of-Home Carers*.

Dr Sarah Meakings has a background in mental health nursing. Her doctoral research examined the service provision for children with serious emotional and behavioural difficulties. She is a research associate in the School for Policy Studies at the University of Bristol, where she has been working on a large UK study providing new insights into informal kinship care.

Dr Graham Music is Consultant Child and Adolescent Psychotherapist at the Tavistock Clinic and an adult psychotherapist in private practice. Formerly Associate Clinical Director at the Tavistock, he has also worked in the Tavistock Fostering, Adoption and Kinship Care Team for over a decade, managed a range of services concerned with the aftermath of child maltreatment and neglect and organised community based therapy services, particularly in schools. He organises training for therapists in CAMHS, leads on teaching about attachment, the brain and child development, and teaches and supervises on the Tavistock Child Psychotherapy Training and other psychotherapy trainings in Britain and abroad. Publications include *Nurturing Natures, Attachment and Children's Emotional, Sociocultural and Brain Development* (2010) and *Affect and Emotion* (2001) and he has a particular interest in exploring the interface between developmental findings and clinical work.

Amy O'Donohoe, together with her younger brother and sister, was brought up by her aunt, Cassie Felton, after being removed from her mother and stepfather's care at the age of 14 because of neglect. Amy, now age 20, is completing a degree in English and Music at Brunel University. Amy's experience was featured in a BBC documentary *Prison, My Family and Me*, which was shown on BBC3 in April 2012. Amy has used her experiences to train social workers.

Dr Don Operario is a faculty member in the School of Public Health at Brown University. Since 2005, he has had the pleasure to collaborate with Drs Caroline Kuo and Lucie Cluver on research addressing the wellbeing of children affected by HIV/AIDS.

Dr David Pitcher is a Children's Guardian and family court adviser. He has researched a number of aspects of grandparenting. He is the Honorary Social Work Adviser to the Grandparents' Association, and one of the founders of Grandparents Plus. In 1999, David set up Parents Again, a support group for grandparent carers in Plymouth. He ran this for seven years, and the group continues to run. David has won two national awards for his work with grandparents.

Dr John Simmonds is Director of Policy, Research and Development for the British Association of Adoption and Fostering (BAAF). He is responsible for BAAF's contribution to the development of policy and practice in social work, health, law and research in family placement, including kinship care.

Dr Andrew Turnell is an independent social worker and clinician with Resolutions Consultancy from Perth, West Australia. Andrew works as a child protection consultant with social services agencies in Europe, Australasia and North America and is the co-creator of the Signs of Safety approach to child protection casework, an approach that is increasingly utilised around the world. Andrew has written two books with two more currently in publication and many articles and chapters on safety-organised child protection practice.

Jackie Wyke is a trustee of the Grandparents' Association. She is a highly qualified and experienced trainer and mentor, and has authored several national training programmes. She is a visiting lecturer for Wolverhampton University. Jackie has three grandchildren, two of whom are adopted.

Dr Sadie Young is a chartered clinical psychologist who developed one of the first assessment and domiciliary services for parents with learning difficulties in the UK, and for 21 years was Head of the Special Parenting Service and lead psychologist for children with learning disabilities for Devon NHS Trust. She has written several articles about the needs of these families including support and kinship care. She has provided training and consultancy to parents, social workers, psychiatrists, nurses, therapists and those in the legal professions. She continues to offer assessment and consultancy as an independent professional.

Dr Jeanne Ziminski is a systemic family psychotherapist with the Child and Adolescent Mental Health Service (CAMHS) in Sutton, Surrey. She has undertaken and published research on kinship care from a systemic perspective, and regularly works with children, families and professional networks in complex kinship care cases.

Subject Index

Author Index